Space Into Light

The Architectural History Foundation/MIT Press Series

Christian F. Otto is editor of the *Journal of the Society of Architectural Historians* and Associate Professor at Cornell University.

The Architectural History Foundation is a publicly supported, not-for-profit foundation. Directors: William Butler, Colin Eisler, Edgar Kaufmann, Jr., Elizabeth G. Miller, Victoria Newhouse, Annalee Newman. Editorial Board: George R. Collins, Columbia University; Henry-Russell Hitchcock, New York University Institute of Fine Arts; Spiro Kostof, University of California at Berkeley; Vincent Scully, Yale University; John Summerson, Sir John Soane's Museum, London.

Special thanks go to the Graham Foundation, whose generous grants made possible the research for this project as well as the color section in the book.

The Foundation gratefully acknowledges the support of the Ford, Hearst and Kaufmann Foundations, The International Telephone and Telegraph Corporation, Skidmore, Owings & Merrill, Samuel I. Newhouse, Jr., and Mrs. Barnett Newman.

Space Into Light

The Churches of Balthasar Neumann

Christian F. Otto

The Architectural History Foundation, New York

The MIT Press, Cambridge, Massachusetts, and London, England

Library of Congress Cataloging in Publication Data

Otto, Christian F
     Space into light.

     Includes index.
     1. Neumann, Balthasar, 1687–1754. 2. Church architecture–Germany. 3. Architecture, Modern–17th– 18th centuries–Germany. 4. Light in architecture.
5. Space (Architecture) I. Title.
NA1088.N4087   726.15′0924   78–27782
ISBN 0–262–15019–0

Designed by Allan Mogel.

Contents

In Memoriam

my mother, Annaliese Schulte Otto
my father, Moritz Karl Friedrich Otto
my teacher, Rudolf Wittkower
my friend, Johannes Taubert

they would have taken great joy in sharing this book with me

Acknowledgments

Work on Neumann and his church architecture was under-
way for an embarrassingly long time. My research began in Germany during 1967; from it came a dissertation accepted by Columbia University in May 1971. I returned to pursue additional
research during the springs of 1972 and 1973. Due to these efforts, the range of questions that I have asked of the subject has
increased significantly: this book is not a revised edition of my
dissertation, but a new investigation more broadly conceived and,
I hope, better in its understanding of the material.

Over the years, the list of those who have helped me has
grown almost beyond bounds. The late Rudolf Wittkower, my
mentor for the dissertation, was an inspiring and deeply humane
scholar; whenever I am involved with architecture and the study
of its history, I feel the presence of his impeccable standards.
Johannes Taubert, from the Bayersche Landesamt für Denkmalpflege until his untimely death, led me to see architecture more in-
tensely than I ever had, and I profited enormously from his sensitivity. From a practical point of view, he facilitated my entry into
buildings and archives, besides introducing me to many helpful
individuals; both services have assisted this undertaking greatly.
Discussions with many people were informative and suggestive,
but special mention should be made of Mark Ashton, Max H. von
Freeden, Jorg Gamer, Walter Haas, Alfred Schädler, P. Norbert
Stoffels, Michael Ulrich, and Peter Vierl. Finally, I owe a collective debt to the members of my dissertation committee: Howard
Hibbard, Henry-Russell Hitchcock, Dorothea Nyberg, Adolf K.
Placzek, Rudolf Wittkower.

Financial support for research and writing was generous,
and for it I wish to thank Columbia University, Cornell University,
the German Academic Exchange Program, and especially the Graham Foundation, which assisted both the research and the production of this book.

11

Space Into Light

Introduction. Space Into Light

Huge, complex, awesome, in places even startling, the abbey church at Neresheim attests to the mastery of its designer, the South German architect Johann Balthasar Neumann (Fig. i). Neresheim was Neumann's last major project, to which he brought a creative imagination coupled with effortless authority.[1] Neumann composed a drama of motion, color, light, and surprise within the stately measure of an ordered whole. In an arena of sober purpose, he exhilarated the beholder with the elegant force of his architecture, matching human scale with monumentality, the pleasure of familiar things with grandeur.

Neumann achieved these effects by supporting oval and circular vaults on an undulating frame of columns, pilasters, arches, and piers. Austere in its elements, this skeletal structure is shaped into several spatial zones. The interior is so lucid and open, the solid parts so reduced, that the whole space is visible from any spot in the church. Despite this transparency, the visitor experiences new impressions with every step: the relationships of parts shift and change, spaces are defined, lead to other areas, are in turn recalled. Direction, counterpoint, and focus are handled with dramatic certainty.

Light deluges the interior, becoming a component of the space. Entering the church through enormous windows, clear light spills into the interior, dematerializing substance by means of highlight and shadow, backlighting and raking light. On gray days, the interior collects light like a gigantic lens, appearing brighter inside than the day outside.

Other art forms intensify the vividness of the experience. Paintings transform vaults and distinguish altars. Color enlivens pilasters and columns, panels, balustrades, and arches. Stucco detailing accents the architecture and the liturgical furniture. Statuary, gilding, metalwork, and wood carving enrich the ensemble. No mere veneer of decoration, this profusion of work is integral to the completed architecture, essential to the aesthetics of the whole, and inseparable from its meaning. Though so complex, the interior is never lost in confusion. Multiplicity is clarified into an integrated whole.

Neumann's abilities as an engineer were considerable, yet in the building of Neresheim, as well as in his other churches,

i. Neresheim, Benedictine abbey church of the Holy Cross, Balthasar
Neumann, begun 1748, view to choir.

structure and technique are straightforward, direct, and basic. This reflects a generally conservative attitude toward building technology common in Central European work of the 17th and 18th centuries. The structural methods often used in church buildings can be summarized briefly. Wall piers—short sections of wall turned at right angles to the nave—replaced load-bearing walls, eliminating the necessity for a solid, continuous outer surface. Vaults were carried by freestanding openworks and three-dimensional arches. On occasion, piers were hollowed out by passageways and niches, and vaults were dissolved by cavernous openings. These structural components seldom were used simultaneously in a single building; one or another was selected that was compatible with the building of a particular ground plan. Controlled lighting and the interplay of formal elements resulted in distinctive interiors that rarely repeated one another.

Neumann's churches, characterized by space, light, and openness, belong to an alternative tradition in western ecclesiastical architecture. From the 4th century, when Christianity became the official religion of the Roman Empire, to the present international position of Catholicism, the church building has served as the physical instrument of spiritual guidance: the mark of Christianity, symbol of its presence and permanence, setting for its liturgy, its arts, its traditions. Commonly the church building was envisioned in terms of durability, with dense construction relatively impervious to the deterioration of age. Built of heavy walls, massive piers, solid masonry vaults, slate roofs, and copper-sheathed domes, these churches supported faith like rock itself. Architecturally, this vision of permanence was expressed by means of the wall, which was treated as a continuous surface that defined the interior. By following the wall, one could understand the configuration of the internal vessel, its perimeters, its zones of focus, the relationship of parts one to the other.

But in certain epochs, an entirely different approach to church building was pursued. Wall as an uninterrupted plane was abandoned, and the interior became transfigured by a special treatment of space and light. The mass of the building was carved away, the necessary structural parts were reduced to what were apparently only frail props or disguised by decoration on their surfaces. Space was transformed by light pouring into the church through huge windows, by the ample use of color, by reflective surfaces that created an immaterial shimmer. These interiors seem suspended above the earth, not supported by it. The church building seen as a part of eternity was replaced by edifices that appeared to be splendid and even miraculous events.

During the early centuries of official church building, this attitude toward church design was realized in several places, notably Constantinople and Ravenna. It emerged again in the architecture of medieval Europe, and occurred a last time before our own era during the late 17th and early 18th centuries. Unfortunately, the historical record of these periods is out of balance. Byzantine and Gothic architecture have been studied by several generations of scholars, whereas 17th- and 18th-century work by Piedmontese and South German architects (to which broad grouping Neumann belongs) has been discovered more recently by historians, and virtually nothing of their writings has been published in English. Before turning to Neumann and his church architecture, these periods should be characterized briefly and the background to Neumann's work sketched in.

Among the monuments of Byzantine architecture, one is spectacularly impressive: Hagia Sophia in Istanbul (Fig. ii).[2] Emperor Justinian initiated its construction as an overt act of political confirmation six weeks after he almost lost his throne in the Nika uprising of 532, and six years later the enormous edifice was consecrated. Justinian exalted in the achievement, claiming that his church overshadowed Solomon's legendary temple in Jerusalem. On the day of consecration, 27 December 537, he is said to have boasted, "Solomon, I have vanquished thee!" His hubris was prompted by an achievement that continues to overwhelm expectations.

From the vast central dome, space expands into half-domes and conchs, flows between straight and curved arcades, and filters through stacks of windows. From every position within the church, views open into spaces seen in whole or in part, along axes or on the diagonal, seeming to expand or to contract. Color and decoration enrich the space, deny mass, disguise structural elements, and visually dissolve solid areas. Light from a multiplicity of sources amplifies these effects, entering the central space directly from clearstory and dome windows, or indirectly through aisles and galleries. Different intensities of light refract on the multiple curved and angled surfaces, denying the presence of mass and material substance.

The special effects of space and light at Hagia Sophia were already observed when the building was first completed. Justinian's house historian, Procopius of Caesarea, wrote that the church was "singularly full of light . . . you would declare that the place is not lighted by the sun from without, but that the rays are produced within itself." And he was overpowered by the weightless altitude of the structure. Describing the central dome, he said, "From the lightness of the building it does not appear to rest upon a solid foundation, but to cover the place beneath as though it were suspended from heaven by the fabled golden chain."

From its 12th-century beginnings through the 13th-century era of great cathedrals and into the 14th and 15th centuries, the

ii. Istanbul, Hagia Sophia, Anthemios of Tralles and Isidorus of Miletus, 532–37, view to choir (lithograph by Gaspard Fossati, *Aya Sofia, Constantinople, as Recently Restored by Order of H. M. the Sultan Abdul Mediid*, London, 1852, pl. 24).

iii. Chartres, Cathedral of Notre Dame, 1194–1221, nave and south transept.

Gothic style dominated sacred and secular building. In a Gothic cathedral, mass is replaced by frail vertical shafts aligned within a vast, light-saturated interior.[3] The sense of too great a height, achieved by means too meager and located within an ambience of color-suffused light, creates an hallucinatory vision (Fig. iii).

Light entering the interior is not clear daylight, which would produce shadow, highlight, and plastic effects, but light washed with many hues and diffused throughout the interior. Drawing space into a continuity, this light emphasizes distances, intensifies the vertical, increases the apparent length of the church from entrance to altar. Consequently, the outer skin of the church is transformed into zones of space and light.[4] Suger, Abbot of St-Denis and the motivating spirit behind the rebuilding of this first "new" church, observed that the stained glass "would shine with the wonderful and uninterrupted light of most sacred windows, pervading the interior beauty."[5]

During the 17th and 18th centuries, many architects who designed churches where space was of primary importance were aware of Byzantine and Gothic architecture. On occasion they acknowledged these buildings in their work and some wrote appreciations of them. Nevertheless, their architecture was determined in the first instance by the classical language of architecture and adhered to its principles of design. They also depended heavily on 16th-century architectural attitudes. The complexity of this involvement with distant and immediate pasts is one aspect of a rich and demanding design situation.

Beginning in the 1630s, François Mansart and Francesco Borromini—working in Paris and Rome respectively—designed buildings based on open frameworks, unified spatial figures, and expansive lighting.[6] By the 1670s, Guarino Guarini had transformed these beginnings into spatial visions of extraordinary intensity. His Turin church of S. Lorenzo, for example, is a centralized structure in which the forms of dome and crossing tower are fused into "an openwork lattice and borne too high in the air on too frail an armature, as if by a miracle" (Fig. iv).[7] During the last quarter of the century, an architecture based on space composition became widespread, and such work can be found in Paris, the Piedmont, London, South Germany, Bohemia, and Austria (Fig. v). Within the course of fifty years, the audacious experiments of the 1630s had developed into a popular mode.

Neumann absorbed some of the design strategies formulated during these decades. But his work is not closely linked to

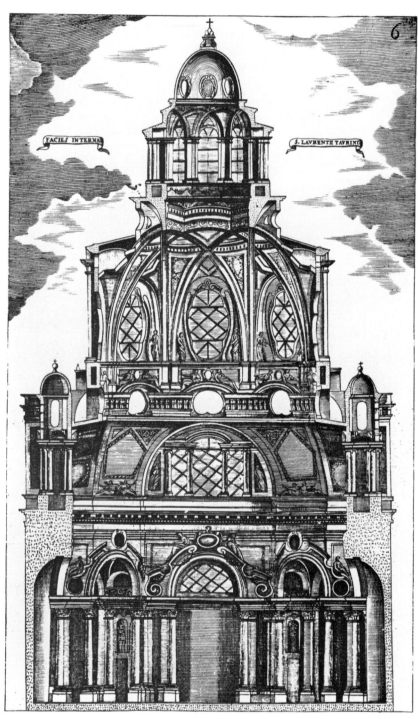

iv. Turin, S. Lorenzo, Guarino Guarini, 1668–87, section (Guarino Guarini, *Architettura civile,* Turin, 1737, pl. 6).

a particular person or approach. His individual projects, both secular and sacred, are marked by their distinctive formal and spatial qualities. In the churches, where designing was little restricted by demands of patron and program, the epic power of his architectural language is boldest, clearest, and richest, and for this reason the churches constitute the subject of this book. Neumann's engineering capacities dominate in the utilitarian structures he built: hydraulic systems, bridges, fortifications, barracks. His city planning, limited in scope, was concerned with reorganizing a small section of Würzburg and the construction of inexpensive rows of standardized housing; this work followed common practice and is not of compelling interest.

Palaces, mostly for the Schönborn family, absorbed much of his time, and he is known as much for his Residenz at Würzburg as for the church at Neresheim. The sequence of public spaces in the Residenz is dramatic and impressive, as is his work at Bruchsal; his proposal for the Hofburg in Vienna was explosive in concept (Figs. vi, vii). But generally in the palace projects Neumann's creative intentions are hemmed in on all sides. These huge enterprises drew on his talents for organization, but made minimal demands on his creative energy. The "designing" was done largely by committee. Patron, interested relatives, and court advisors specified what functions had to be accommodated, what rooms were necessary for them, where they should be located within the building, what amenities must be included, and so forth. For these meetings, individual cliques often arrived with their own archi-

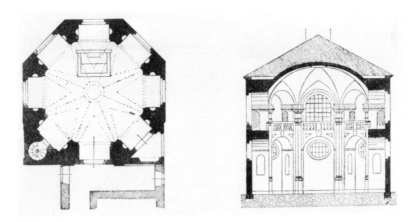

v. Teplá, hospital church of the Holy Trinity, Christoph Dientzenhofer, 1692–99, plan and section.

23

tects in tow, who in turn argued for their personal vision of those few areas that could be designed more freely. Hildebrandt, von Welsch, Johann Dientzenhofer, de Cotte, and Boffrand all had their say about the design of the Residenz. The solution emerged through give and take. Once protocol and function were worked out, once the design compromises were struck, Neumann would oversee construction of the building. And once the fabric was up, he would organize the necessary logistics of interior finishing by various artists and artisans.

Only in the design of the facades and in the ceremonial parts of the palace could he work more independently. Here Neumann gave voice to concepts similar to those expressed in his churches: transparent and light-saturated space, form within form, layering, relation of plan to vault. The opportunity to move the spectator up through space by means of stairs is unique to the palace designs, and Neumann orchestrated this dynamic moment with dramatic variation in different projects. On the other hand, the individual rooms are shut off from one another by walls, eliminating precisely that area of design which most distinguishes the churches: the relation of spatial figures to one another, their arrangement within a differently shaped outer shell, and the lucid transparency of the whole. In church after church, we can document Neumann's confrontation with these design issues. He was largely indifferent to the church exteriors—internal space brought into light was his concern. Because the large number of churches provide a range of responses that contrasts decisively with his few public spaces in the palaces, Neumann's ecclesiastic interiors are the focus of this study.

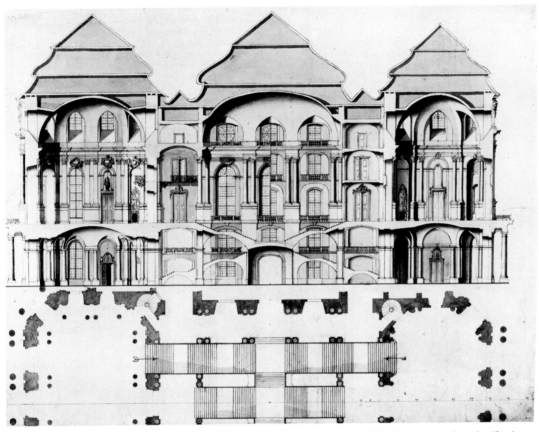

vi. Vienna, Hofburg, Balthasar Neumann, 1747–48, project: longitudinal section of main stair in two alternatives (Berlin, Kunstbibliothek, Hdz. 4730).

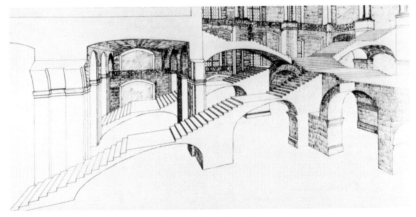

vii. Perspective rendering of Hdz. 4730 (Fig. vi).

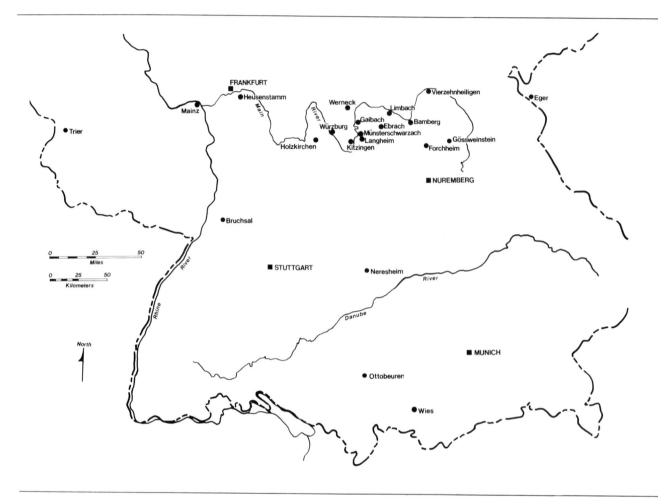

Map of Southern Germany, with sites of Neumann's churches.

I.
Training
and
Patronage

Neumann's career appears to be riddled with contradictions. One of the most prolific architects in Europe, officially he was an officer in the engineers corps of the Franconian military (Fig. 1). His extraordinary talents did not alter the daily routine of a civil servant. He produced voluminous building reports without ever stating or even suggesting his architectural principles. He immersed himself in the study of architecture from other places and periods, yet it is impossible to pinpoint specific influences in his buildings. At a time when architecture was determined by illusionism and the lavish integration of other arts, he created clear, logical spaces that were effective in their own right. To bring Neumann and these apparent discrepancies closer to us, we must begin by considering his immediate background as a designer, and the context of patronage, program, and practice within which he worked.

Born on 27 January 1687, the seventh of eight children from an impoverished family, Balthasar Neumann was trained in his home town of Eger (Cheb) as a bell and artillery founder.[1] With journeyman's papers in hand, he arrived at Würzburg in 1711 to seek employment at the famous foundry of Ignaz Kopp. These were busy years for Kopp, where in addition to bells and ornamental pieces, all armaments for the Franconian military were produced. Neumann's personality was not submerged by the demands of foundry work, however. The sparse information we possess about these early years suggests that a relentless ambition drove him.

During his first year in Würzburg, he was already indentured as fireworks artificer (Fig. 2). He also struck up an acquaintance with Andreas Müller, who became his architecture teacher. A captain in the engineers corps, Müller was sufficiently established within the court hierarchy to serve as personal guide for Emperor Charles VI on the occasion of his visit to Würzburg in 1712. Müller encouraged and coached Neumann in the study of geometry and surveying. As these were mastered, he offered him further information in civil and military architecture. Neumann's deepening involvement with these studies is reflected by three loans he solicited from the Eger city fathers (17 June 1711, 30 March 1712, 8 June 1712), initially for books and materials, and finally so that he could devote himself full time to his studies. Giving up his job with Kopp, he assured his Eger benefactors that he was making considerable progress and would be able to show them "something extraordinary." [2]

Due perhaps to Müller's influence, Neumann became a private in the Franconian artillery. By 1713 he was evidently well versed in mathematics. In this year he also produced his "Instrumentum Architecturae," a device that provided the different diameters for Tuscan, Doric, and Ionic orders at a given height (Fig. 3). This method contrasted with the usual practice of establishing a set diameter as the generator of various column heights, and demonstrated already at this early stage Neumann's individual turn of mind. Commissioned on 8 May 1714 as cornet in the Prince-Bishop's personal guard, where he served essentially as Müller's adjunct, Neumann began in this year the project that was to test the application of his studies in practical experience—drawing up a map of Würzburg (Fig. 4). It was completed the following year.

As for many architects, engineers, and master craftsmen of the era, the military remained an "official" career. By providing instruction in drawing and surveying, in geometry and mathematics, it offered excellent basic disciplines for architecture.[3] Returning from the siege of Belgrade under Prince Eugene in 1717, Neumann was promoted rapidly, to captain in the engineers in 1718, to artillery captain in 1720; four years later he was commissioned artillery and engineer major, in 1729 lieutenant colonel, in 1744 full colonel. A portrait by Kleinert of 1727 and one by Tiepolo in the early 1750s depict Neumann in full military dress, surrounded by military attributes. He was clearly in command of professional military training [4] and work on fortifications occupied him throughout his life. But history's significant memory of him is as an architect; in this regard, his chosen city assumes importance.

For a full half-century, 1651–1701, Antonio Petrini's work in Würzburg determined the scope of design attitudes.[5] Though severe in detail, his projects were consistent in conception, monumental in realization (Figs. 5–7). Their authority remained inescapable, and their influence established Würzburg as an architectural center. After Petrini's death a scattering of masters and craftsmen were sucked into the vortex, none of whom emerged as a convincing successor, so that a Bamberg master had to be called in for consultation on the Neumünster, the major commission of the following year (Fig. 8). Locally, the master carpenter Josef Greising was responsible for supervising this enterprise.[6] He represents the strongest talent to succeed Petrini and is associated with all the on-going larger projects in addition to Neumünster, the Ebrach and Münsterschwarzach monasteries, parts of the Julius hospital, St. Peter (Würzburg), the church at Obertheres, and many city houses.

We find Neumann in Greising's company on several occasions from 1715 on, but apparently working as a hydraulics engineer, and not on architectural matters. By 1709 Neumann was involved with the construction of fountains in Eger. He returned there from Würzburg in 1713 to undertake work on the mineral water spring of the Franzensbad. The Gaibach waterworks occupied him in 1715. During this year and the next he was responsible for the large subterranean canalization project at Ebrach monastery (Fig. 9), where Greising served as coordinating architect.[7]

These efforts were broadened by military obligations in 1717 when Neumann accompanied the armies of Prince Eugene in the siege of Belgrade. Offered a captain's commission by the Viennese *Hofkreigsrat* upon his return, Neumann turned it down, indicating that he needed to travel and study. After a stay in Milan on the staff of the Emperor's governor general, he returned to Würzburg. Boasting training, travel, and experience, his credentials as an architect were irrefutable. Agitated by the desire to build elaborately and in profusion, Johann Philipp Franz von Schönborn, Prince-Bishop of Würzburg, appointed him his personal architectural advisor, a position Neumann quickly consolidated. In 1721 both Müller and Greising died, leaving him the major designer in Würzburg. In this year, under the umbrella of his patron's authority, Neumann formulated a document that granted the court jurisdiction over all civilian construction. The following year a building commission was created that required Neumann's approval for all construction undertaken in the city. The trainee of five years before was now established as the final architectural authority within the bishopric.

Though great, Neumann's authority was limited by the restrictions inherent in the nature of Schönborn patronage. The enthusiastic but demanding sponsorship of this family continues to delight observers of the South German scene. Spouting an eccentric and amusing jargon characterized by personal formulations and Latin, French, and Italian idioms,[8] they pursued their extensive building enterprises with superabundant vitality. Three Schönborns interest us: Lothar Franz, Archbishop and Elector of Mainz, 1695–1729, Prince-Bishop of Bamberg, 1693–1729; and his two nephews, Johann Philipp Franz, Prince-Bishop of Würzburg, 1719–24, and Friedrich Karl, Imperial Vice Chancellor, 1705–34, Prince-Bishop of Würzburg and Bamberg, 1729–46.[9]

Lothar Franz (Fig. 10) was the architectural patriarch of the family, the "arch-architect" (*Erzbaumeister*) as his nephews referred to him. Any building enterprise with which he could in some way involve himself, he pursued with passion. His lengthy and frequent conferences with his personal architect, Maximilian von Welsch, often lasted into the small hours of the morning. He tried his own hand at designing, though with minimal success.[10] His nephews were quick to solicit advice from him, which was proffered frequently and ranged across a wide spectrum of particulars.

Raised and educated together, thirteen months apart in age, these nephews possessed very different personalities. They grew up in Würzburg, studied at the university in Mainz for a short time, and were sent for several years to the Collegium Germanicum, a Jesuit school in Rome. Their travels in Italy took them to Venice, Ferrara, Bologna, Loreto, Naples, Siena, and Genoa. Leaving Rome in 1693, they studied at the university in Würzburg before setting out in 1697 on travels intended to lend them political insight and diplomatic experience. They journeyed through Germany to The Hague, from there to London, back through France to Paris where they remained for half a year. Friedrich Karl listened to law and theology lectures at the Sorbonne, both brothers explored Paris, Versailles, and Marly. During the following year, and until they were elected to their respective posts as Prince-Bishop of Würzburg and Imperial Vice Chancellor in Vienna, the nephews were sent on various political missions throughout Central Europe.

Johann Philipp Franz (Fig. 11), egotistic and with an irritating sense of his own superiority, was a vital, impulsive character. He engaged in a relentless quest for funds in order to indulge himself with pleasures and splendid things. His Residenz in Würzburg was conceived on a scale out of all proportion to the size of the bishopric supporting it; Lothar Franz moaned that it would ruin the family. His activities were fraught with intrigue, his enemies countless. For months he would follow the hunt, indifferently tearing up the countryside and embittering his subjects. With melodramatic justice, he died poisoned while hunting.

Friedrich Karl (Fig. 12), by contrast, was a reserved, gentle, and prudent personality. Possessing an excellent understanding of the law, he dispatched his obligations as Imperial Vice Chancellor with responsibility and enormous industry. His interest in politics was lively, his conversation witty. If Lothar Franz saw Johann Philipp Franz leading the house of Schönborn to ruin, he might take comfort in the common sense, dignity, and fortitude of Friedrich Karl, which strengthened it and contributed to its continued significance.

Both brothers received some architectural training as part of their education. They took advantage of their extensive travels to see as much architecture as possible. Evidently the passions of their uncle were contagious, for the brothers acquired an architectural awareness that was European in range.

Schönborn patronage set limits to Neumann's creative activity, as it did for other artists. When the architect returned to Würzburg in 1719, Lothar Franz doubted his aesthetic maturity. He saw in the young man the potential of a strong designer, but recommended that he be sent to Italy and France for two years of study. There, Lothar Franz felt, Neumann would gain the appropriate architectural experience to become a first-rate artist in his own right. Neumann was a sound architectural investment, concluded the Elector practically, one that would eventually pay excellent dividends.[11]

Presumably Johann Philipp Franz was reluctant to lose his personal architect for any time at all, not to mention two years. At this moment work on plans for the Residenz (Fig. 4) was intense, with Neumann plunged into the middle of things. The start of construction was imminent. Designing for the Schönborn chapel was about to begin (Fig. 27). Neumann was essential for both undertakings. How could he be released from this demanding situation? Besides, nephew could point out to uncle that Neumann had just returned from Italy. Apparently pressure from Lothar Franz mounted, and by December 1720 Johann Philipp Franz had agreed to release the architect for several years of study.

In April Neumann was sent off to the famous Uffenbach libraries in Frankfurt, perhaps as preliminary orientation for his trip.[12] Yet this study-voyage never materialized. When he arrived in Paris two years later, it was more to consult with de Cotte and Boffrand on the Würzburg Residenz plans than to absorb architectural lessons from the French. Until his death in 1724, Johann Philipp Franz built with an abandon that bordered on the compulsive. He recognized that Neumann's involvement was essential to success. A long-term study leave was clearly out of the question.

Another limitation imposed by Schönborn patronage was their recourse to more than one designer for larger projects. In the discussion of specific undertakings, below, the complexities and implications of this penchant for collective design will be demonstrated. Here it should be noted that these situations demanded adroit argument and diplomatic skill from the architect who hoped to defend a personal project successfully. In the initial stages of planning for the Residenz, for instance, Neumann not only had to record Johann Philipp Franz's personal ideas, but was obligated to integrate material from Mainz (Lothar Franz and Maximilian von Welsch), Vienna (Friedrich Karl and Johann Lucas von Hildebrandt), and even from others within the bishopric (Johann Dientzenhofer). In addition, Johann Philipp Franz requested material from ten different cities, and when the cornerstone was laid for the structure, Neumann shared supervision of construction with Johann Dientzenhofer.

Crucial to Schönborn building operations was an extensive exchange of information. *"Oculi plus et facilius vident quam oculus,"* noted Johann Philipp Franz—many eyes see better than a single pair.[13] Designs were sent back and forth for suggestions, corrections, or confirmation. On occasion the architect of a project traveled with his designs to the courts of other family members and their architects: with Residenz plans in hand, Neumann visited Mainz in 1719, Paris in 1723, Vienna in 1730 and 1734. Perhaps most productive were the larger architectural conferences that drew on the participation of family members or their delegates, sent to argue particular positions. The conferences cannot be recreated today, since no minutes survive, if indeed they were taken at all. But available correspondence and surviving notes help to illuminate the nature of these discussions.[14] For secular projects, lively and detailed debate focused on the arrangement and sequence of rooms, on the placement of courts, stairs, and public spaces, on problems of circulation and related programmatic considerations. Facade design, on the other hand, was little discussed; this remained the architect's realm of creative responsibility.[15] An intelligent reorganization of an architect's project was probably beyond the capabilities of most clients. Even the Schönborn, who received some architectural training as part of their education, appear to have run into trouble when they turned their hands to designing.[16]

Church architecture was treated in a similar manner: plan and elevation remained concerns of the architect. The Schönborn limited the range of their insistent questions to other matters. Architectural detail occupied them, such as the frame of a door or window, the profile of a base. They determined, to a great extent, the nature of decoration: how much painting, sculpture, stucco; according to what theme; placed where. Technical questions were of interest, such as the ingredients of plaster or the manufacture of porcelain. But the Schönborn never attempted to establish the basics of a church design, nor did they suggest reworking a design that had been presented. The aesthetic concept was accepted or rejected as a whole. With amused irony, they referred to their architects as gods of construction supervision (*Baudirigierungs-götter*).[17] The Schönborn exerted their influence by requesting designs from several architects, before and during the planning stage, at times even after construction had begun. Rather than manipulating the elements of one master's design, dissatisfactions or uncertainties were expressed by requesting alternatives from other masters. The Schönborn then selected what appeared to them to be the more successful solution.

Was this hands-off attitude the result of ecclesiastical traditions that determined the nature of church design? Were church solutions the inevitable consequence of theological programs? The answer appears to be a simple no; a free creative spirit guided church design in South Germany. This question will be reviewed more thoroughly in Chapter V. For the moment, a few of Neumann's church projects reveal the nature of the situation.

During his 1703 visit to Florence, Johann Philipp Franz was struck by the tradition of the mortuary chapel.[18] Back in

Würzburg, and before his elevation to Prince-Bishop, he broached the notion of a similar Schönborn structure. Significantly, though confronting a specific architectural tradition, he requested that his chapel meet only two conditions: it must be domed and the interior finished in marble (Fig. 26). The plan and internal elevation were never discussed, possible symbolic implications of the architecture were of no concern, even the number and disposition of memorials did not emerge as an issue until the plan had been established. In short, Johann Philipp Franz did not pose questions with architectural implications.

His brother, Friedrich Karl, appears similarly disposed. For the design of his palace church in the Residenz, one might assume that the matter of prototype was of major importance (Fig. 74). There existed a long pedigree, extending from the 12th-century Whitehall chapel to the Versailles chapel of the 1680s, for longitudinal, double-level structures—aisle below, balcony above, and a special place for the patron fitted out in the west opposite the altar.[19] Discussion of the Würzburg church never acknowledged these prototypes. Silence might be interpreted as recognition of a well-established tradition, except that Neumann's design remained unconventional. He did not employ a continuous upper level; instead, separate loggia-like compartments are entered through individual doors from palace corridors; the west end of the church is left empty. Only at a late stage in the design process, when the church was already in construction, did Neumann insert two oratories for Friedrich Karl and his family into the east end of the building, flanking the choir. Friedrich Karl's concerns about the church had to do with its location within the Residenz (close to his personal rooms) and the nature of its interior decoration. His attitude was similar to his brother's: although involved with a project that had personal significance for him and at the same time clear prototypical implications, he argued neither for convention nor against novelty.

Friedrich Karl also sponsored the pilgrimage church at Gössweinstein (Fig. 55). Of the several architects who submitted designs for the structure, only those by A. F. Freiherr von Ritter zu Grünstein [20] and Neumann survive; Johann Dientzenhofer's description of his submission indicates what its basic arrangement of parts was to be. None of these projects addressed the problems peculiar to the pilgrimage church: circulation, number of chapels, disposition of relics. What does appear to have aroused interest was symbolic reference to the Trinity. Dientzenhofer's design is explicit in this regard—a centralized structure comprising three units divided into three parts. Ritter zu Grünstein's project contains three bays, each bay with three parts. And the east end of Neumann's church recognizes this numeric symbolism. In the extensive surviving documentation for the building—financial records, letters, protocols by various parties—one searches in vain for any mention of the use to which the building was to be put. Matters of finance, materials, and work schedules were pursued in elaborate detail. Questions of the content and to a degree the form of the paintings and altars received exhaustive exposure. In stark contrast, issues of architectural form and accommodation to use remained unmentioned.

But did this situation hold for monastic commissions, where the client was a distinct religious order, serving a particular purpose, located in a specific place? It would appear to have. The monumental Latin cross plan employed for the Benedictine monastery church at Münsterschwarzach (Fig. 46) was specifically rejected later for the Benedictine monastery church at Neresheim (Fig. 145). After receiving the commission, Neumann complied with the Neresheim abbot's request to show him the plan of the newly completed Münsterschwarzach. But he also made it clear that he had no intention of designing anything similar: "Your church cannot become a mere copy" ("... just eine Kirche wie die andere herauskommen").[21] The abbot accepted this position with an equanimity which suggests that he expected it. He requested only that Neumann's project acknowledge certain conditions of site. Interestingly, Neumann's first designs for Neresheim were based on his scheme for the Cistercian monastic foundation at Langheim (Figs. 107, 139). He soon departed from this formula, but his approach demonstrates the persuasions of formal, not programmatic, imperatives.

The absence of programmatic restraints from Neumann's church commissions was not unusual. The functional and formal requirements for western Catholic churches had produced a few basic forms to accommodate the demands of liturgy, theology, tradition, and symbol—demands that changed slowly and rarely altered the function and layout of the buildings. The last major liturgical amplifications had occurred during the Middle Ages, and no theological, liturgical, or administrative discussions in the 17th and 18th centuries addressed architectural problems.[22] Once general functional requirements had been determined, such as the inclusion of a monk's choir or separate chapels, the patron's involvement centered on disposing altars, their number and sequence, pulpit, choir stalls, baptismal font, seating, and so on within the planned space, which was usually large enough to hold liturgical furniture and the faithful with room to spare.

Even churches serving specialized purposes did not subscribe necessarily to predetermined forms. The choirs of South German pilgrimage churches, for instance, in order to accommodate heavy traffic around the altars and relics, commonly had a lower altar placed before an aisle and another altar on a balcony above. This allowed two streams of pilgrims to circulate simultaneously into and out of the sacred area. At Die Wies, however, the Zimmermann brothers designed the choir visually, but not functionally, in this manner (Fig. 13). The lower aisle leads past the altar only through a cumbersome route, and the balcony is inaccessible to the public. By contrast, the former Benedictine monastery church of SS. George and Jacob the Elder at Isny employs this double-tiered circulation system, though it never served the pilgrimage (Fig. 14).

This freedom from programmatic limitations put the designer in a commanding position: any given church project offered the potential of demonstrating without compromise his ability as form giver. On the other hand, if the architect entertained the hope of receiving and realizing a commission, his project had to recognize limitations. Site considerations and structural feasibility represented obvious problems. The most frequently felt difficulty, however, was financial. A good design did not exceed its projected budget, and to this demand Neumann was always responsive. He envisioned Heusenstamm (Figs. 64–67) with two towers and a nave containing three bays, but he executed a one-tower facade located before a nave of two bays. For Gössweinstein (Figs. 52, 53, Pl. VI) he proposed a full dome over the crossing that punched through the roof and was crowned by a lantern. Instead a saucer dome of reduced diameter was constructed, tucked well inside the roof and without a lantern. This does not imply that Neumann was content with these economy measures, or that he accepted them easily. When the Neresheim abbot requested him to design a cheaper version of the church with a small choir, he did so. But he accompanied the design with a strong letter demanding that the abbot decide whether he intended to erect an impressive monastery church or a mean parish building. Neumann's large choir was realized, but during construction the abbot was voted out of office by his fellow monks due to the extraordinary expense of the undertaking.

II.
Design and Construction Practice

To consider how a building came into being, both office and construction practice must be reviewed. This discussion, distilled from specific designs, focuses on procedure and the materials generally employed by the architectural profession.

Often architects jot down ideas for buildings on scraps of paper and experiment with tentative solutions in sketches (Fig. 15). Material of this sort by Italian masters is preserved from Sangallo to Juvarra, and a few collections by German designers are known.[1] Within Central Europe, architectural sketches are rare in the 17th century and virtually nonexistent during the first half of the 18th. Nothing of this nature survives from Neumann's hand. If it ever existed it must have been considered completely insignificant, a base expediency that was soon discarded. Enthusiasm for the artist's sketch as a primary, spontaneous expression began to develop in the 16th century. In Germany, this attitude excluded architectural renderings almost entirely; I have found no letter, no note, no record that breathes a word about them. Exact parallels are found elsewhere in Central Europe.[2]

What does survive in greater numbers is scaled drawings —in a sense sketches produced with straightedge and compass (e.g., Figs. 69, 70). These served both architect and client, and

37

were employed for problem-solving as well as for presentation. It appears odd to suggest that an elaborately constructed plan could be the mode for working out a solution. That this was so is indicated by the inaccuracies, corrections, and missing parts in many drawings (e.g., Figs. 95, 108, 141). They were reworked when problems arose, and abandoned when basic, unresolvable difficulties emerged. The matter is further confirmed by Neumann's method of developing a design by means of plans. A scaled plan (although the scale is not always on a sheet, the drawings are obviously realized according to a scale) would be drawn, at times with a left and right variation (e.g., Fig. 140). A projection of the vault base shown in dotted line often was included (e.g., Figs. 52, 113, 138). The resolution of specific problems, such as the demands of site or effectiveness of circulation patterns, was examined on the basis of this plan.[3] If changes appeared necessary, they were either laid in directly over the errors with graphite or ink, or parts of the sheet were pasted over and redrawn, or written notes on alterations were included (e.g., Figs. 141, 143). This provided the basis for a new plan. The more complex the difficulties in a project, the more plans would be produced until an apparent solution was attained. Only then would Neumann design longitudinal and cross sections, and at times external elevations. This material was composed as orthogonal projections so that accurate dimensions of every element in the design could be established (e.g., Figs. 101, 115, 116, Pl. I). Walls and vaults were recorded without details of construction or material. The framework for the roof often was depicted in detail, though it seldom agreed with what was actually built. Perspective renderings, that is bird's-eye views with vanishing lines set on raking diagonals, or central, one-point perspectives, seldom were employed except to document a completed structure (e.g., Figs. 27, 47, 86). If no difficulties either of an aesthetic or technical nature were revealed by the sections, the design was ready for presentation.

Usually a model accompanied the renderings, offering the client a more accessible three-dimensional image of the proposed building. Sometimes Neumann personally prepared the model, though often he had it done for him. Wood, plaster, or wax was the usual material. Though many are mentioned in the documents, only two models survive, one for Münsterschwarzach and one for Vierzehnheiligen (Figs. 48, 49, 132). Both are wooden constructions that can be opened to show the interior. If the presentation pieces revealed problems, Neumann returned to making plans.

Neumann personally authored many renderings (e.g., Figs. 69, 70, 108–111). These range from factual, prosaic plans to extraordinarily sensitive elevations of stunning beauty, to dramatic, exaggerated perspectives.[4] Most drawings in the surviving corpus, however, were produced by office draftsmen.[5] As the volume of Neumann's work increased, this became a necessity. Presumably a draftsman would receive detailed verbal instruction and proceed to draw on the basis of this information. Additional or more detailed explanations or corrections were given as the project progressed. At times, control of this sort was not possible. Neumann then sketched in changes on the finished sheet, and a fresh rendering was produced.

Drawings were first constructed in graphite or with a stylus that engraved line into the paper. Lines then were inked in, and the rendering frequently completed with ink or pastel washes to indicate plasticity and volume; the exact construction of shadow enhances these qualities.[6] Subtle blue, pink, green, and yellow tones commonly seen in the drawings are delicate and transparent in quality, filling the representation with space and light (Pl. I).

Many renderings reveal the points and axes employed to build up a plan or elevation. These make it clear that Neumann's designs are derived from basic geometric figures and numerical ratios. For example, an arrangement of squares, circles, and ovals [7] determined the plan of Vierzehnheiligen (Fig. 130).[8] At Langheim, quadrangulation, specifically in this instance a row of tangent squares, established the placement of supports, the size of the bay unit, the width of the aisles. Triangulation was employed at Mainz to arrive at nave and aisle height, the width of nave and aisles, and wall thickness (Fig. 118).[9] In elevation, Münsterschwarzach (Fig. 47) is divided into sixths (the pedestal zone equals one-sixth; the zone containing the order, three-sixths; that of the vault, two-sixths), whereas Holzkirchen (Fig. 34) is precisely halved by the springing point of the dome (marked by the top of the strongly projecting entablature). These geometric and proportional systems represent pragmatic concerns. They do not bespeak a theoretical or conceptual point of departure, but are practical arrangements that help organize the basic measurements of plan and elevation. This factual, common-sense approach to architecture is found in Neumann's work time and again.

Once a solution was approved for construction, the project was considered final, subject to no further change.[10] Architectural tracts [11] insist on this procedure, ominously citing substantially increased construction costs and future unemployment for the architect if violated. Hammer out all problems on paper and in models together with the client, they warn, or the consequences in faulty and rebuilt construction may be disastrous. Neumann held fast to these prescriptions. His written reports confirm that execution was based without deviation on a final project.

Construction was a collective undertaking, committed to traditional methods and dependent on the talent of specialized craftsmen. Stucco and gilt, woodworking and iron-smithing demanded training as particularized as the heavier construction work of stonecutters, stonemasons, and roofing carpenters. Neumann's task was to organize these talents effectively into a sequence that led to realization. For a monthly fee he would appoint a local foreman, usually a master stonecutter or stonemason, to oversee day-to-day operations. Responsible for organizing the labor force, the foreman could hire and fire as necessary. He administered the funds for construction, procured building materials, determined the sequence of jobs, and maintained a review of quality in the workmanship. He was obligated to remain on the site and could not simultaneously supervise another building. Following him in the hierarchy stood a stonecutter and a stonemason, each responsible for a crew of workmen. The former received a monthly sum, while the latter was paid different fees for each running foot of wall, entablature, molding, etc. The labor force was filled out by unskilled laborers, volunteers, and the numerous artisans who attended to a large number of specialized productions, ranging from door locks and handles to stucco, furniture, and roof tiles.

The foreman was provided with a measured plan from which to work. At Gössweinstein this was glued onto a large wooden board to preserve it through the rigors of work and weather. A second plan, reportedly delivered after the fabric was already standing, presumably indicated the placement of balconies, balustrades, and altars. A plan contained no information about materials or construction procedure (e.g., Figs. 52, 107). It depicted an aesthetic concept; the practical matter of translating this idea into a building was determined by tradition and discussion. Neumann's office drew up measured details for specific parts of the structure when required. Models were prepared to illustrate elements such as door and window frames, entablature profiles, capital details, and to help solve difficult structural problems. The large wooden model for the Neresheim roof is made exactly to a 1:33⅓ scale, and exhibits the precise nature of each joint (Fig.

154). It served two purposes: first to demonstrate the feasibility of the design, secondly to give the carpenters a source from which they could take exact measurements during construction for the size and shape of the different timbers. Several times during the building year, which generally ran from April to October, Neumann would inspect the site. In these visits he ascertained that construction was being realized properly, discussed and worked out problems with the foreman.

At the outset Neumann selected an appropriate quarry and during construction it was the foreman's responsibility to maintain a supply of necessary materials on site.[12] While stone rubble could be drawn from convenient local deposits, Neumann commonly had large, quality ashlar shipped in from the Abtswind quarry. If good stone was available on site, as at Vierzehnheiligen, this was considered particularly advantageous. Even in this case, however, tuff for the vaults was brought in from Utzing. Special stones often were drawn from a distance, such as the particularly light but tenacious tuff from Homburg am Main for the enormous vault over the Residenz staircase, or the Lahn marble from Kostheim am Main to finish the interior of the Schönborn chapel. Wood was plentiful in Franconia and presented no problems of supply. Neumann ran his own glass and mirror manufacture for the churches and palaces. Window glass was produced in Fabrikschleichach in the Steigerwald; mirrors—lavishly incorporated into palace interiors—were supplied from Würzburg. His glass and mirrors were exported as far away as Holland, and seem to have provided him with tidy profits.

Large work crews were used (almost a hundred men were employed at Gössweinstein, a medium-sized structure, during the raising of the fabric), erecting masonry shell and roof at an impressive clip. Often, building campaigns of three or four years were sufficient to complete walls, vaults, and roof. Construction of towers and finishing of the interior added years to the final completion; stucco, paintings, altars, gates, and benches, each the domain of one or two artisans, consumed large blocks of time. Not infrequently, a church was consecrated with considerable inside work still to be finished.

With foreman and crew hired, quarry selected, and delivery of materials contracted for, Neumann would lay out the site. Now the heavy construction began. After trenching, foundation ashlar was set. For walls and vaults, Neumann worked with a few standard options, decided specifics on the basis of client demand, budget, size, and significance of the undertaking. Wall construction was ashlar or rubble. The Schönborn chapel (Fig. 27), Gössweinstein (Fig. 51), Vierzehnheiligen (Fig. 133), Maria-Limbach (Fig. 119), for instance, employ the former, Münsterschwarzach (Fig. 45) and Neresheim (Fig. 151) the latter. Ashlar walls were finished inside by means of brick or rubble surface, or were covered with plaster. Stone blocks would be finished crudely at the quarry to reduce transportation weight. A stonecutters' hut, set up on site to provide final shaping and smoothing, remained active through the winter to ensure adequate material for the summer building campaign. In contrast, rubble wall construction, even if strengthened by ashlar corners, could be raised faster and at less expense. Irregular stones were built up into a solid wall by using generous amounts of mortar to accommodate the heterogeneous material. In such operations, door and window apertures could be framed in cut stone, although, as at Gaibach (Pl. VII) and Kitzingen (Pl. IV), this was not always the case.

With walls up, a specialized master (*Zimmermeister*) began the wooden framework for the roof (Fig. 16). This locked into the walls, spanning the area between them, and often was put up before work began on the vault.[13]

Complex, ingenious, and sophisticated, these constructions appear to our eyes as artworks in their own right (Fig. 155). If the vault was to be low set, this timberwork could be arranged as a truss placed on the wall tops. But often vaults crested high above the wall top; then the timberwork had to be umbrellaed over the curvature of the vault. The two systems could be fitted snugly together, leaving a narrow crawl space between them. Unless the roof is being replaced, it is physically difficult to study the timberwork in these buildings. The great cartwheel of wood above the crossing dome of Kitzingen and the low-slung saucer nestled over the Käppele crossing indicate a range of solutions.[14]

For construction of the dome, two basic techniques were current in South Germany—brick shells and lath and plaster units. To construct the first, centering, or wooden formwork in the shape of the vault to be built, was assembled in place as the mold for the vault. On it, large bricks[15] were laid in horizontal rows in thick mortar beds (Figs. 76, 82). Starting at the dome base, the bricks were arranged row upon row to create the shape of the vault, gradually closing the open space toward the center. The shell of Neumann's vaults was one brick thick with deeper ribs disposed over it in an imprecise way.[16] One and a half brick lengths in width, one of the ribs followed the long axis of the vault, with others branching off from it at approximately 45 degrees, creating a herringbone pattern. The ribs do not provide structural support for the unit in the manner of a Gothic rib vault, but are laid on top of the shell, often in wavy, irregular fashion, presumably as stiffeners. The bottom third of the vault was usually strengthened by an extra layer, two bricks in depth, establishing a solid base, and on occasion an iron band was wrapped around the shell two-thirds of the way up. This procedure was varied sometimes by the use of tuff for the upper sections in order to reduce weight. The vaults at Vierzehnheiligen are primarily tuff blocks irregularly arranged on the centering and clamped together by iron pieces; mortar was poured over the whole, producing a crude form of reinforced concrete. A similar technique was intended for Neresheim.[17] At Maria-Limbach, rubble was used in constructing the vaults.

By avoiding cut-stone vaults in his buildings, Neumann sided with a technique that was familiar, uncomplicated, inexpensive, and quickly built. Stone block of proper quality, quarried and transported to the site, was eliminated. The precise calculation of stone carving, the highly specialized masons, the time and expense required to produce the vaults of a Mansart or Borromini were unnecessary. Inexpensive brick was arranged into the shape of a vault with a minimum of fuss,[18] and the results were fireproof, stone vaults. Centering was necessary [19] but represented the most elaborate piece of construction on the site. Otherwise ladders and simple lifts provided vertical transportation for workers and materials.

Another advantage of the system: it required little technology. German treatise writers were indifferent to construction apparatus. The prolific author, Joseph Furttenbach, proud of his ingenious technical solutions for the stage, discussed no building machinery; Johann Wilhelm, another author concerned with more technical aspects of the architectural scene, illustrated a crane and pulleys (Fig. 17).

Finally, the system was marvelously flexible. Oddly shaped, fragmented, and bent vaults required only centering as preparation. The brick and mortar shells could be assembled rapidly, and they hardened in a few weeks, when finishing plaster could be applied over the inner surface.

It could even be argued that this process represents an effective relationship between material, method, and product. Take, for example, the three-dimensionally curved vault edges at Nere-sheim (Fig. 150). These define the central dome and distinguish it from the oval transepts at either side. The torsion arch describes a complex, solid geometrical figure which, from both a mathematical and aesthetic point of view, is a highly sophisticated statement. As a design on paper and as built construction, however, this form was simple and direct. On paper, Neumann placed ovals tangent to one another. To construct this project, arches were cut out of the crossing and transept centerings, and the two units joined. The masons then built up bricks and mortar on these forms. When the shell hardened and the centering was removed, the torsion arch resulted as the line of juncture between ovals—the complex consequence of a straightforward approach.

Brick vaults had a long and venerable pedigree in South Germany.[20] The Romanesque cathedral in Würzburg used them, and they are found often during the following centuries. Indeed, they were apparently so obvious and traditional that no German architectural theoretician discussed vaulting. Some writers devoted entire tracts to the wooden support systems for roofs,[21] which posed a compelling problem for the time, and a variety of fascinating solutions were demonstrated, with detailed methods for construction. Even Sturm could not resist displaying his expertise, noting that he was unable to gain access to Parisian church roofs to understand them sufficiently, so that his examples derive from German work.[22] In blatant contrast, the construction of vaults (and, for that matter, walls as well) was neglected. In his quest for encyclopedic completeness, Sturm made an initial stab at the problem, prefacing his remarks with a lament that no one else has written on the matter.[23]

At this time in South Germany, the alternative to brick vaults was lath and plaster units. These required a wooden construction in the shape of the vault, which was finished with a plaster surface (Fig. 18). Light in weight and largely free of problems of statics, these units were placed on a ring base, which in turn required support at only a few points. Pieces of the vault could be dropped into the space below or cut away above the ring base. The first use of the technique is Johann Jakob Herkomer's Benedictine church, St. Mang in Füssen, begun in 1701. Why this system was employed here is not clear, since the piers are sufficient to support stone vaults. It was not until the 1730s that lath and plaster vaults came into their own. The technique was used by some of the great masters of this generation, such as the Asam

brothers, Peter Thumb, and J. M. Fischer. The aesthetic consequences of this procedure can be demonstrated at Die Wies, where
the Zimmermanns carved away and hollowed out the lower zones
of the vaults to produce a hallucinatory effect in terms of stone
technology (Fig. 19). Neumann never accepted this method. He
prided himself on the use of "stone" vaulting, presumably due to
its strength and fireproof qualities, perhaps because it still represented to him the grand tradition in design.[24]

Construction of a building's fabric constituted but one step
toward completion of a church. "Pure" architecture was considered unfinished; the necessary liturgical furniture (such as altars,
pulpit, seating, baptismal font, faldstools) was needed to complete
an architectural space. Other major elements were frescoes, statuary, stucco, gilding, metalwork, and color (Fig. 20). The complex,
multifaceted nature of a "completed" enterprise raises an important aesthetic issue.

In the 20th century, architecture as the composition of
space is generally distinguished from "decorative" elements included within this space.[25] Recognizing the art of architecture as
self-sufficient, a range of relations between "architecture" and
"decoration" is posited: they may be placed passively side by side,
they may be integrated, or they may be arranged so that one effectively overwhelms or masks the other. The possibility of such a
distinction was foreign to the taste of much of the 18th century.
For artist teams like the Asam or Zimmermann brothers, architecture meant responsibility for everything from foundation ashlar
to stucco gilding. Neumann's attitude toward this issue was similar.

In many of Neumann's works, the "decorative" completion
of a church required as much or more time than its construction.
Gössweinstein (Fig. 55) was built in five years from 1730–34, but
the interior was still being worked on in 1745; Heusenstamm
(Fig. 66) was put up in 1739–40, and was not yet complete when
consecrated in 1756; two years were required to erect the fabric
of the Schönborn chapel in Würzburg (Pl. II), but eight to finish
the interior.

How did completion take place? Usually the architect, in
consultation with the patron, decided what and how much was to
be included, and where these elements were to be located (de-
cisions such as stucco around the fresco fields and on the window
frames, gilding on the fresco frames). For each medium a specialized master was selected. This person priced the job, and if the
bid was accepted he began work. A case in point demonstrates the

mechanics of the process. For the Gössweinstein main altar (Fig. 57), Neumann designed an imposing, six-column unit that would fill out the apse and dramatically resolve the processional impact of the church. Monies were scarce however, and Friedrich Karl suggested an altar without columns in the shape of a tabernacle. Neumann's assistant, J. M. Küchel, was entrusted with the new project, and during the summer of 1737, Friedrich Karl sent him on a trip to Munich, Vienna, Prague, Dresden, and Berlin to study similar altar types. Early in 1738 Küchel's design was approved. He then sketched it in full size onto the apse wall of the church to ascertain the effectiveness of the design for that specific place. Incorporating the necessary adjustments of scale, a model was prepared for Friedrich Karl's approval. He requested certain changes: the four cherubs were to be replaced with the symbols of the Evangelists, the statues of Saints Borromeo and Otto, located on either side of the altar, were to be set farther back, the major statues were to be 8 *Schuhe* (a measurement, almost equivalent to 1 foot or 30.5 cms.) tall and finished in white so that they could be seen clearly from the church entrance, and so on. After the modified model was approved, contracts were made with specialists for each medium, such as sculptor, stuccoer, marbler. Not all of Friedrich Karl's proposed changes were incorporated into the finished product, however. As work progressed, modifications continued to be made. After four years, the altar was complete. Construction of the entire church, including the two-tower facade, had taken five years.

Neumann was no exception to these traditions. He presented his buildings to sculptors and stuccoers, painters and gilders, woodworkers and metalsmiths to receive their efforts.[26] He was extremely successful at recruiting appropriate talent and organizing the work programs of these many individuals. Neumann possessed a keen sense not only for native ability, but also for an artisan's inherent sensitivity toward architecture. His letters often report on the progress of his hiring efforts. He also stressed the importance of managing this army of independent workers: of his work at the Residenz, he noted that "one of the most important matters is organizing everything." [27] During the process of "decorating" a church, Friedrich Karl discussed matters of form and content directly with the individual artists involved. He rarely received Neumann's opinion on interior work, assigning him the task of coordinator.[28]

Neumann's personal responses to the aesthetics of other

media varied from project to project. On occasion he included a considerable amount of "ornamentation," orchestrating materials into integral components of the design, as in his Langheim project (Figs. 109–111). Yet he also considered his architecture effective without the addition of other art forms. In this he is unusual, revealing a deeply rooted concern for pure construction. When confronted at Gaibach (Pl. VII), due to a restricted budget, with a choice of stone vaults and no decoration, or less expensive wooden vaults and the use of decoration, he chose the former without hesitation. But Langheim and Gaibach are extreme instances; more commonly, Neumann created a space assuming that many artists would contribute to it. Vierzehnheiligen (Fig. 131, Pl. XI), for example, was designed with clean surfaces intended for the stucco, fresco, and statuary of others. This work does not transform the basic spatial purposes of the church, though it does create a richer, more demanding space. The absence of the Shrine of the Fourteen Helper Saints (*Nothelfer*) in his Vierzehnheiligen projects is even more demonstrative of this situation. The shrine served the supreme purpose of the church. Neumann recognized it as a prime element of the interior, and he focused the architecture of the entire building toward this spot, but he assigned its design to another.[29] This is all the more striking, since he was actively engaged in the design of altars.

The altars in Neumann churches can be grouped into different categories.[30] Some are constructions that fit into niches and are minimally responsive to the surroundings (Holzkirchen; Schönborn chapel in Würzburg, Figs. 21–23); others are located more assertively on high platforms and include monumental, free-standing sculptural pieces (Kitzingen, Pl. IV; Heusenstamm, Fig. 66). But the type of altar Neumann designed most frequently consisted of columns with a baldachin-like central unit and spreading wings (Figs. 43, 63). We find this first fully developed in the cathedral of Worms (1738), with forerunners at Münsterschwarzach (1727), the Würzburg court church (1734), Gössweinstein (1734–36), and with major variations for Altspeyer (1739), Vierzehnheiligen (1744), Brühl (1745), Trier (1745), Bruchsal (1746), Neresheim (1749), and in a 1746 project (S.E. 236). These altars have a powerful effect on a church interior. Neumann conceived them as small, open structures, and arranged them to reiterate and synthesize the surrounding architecture—a responsiveness that makes them a focus for prayer and contemplation.[31]

From these projects, it is evident that Neumann was fascinated by the architectonic concept of the altar. To complete each one, he let others design the required sculpture, painting, and decorations. As a result, altars subscribing to very similar concepts, such as those for Brühl and Trier, may possess very different qualities; Johann Wolfgang van der Auvera's completion makes the former jaunty and pointy, while for the latter, Ferdinand Tietz employed languid and rounded forms. This process parallels Neumann's design procedure for his churches, for which individual, specialized craftsmen were in large part responsible for the overall decorative effect. We have therefore come full circle, and with their setting established, we may turn to a consideration of the churches themselves.

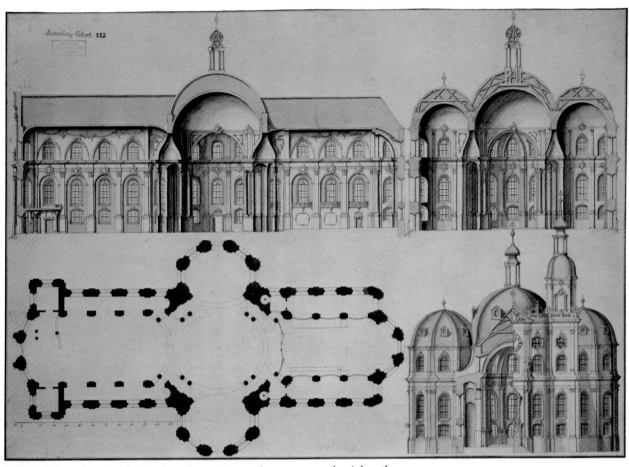

I. Neresheim, plan, longitudinal section, cross section, cross section/elevation
(Würzburg, Mainfränkisches Museum, S.E. 112).

II. Würzburg, palace church, view to entrance.

III. Bruchsal, view to choir, altar designed by Neumann.

IV. Kitzingen, detail of choir.

V. Kitzingen, exterior.

VI. Gössweinstein, crossing, vault.

VII. Gaibach, view to choir, altar by Antonio Bossi, 1747–48.

VIII. Neresheim, crossing.

IX. Neresheim, detail of nave elevation.

X. Werneck, main altar to right, side altar to left: stucco and main altar by
Antonio Bossi, side altar by Materno Bossi, 1780.

XI. Vierzehnheiligen, view to choir, stucco by Johann Michael Feichtmayr,
Franz Zaver, Johann Georg Übelhör, 1764–71: frescoes by Giuseppe Appiani,
1764–70: altar designed by Johann Jacob Michael Küchel.

III.
The
Twenties and
Thirties

Historians of Neumann's architecture have attempted to impose a logical development on the churches, postulating that his work progressed throughout his life toward the grandiose culminations of Vierzehnheiligen and Neresheim. To align his designs into a chronologically determined linear development is to deny them their individuality, variety, and vitality for the dubious gain of abstract order. Accordingly, each building is studied here on its own terms, on the basis of its specific design strategy. From these individual monographs, a synthetic view of Neumann's architecture can be brought into focus.

In the churches, Neumann's primary and consuming interest was the making of space. The exterior shells are plain, with little attention paid to them. Documentation for the buildings confirms this impression: in the drawings, plans and sections overwhelmingly outnumber exterior elevations. Moreover, renderings for exteriors always appear late in the design process, after the interior has been thoroughly worked out. When Neumann writes about his buildings, it is to report on their progress and on what is happening inside—scarcely a word survives about the outside shell.

This attitude relates to a long-standing tradition. From

Early Christian times on, the interior of the church was important as an indication of the heavenly paradise on earth, as a vessel for the celebration of the mass.[1] Many 17th-century architects—that is, the generations immediately preceding Neumann's—attached importance to the church exterior, but interiors remained their prime concern. Because architecture to Neumann meant space composition and all its ramifications—movement, unity, light—the discussion of his churches here and in Chapter IV addresses primarily the architect's spatial concerns. This approach is dictated by the nature of the work and offers the most informative understanding of it.[2]

During the 1720s and 30s, Neumann broached a range of themes. He formulated several decisive statements of a high order, others were merely satisfactory, a few remained pedestrian. Neumann's first church project, the Schönborn chapel attached to Würzburg cathedral, is the logical starting point. The history of this design reveals both the subordinate position the architect still held and his already keen creative instincts. His second, less ambitious undertaking, Holzkirchen, will be considered in relation to the later centralized designs of Bamberg and Bruchsal. The Latin cross churches of Münsterschwarzach and Gössweinstein constitute his third and fourth efforts; Trier and Heusenstamm, later but less demanding longitudinal interpretations, can reasonably be grouped with them. The ovoid spaces of the Residenz court church and the later, abbreviated version of this design, the Werneck court chapel, round out Neumann's work on church design during these years.

The Schönborn
Chapel
at Würzburg

Walter Boll chronicled the history of the Schönborn chapel (Figs. 21–23) almost fifty years ago and his scholarship remains definitive in many respects.[3] But he characterized the final design as "impersonal," an assemblage by various architects, none of whom determined the character of the building decisively. Today this situation can be defined more precisely.

In 1718 Johann Philipp Franz considered attaching to the north transept arm of the cathedral a replacement of the ruined Crispinus chapel, to serve as a mausoleum and memorial for the Schönborn. Two pedantic projects were submitted, one by Georg Bayer, the other by Georg Hennicke. No action was taken, since the cathedral chapter withheld approval for building until Johann Philipp Franz was elected Prince-Bishop in 1719. When the idea was resurrected the following year, this time with Johann Philipp

Franz in a position of authority, the earlier proposals appear to have been forgotten. Lothar Franz's personal architect, Maximilian von Welsch, now took charge of the operation. During the winter of 1720–21, he designed a building that established the basic format and size of all later variations: a circular domed space with rectangular chapels placed on the cross axis (Fig. 24). Presumably after construction stopped for the winter, and certainly before April 1722, Neumann suggested a reorganization of the interior which decisively altered the internal space (Fig. 25). He inserted four pairs of columns into the circular area and joined them with torsion arches [4] in order to create the pendentive zone for the dome. This translated the circular plan into the elevation: columns, the horizontal line of the entablature and the stilted elements above this, the torsion arches, the pendentives, and the base of the dome conform to the same curved shape (Fig. 26). The result is an independent, tholos-like form, extensively open to, yet clearly distinguished from, the surrounding spaces and wall.[5] The curving outer wall that defines the ancillary areas bulges around the tholos, remaining physically distinct from it. The torsion arches cut away the vaulting over the ovoid side spaces, framing the round shape of the dome. The circular domed unit is inserted into a continuous shell, one form within another, like a bolt slid into its casing.

Although there is an initial resemblance, the projects by von Welsch and Neumann are very different conceptually. Von Welsch designed a single space defined by continuous, undulating walls; Neumann located one circular unit within a second larger and different spatial configuration. The centralizing impact of this independent tholos remains unquestionably sovereign and is convincingly integrated with the whole interior. Not only does it open to the surrounding spaces, but articulation (entablature, pilasters, columns), decoration, and coloring are consistent throughout. Neumann holds distinction and unity in dynamic balance.

Within this unusual space, lighting remains conventional. The dome apex opens into a lantern. Three arched windows are carved into the bottom of the vaults over the ancillary spaces, one at each end and one in the middle; another opens the wall above the side altar, and a similar unit is located in the west wall. There is a modest oculus above the main entrance. This fenestration illuminates the chapel sufficiently, though without distinction. Having constructed the outer fabric, von Welsch determined this conventional fenestration; Neumann's unusual internal interpretation generates a vivid contrast.

Standing at the forefront of Neumann's sacred work, the Schönborn chapel reveals characteristic procedures and attitudes. First, confronted with a large number of givens, Neumann nevertheless realized an individual interpretation. The patron had insisted on a domed structure finished internally with marble veneer. As carried out, von Welsch designed the outline of the structure, several hands were involved in designing the marble cladding, yet the basic character of the internal space was created by Neumann. Secondly, a number of buildings in Italy, France, and Bohemia may have suggested this interpretation to him.[6] The list of possible sources reflects his broad acquaintance with European architecture, yet only the most generalized relations to any specific prototype can be ascertained. The chapel remains distinctive and personal. And finally, the aspect of the design that intrigued Neumann was the interior. Though located at a strategic urban focal point between cathedral and Residenz, the external fabric of the structure did not prod him into action; it is by von Welsch alone (Fig. 27). He did feel challenged by spatial problems, however, and here his response was imaginative, unorthodox, consequent, and mature.

A parallel with the early work of Borromini comes to mind. While still employed by Maderno, albeit working quite independently, Borromini changed his master's plan for S. Ignazio (Fig. 28). He hollowed out the pier corners and inserted pairs of freestanding columns, so that space—and not the continuity of wall—became the prime component of the interior. This reversal of traditional values in architecture was pursued in his later work. One hundred years later, also within the context of another master's work, Neumann introduced pairs of freestanding columns as a major design change, creating an interior controlled by space. He also was to follow this concern in his own architecture.

The Schönborn chapel also evokes Bernini's S. Andrea al Quirinale (Fig. 29) by employing a short major and a long cross axis, in a reversal of initial expectations. Bernini tempered this opposition by excluding the side chapels from the axial tensions: his cross axis is stopped by the piers of the central space. Neumann exaggerates the composition by broadly opening this cross axis into ancillary spaces. But these oval areas are placed parallel to the entrance-altar axis, emphasizing this orientation as well. And finally, the centrality of the area is marked vividly by the tholos, which contains the altar and into which the main entrance opens.

The Priory Church at Holzkirchen

The priory church at Holzkirchen is the first project Neumann pursued by himself from start to finish.[7] Johann Dientzenhofer was given the commission originally in 1723, but no construction was begun. When he died three years later, Prince-Bishop Hutten (1724–29), Johann Philipp Franz's successor in Würzburg, transferred the operation to Neumann. Dientzenhofer had proposed two types of centralized designs in his Holzkirchen projects. In one a circular unit was expanded by curved ancillary spaces on the cross axis (Fig. 30); in the other a four-leaf-clover plan, lengthened in the entrance-altar axis and narrowed in the cross axis, employed torsion arches to establish various spatial figures (Fig. 31). All the proposals were heavily indebted to Bohemian work of the preceding decade. Neumann introduced a different concept. He designed a single, cylindrical, domed interior shaped on the outside as a slightly irregular octagon (Figs. 32–34). Eight columns, barely engaged in the wall, rise beneath a strongly projecting entablature and hemispherical dome. One large window opens the wall between each two columns, while four oculi are inserted into the lower half of the dome on the main axis. An organ tribune frames the entrance, opposite which the altar stands on a raised platform. Limiting himself to this modest collection of architectural elements, Neumann enriches the circular form by rhythm and contrast.

The eight windows are set into wider and narrower areas, and contain respectively concave and splayed frames. They establish a rhythm of shallow, wide, curved zones, and deep, narrow, angular zones. The figure of a Greek cross is implicit in this arrangement, further emphasizing the entrance-altar axis. Vertically, the interior is divided into two halves, with the height of the order equal to that of entablature and dome (Fig. 34). Set on high pedestals, the columns stand half before the entablature rather than solidly under it. This labile relationship is underlined by the vigorous projection of the entablature into the interior. In addition, the dome, rising from a stilting band above the entablature, is stepped back so far that its base lies just outside the order. These shifts, obvious to the eye even if their exact nature can be established only by measurement, dissipate the traditional notion of columns firmly supporting a dome.

By arranging the elevation in this manner, giving each architectural element a high degree of independence, Neumann creates a collage of distinct, sharp-edged units united by rhythms and contrasts (Fig. 35). The notion of separable components, proposed by the Schönborn tholos, again emerges strongly, though the vocabulary is different and the spatial vision less adventurous.

The lighting at Holzkirchen remains simple. Large windows open the walls extensively, and four *oeil-de-boeuf* windows —and possibly a lantern [8]—are set in the dome, filling the interior with ample, clear light. This constant brightness produces luminous shadow areas that accent the plasticity of curving and projecting frames and the round column shafts. Directness and regularity of light sources, a brightly lit interior, and gleaming sculptural elements will continue to fascinate Neumann.

The Palace Church at Bamberg

He experimented with two other centralized buildings during these decades, one at Bamberg, the other in Bruchsal. For the first, the court church in the Bamberg Residenz, a 1730 project is lost and a second project of 1733 remained unrealized.[9] Embedded mostly within the palace, the exterior of the building would have remained of little importance. Since only one plan survives for the project (Fig. 36), the intended interior and vaulting cannot be established with certainty.[10] This plan shows a dominating circular core from which four rectangular units project to the cardinal points. Equal in size, they serve as vestibule, choir, and transept arms. These angular spaces, breaking out through the walls, seem at first glance to weaken the circular form. But the vaulting presumably offered a vigorous counterforce to these extensions. Supported by eight columns, the round cupola appears to be arranged within the circular church like a space-creating tholos. This unit would establish the key impression of the interior; its effectiveness would be further emphasized by windows set into the wall behind the columns. The vision of an open form (tholos) placed within a zone of space and light (ancillary spaces and windows) is clearly implied in the plan. Neumann used similar concepts in his designs for the crossing units of Münsterschwarzach and Etwashausen.

The basic compositional elements of Holzkirchen and Bamberg are the same: a circular core, eight columns surmounted by a vault, and a cross axis worked into this centralized space. But in the latter church, the columns are freestanding and grouped into four pairs, heightening the plasticity of the interior. This is complemented by the much more robustly contrasted cross and circular forms, creating a space charged with movement. The deeper secondary areas and the independence of the freestanding tholos would certainly have increased the richness of the lighting as well. In this way Neumann shifted his interpretation decisively. The consistent unity of Holzkirchen is an effective contrast to the complex unity of Bamberg. The circle-cross theme is interpreted once with reserve and subtlety, once overtly and with dynamic movement.

St. Peter at Bruchsal   The second centralized church is St. Peter in Bruchsal. By far the largest building in this group, it is also a design with inexplicable qualities. The plan (Fig. 37) proposes voluminous spaces charged with powerful axes and dynamic counterpoint, yet the interior (Pl. III) is papery and passive. Window frames, entablature, and moldings are all flat. Large niches in the arms do not gouge out mass, but fold back effortlessly. The vaults (Fig. 40) are presented as thin sheets, and the dome is perched weightlessly over the crossing, its springing point and light sources hidden from sight. In short, a Neumann design appears to have undergone a quixotic transformation in construction, resulting in a structure that is not what one imagines it ought to be. To address this paradox, we will first discuss the characteristics of the church, and then consider its history.

The Greek cross plan of Bruchsal has arms of approximately equal size.[11] These open out from the domed crossing to the polygonal terminations. Squarish towers to the west, and two-story oratories in the east, occupy the outside corners between arms. Inside, the crossing corners are beveled to a 45° angle, producing narrow faces which rise through an abbreviated entablature into pendentives (Pl. III). These are surmounted by a hemispherical dome without lantern, substantially larger in diameter than the "supporting" pendentive ring. As a result, the dome springs from behind the pendentives, actually from a point outside the crossing corners altogether (Figs. 41, 42). The dome "base" is opened by eight large windows, made invisible from almost every point within the church by the protruding pendentives.

Broad arches separate crossing from arms (Fig. 42). Barrel vaults terminating in groined half-domes cover the latter. In each arm two monumental niches stretch from the floor high into the vault. All windows are the same height and shape. The floor level of the altar arm rises two steps above that of the others, and the altar stands on a platform of three additional steps. An organ balcony frames the entrance opposite the altar.

Axes and the particulars of wall and vault articulation introduce persuasive life into this framework. The wider entrance-altar arms are played off against the narrower units of the cross axis (Fig. 37). The former develop spatially from entrance to altar: one passes beneath the low organ balcony into the entrance arm with its broadly billowing niches to the crossing. Here altars placed against the beveled corners to the east lead into the choir, where a niched wall proceeds to the raised high altar.

In contrast, the cross arms are devoid of axial development. Nothing specifically draws the spectator into them. They mirror one another as contained, static spaces.

This distinction is further intensified by the niches in each axis. Those of the altar-entrance arms are broad and deep, set basically in the middle of the arm, and emphasized by a window. In the transept arms, the niches are narrower and less deep, set close to the crossing and clearly separated from the window area. The contrast between the more spacious and the more lean, between the wide and the narrow, between a self-lit and an unlit unit, between a form located centrally within the arm and one set at the beginning, establishes a counterpoint which further enriches the distinction between arms. Rising through the entire elevation and well into the vault, the niches bind together these areas which are otherwise distinguished by a modest entablature. They create a vertical balance to the horizontals of the entablature and the uniform height and placement of the windows.

Within this activity of axes and counterpoint, the crossing, central to every Greek cross church, is not forsaken (Pl. III). Though beveled, the crossing corners do not open easily into the arms. Three niches placed one above the other draw the eye upward in a rapid rhythm, establishing decisive vertical accents.

As the spectator's glance passes to the dome, the forceful dynamics that existed below are dramatically altered (Fig. 41). Illuminated largely by hidden sources and rising from an invisible base, the dome seems to float miraculously above the church. Elsewhere the articulation is firm, direct, and clearly lit; then the visitor discovers this hovering shell. The climactic emphasis of the crossing is achieved by introducing this unexpected note into the composition, vividly stressing the interior's fulcrum.

The history of Neumann's involvement with St. Peter is problematic. The church replaced a Gothic structure of the early 14th century (Fig. 39). Prince-Bishop Damian Hugo von Schönborn, who sponsored the undertaking, apparently was considering erecting a new church circa 1736.[12] When most of the old building was destroyed, 22 March 1738, Neumann had already designed a new project.[13] The work of clearing the site lasted into the summer of 1739; construction began in the spring of 1740 under the supervision of contractor Johann Georg Stahl, though the official cornerstone ceremony occurred only on 26 March 1742. Structurally complete by late 1746, the interior was finished during the next decades.

Documentation indicates that Neumann submitted a project for the church and observed the initial stages of work. In 1738, he watched while the defective parts of the old building were dynamited; in 1739 and 1740 he visited Bruchsal to confer with the foreman, Johann Georg Stahl. He did not return there until 1746 when the church was complete. In brief, he could have supervised only the very start of construction. Regrettably, no visual material from Neumann's office survives for the undertaking. The building contains qualities foreign to Neumann's oeuvre: the papery nature of the walls, the large niches, the stiff articulation of the crossing corners, the illusionism of the dome. The vaults are lath and plaster, a method Neumann never accepted. On the other hand, the axial dynamics, the dramatic nature of progression, and the basic concept of plan record Neumann's sensibilities.

In the absence of further evidence, a definitive solution to these contradictions is not possible. Yet a scenario may be suggested. Neumann may have submitted a design which became the basis for the undertaking. Local talent modified this project (the surviving drawings for St. Peter are not by Neumann, yet were done before construction began) and Stahl supervised construction of the building without on-site consultation with Neumann. He acknowledged local variations and interpreted and adjusted the design. The plans, for example, do not reveal how high and in what manner the niches were to be terminated, or how the entablature was to look. The crossing could be simplified. Lath and plaster vaults might appeal due to lower cost and simplified structural procedures. The consequences would be a Neumann building with qualities unlike Neumann's work—in short, St. Peter as we experience it today.

From the exterior, Neumann suggests a basilica with a two-tower facade (Fig. 37). Although the towers are placed in the corners between nave and crossing, and consequently well behind the elaborately articulated facade, the higher roofs of nave, crossing, and choir establish an axis that dominates the lower and smaller roofs of the cross arms. This longitudinal sequence of facade, towers, and roofs alludes to a basilical format when the building is seen as a whole from afar. By establishing these expectations on the exterior, the impact of the Greek cross plan is heightened when the visitor enters the building.

The detour through Neumann's centralized churches of the twenties and thirties led us to a project of 1738, chronologically

The Benedictine Monastery Church at Münsterschwarzach

far beyond our starting point. We now return to Neumann's second independent design after the modest Holzkirchen, the Benedictine monastery church of Münsterschwarzach.

In 1821, less than eighty years after its consecration, a twenty-year process of leveling the church (Fig. 45) and monastery buildings was begun as a consequence of Napoleon's destruction of the Holy Roman Empire, officially initiated on 25 February 1803. The *Reichsdeputationshauptschluss* of this date eliminated, among other things, all the ecclesiastical states in Germany (with the exception of the Electorate of Mainz), dragging down imperial monasteries and dispersing their wealth among secular powers.

The cornerstone for Münsterschwarzach had been laid in 1727.[14] With this design, coming at the outset of his career and when Neumann was forty years old,[15] he asserted his enormous creative abilities, producing an edifice of colossal size and aesthetic conviction. The design of Münsterschwarzach can be studied in the projects and views of the razed building that remain in six plans, twelve elevations, a wooden model, and two engravings printed for the 1743 consecration ceremony. In his excellent monograph on the church, P. Salesius Hess investigates this material meticulously. He arranges the drawings in a sequence which he feels illustrates the development of Neumann's design. This passes from a modest dome without lantern and contained within the roof, through a series culminating in a huge dome on pendentives recorded in the consecration engravings. Postsecularization material confirms that when built the building corresponded basically to the engravings.[16]

Illustrated in the engravings is an immense church consisting of a two-tower facade containing the vestibule, a four-bay nave, crossing and transept arms, and a two-bay choir terminated by a narrower apse (Figs. 46–49). Externally, the facade is enriched by a tall, tower-like lantern located above the steep profile of the crossing dome, and by a single tower rising above the apse (this is Neumann's first use of an apse tower, which he was to work with in some later churches as well). These verticals are played off against the massive forms of the elevation: a two-story facade combining a rich assemblage of pilasters, engaged and freestanding columns, paired pilasters on the aisle flanks, and solid, curved buttresses along the clearstory. The looming presence of these massive and simple forms is revealed in Müller's 1825 lithograph: a monumental exterior announcing the stately majesty of the Münsterschwarzach interior.

Nave and choir bays employ massive wall piers joined by arcades and faced with paired pilasters placed on monumental pedestals. A strong entablature, projecting over the orders, is surmounted by a stilting band. Broad ribs curve over the semicircular barrel vault, while wide lunettes with steep profiles span the entire area between them, opening the vault extensively. Chapels located between the wall piers are linked by a narrow passageway, which continues through the western crossing piers, curving into the transept arms. Large windows, commencing at pedestal height and rising to the entablature, constitute most of the outer wall in each chapel.

The faces of the crossing piers curve back according to the radius of a circle drawn from the crossing's center (Fig. 46). Paired, engaged columns on monumental pedestals are placed against these piers. Above their projecting entablature and stilting band, pendentives rise vertically, maintaining the circular figure of the crossing. The four pendentives come together in a ring at a height above that of the nave and choir barrel vaults. Stepped back from the molding of this ring, a dome with steep profile lifts to a large lantern.

The spacious, rectangular transept arms are articulated by pilasters and columns on monumental pedestals and surmounted by ribbed barrel vaults similar to those in the nave and choir. Elevation and clearstory windows of the same size and shape as those in the nave puncture walls and vault.

The articulation of the two choir bays is like that of their nave counterparts, except that balconies, supported by walls running between piers, are included beneath the windows. A small apse curves out from the straight east-end wall. The corners where this wall joins the bay pier are marked by single, freestanding columns.

As revealed in the engravings (Figs. 46, 47), the space at Münsterschwarzach was similar in spirit to such huge structures as the Basilica of Constantine or St. Peter. Rising 12 feet, the pedestals alone would dwarf the spectator. One would have gazed up at them as if prostrate on the floor, along the towering columns they support, and into the cavernous interior spaces. From the vestibule, progress toward the altar would have been beneath a processional avenue of monumental arches, with the powerful verticals of pedestals, pilasters, *ressauts,* and broad ribs arranged with imposing majesty along the length of Münsterschwarzach. The rhythmic advance of these elements expands into the stately grandeur of the crossing before the choir bays lead to the altar.

The vertical thrust of the arches is tempered by horizontals. Entablature and a tripartite division of the pedestals create effective horizontal bands drawn about the entire interior. They bind together and moderate the robust verticals. These accents are further augmented by a strong rise of the projecting verticals and the fall (or recess from this plane) of chapels, arcade, entablature, and lunettes with clearstory windows. The systole, diastole of this pulse, based on the verticals but progressing down the nave with the horizontals, intensifies the dynamics of the interior.

Assembled of standard components in elevation and vaults, the resulting interior appears unconventional (Fig. 49). In balance with plastic mass—verticals, entablature, vaults—stand the imposing spatial shaft of the chapels and the volume of the lunettes. These plastic qualities are emphasized by the huge chapel windows which practically eliminate an outer solid plane, filling the depth of the wall with light.[17] This is no longer an architecture of solid, continuous mass and contained space. A muscular supportive framework replaces the masonry, defining enormous, cave-like spaces. Light spills through the voluminous chapels and lunettes, further dematerializing substance. Nave, choir, and transept arms are no longer articulated by walls in the traditional sense; Neumann has interpreted them instead as deep, luminous reliefs of monumental dimensions.

The crossing rises to a powerful climax within the interior. Its elements all subscribe to the same circular form and are detached from adjoining piers and arches. Pedestals and entablature step in from the pier behind, which the columns barely touch. An indentation distinguishes stilting and pendentives from the adjoining arches. Contained within a circle and separated from surrounding mass, this unit becomes an independent tholos set within the crossing. The steep dome gradually draws this cylinder closed. Entirely frescoed, the immense, smooth dome shell remains bright throughout its elevation, illuminated from below by four oculi set within lunettes located at its base and by a lantern of towering height that creates a magnificent climax for this imposing interior.

The grand and stately monumentality of Münsterschwarzach, its rich rhythms, space, and masonry, are composed with mastery and sophistication. Considering that he began this church only one year after Holzkirchen, it is all the more remarkable. Neumann would not return to this concept again.

The Holy Trinity Church at Gössweinstein

While Münsterschwarzach was in construction, Neumann began a second basilica based on a similar plan, the pilgrimage and parish church of the Holy Trinity in Gössweinstein.[18] Between 1715 and 1727 four architects had submitted projects which for one reason or another were never realized: J. L. Dientzenhofer, J. G. Christian, A. F. Freiherr von Ritter zu Grünstein, and Wenzell Berner. Neumann's project, begun possibly in 1729, but definitely complete by May 1730, has nothing in common with these. Instead, it reflects the far larger Münsterschwarzach. The Münsterschwarzach facade in S.E. 50, S.E. 70, and on the Munich model is similar to the Gössweinstein facade; the crossing vault depicted on S.E. 61 for Münsterschwarzach resembles the unit built at Gössweinstein, though the Gössweinstein plans all indicate a pendentive dome; in placing the order on high pedestals, Neumann alludes to a monumentalized interior at Gössweinstein. Yet, by and large, he addresses different considerations here: similar shells encase dissimilar interpretations.

Gössweinstein consists of a vestibule located between two facade towers, a two-bay nave, crossing and transept arms, and a choir with chancel bay and apse. Although a pilgrimage church, and therefore large enough to be visible from a distance, Gössweinstein is kept simple on the outside. The two-story facade (Fig. 50) is placed on a tall plinth. Two towers rise only one additional story to continue this planar quality; their verticality is established mostly by tall lanterns above domed roofs, and by beveled corners which somewhat reduce their width. Pilasters on the facade below the towers reinforce the vertical accent, but the decisive horizontals of plinth and entablatures effectively reduce its impact. Compared to the monumental, plastic, towering qualities of Münsterschwarzach, the Gössweinstein facade is flat and contained. The elevation of flanks and choir (Fig. 51), treated more simply with barely projecting pilasters, is topped by steep, unarticulated roofs.

Inside, a low-set organ balcony fills the vestibule, curving out from it into the western section of the nave (Figs. 52–55). Six-wall piers surmounted by a semicircular barrel vault constitute the nave. Proscenium-like arrangements, which consist of concave corners and vaulting bands, frame this space as a distinct unit. Flanking, shallow chapels are separated from the nave by arcades, piers, railings, and a rise in floor level. Physically excluding the visitor, these read as colossal niches, a space-containing elevation of several layers. A first plane is indicated by the monumental paired pilasters attached to each pier face, together with the barrel vault they support. The arcades, springing from a vertical wall band placed against the pier sides, establish a second plane. Behind these frames rise the monumental niches. The expansive, space-impregnated "wall" gives the nave an open and spacious feeling.

Wide arches springing from paired pilasters define the crossing to the east and west, narrow arches over single pilasters to the north and south (Fig. 54, Pl. VI). Between these sets of pilasters, the crossing piers are planed off to a 45° angle. Pendentives rise from these beveled corners to a shallow saucer dome that does not extend to the crossing arches, leaving the area between arches and pendentives filled out with triangular vault segments. A flat vault results. The shallow, tilting surfaces have the papery quality of folded, bent, and embossed cardboard.

The vaulting of the arms is treated differently (Fig. 56). Each arm is surmounted by a hemisphere rising from the circular wall. But these are cut away so extensively that they cover the area only partially. Large lunettes over the three windows of the wall slice away the dome base. And the dome, rather than running up to the crossing arch, as would be customary, is separated from it by raised, crescent-shaped vault segments. This hiatus continues down into the elevation, where a section of curved wall splits apart the pilasters supporting arch and dome. The result of these cuts and shifts is to create the impression of a double-layered vault. The fragmented sphere appears to be placed against a second, capping layer. Franz has observed and analyzed the use of a double-layered vault by Christoph Dientzenhofer at Brevnov,[19] where two layers run down the entire length of nave and choir, one alternating with the other. Neumann's interpretation here is similar, but on a smaller scale and within a circular unit.

There are allusions to layering in the arm elevations as well. Since the inner wall is semicircular and the outside polygonal, changes in wall thickness inevitably occur. Neumann exploits these contrasts by treating placement and framing of the central windows differently from the flanking pair. He further establishes the surfaces of the inner wall and pilasters attached to it as distinct layers. Springing from four pilasters framing the windows, the triangular vault sections between the lunettes look very much like pendentives. Closely tied to the dome, the pilasters thus continue that plane as a supporting frame, which is set against the unadorned, continuous inner surface of the wall. In sum, Neumann indicates a distinction between the outer and inner wall surfaces, and divides the inner boundary into separate layers.

The apse vaulting is similar to that of the arms (Fig. 57). But here a chancel bay stands between apse and crossing; wider than the apse, the barrel vault surmounting it is higher than the adjoining dome. Neumann joins these vaults directly to one another, again producing a double-layered effect. The chancel bay is stepped out from the apse in relation to its higher vault. An elaborate balcony masks the bottom half of the window set into the wall, adding a robust sculptural note to this area. The apse wall is separated into pilaster and wall layers as was the case in the transept arms.

Gössweinstein is a pilgrimage church dedicated to the Holy Trinity. Neumann designed the building to acknowledge this purpose. From the vestibule, the visitor experiences a peaceful, harmonious, radiant space (Fig. 55). The vaults, all about the same height, pass from entrance to altar as a continuous, gently undulating surface. Curving into the nave, the western crossing piers obscure the transept arms. Their concave elevation and pilaster articulation are repeated by the beveled corner of the eastern pier and its pilasters, binding different sections of the interior together optically and confirming the unified impression conveyed by the vaults. As one passes forward, this sense of totality disintegrates and the building separates into its functioning parts. Distinguished as a separate unit by its architecture, the nave affords the pilgrim a place where he can collect and prepare himself before attaining the final goal of his journey. Here, in the area of crossing, transept, and choir, the symbolism of the Trinity is everywhere manifest. The plan of this section is trilobed, with each lobe opened by three windows marked by a lunette; three altars, one in each lobe, give spiritual focus; the main altar is composed of three triangles; and so on. The articulation of this area also is intensified; the layering of vaults and elevations creates a distinguishing elaboration of forms. Employing not only more, but larger windows, this section is far brighter than the more reserved nave. Together with symbolic numbers, Neumann here expands the richness of forms and light in the church.

This detailed description of Gössweinstein may give the impression that it is stocked with a bewildering multiplicity of elements. The different vaults are an example. Three systems are employed: the barrel vaults of nave, monumental niches, and apse; the hemispheres of arms and apse; and the crossing vault of several cardboard-like planes—a variety further exaggerated by differences between the barrel vaults. The chancel bay vault is not as wide as that over the nave, and it has smaller lunettes. The niche vaults, placed at right angles to the others, are little more than broad bands. And finally, each of the barrel vaults subscribes to a different arch.

Yet what happens in fact? The three lobes containing the three main altars of the church are related by common vaults. Within these corresponding areas, the larger high altar is distinguished by the added space of chancel bay with its rich loggias. But the barrel vaults of this bay are nothing more than a development of a form inherent within the transept arms. If the arch of the arm crossing and the dome were pulled apart, the crescent-shaped vault segments presently separating the two units would become barrel vaults as in the chancel bay. These fragments and the barrel vault itself relate to the nave. They constitute the upper, continuous shell against which the hemispherical dome shells of the lobes are placed; thus, distinction is imposed upon the continuity of covering. The crossing is just as surely integrated into the whole. It is clearly set apart by its papery quality, tilting planes, and saucer dome, but its independence is minimized. The triangular sections are another variation of the different lunette shapes in the other vaults. Flat, rather than voluminous, the crossing opens generously to all sides, establishing a focus for the three altars placed in adjoining spaces without distracting from their importance.

This harmony of parts is complemented by the decoration of the interior. J. J. M. Küchel's altar and pulpit are the most elaborate elements in the church; the other altars are simpler, and the tonality and finishing of the walls and vaults are reserved. The elevation is white, the vaults and window jambs white stucco against a blue ground. Paintings in the vaults are restricted to smaller, contained fields (programs for the paintings, proposed in 1734 and 1768, were never realized, and the present work was done in 1928 as part of the 1913–28 restoration of the church). The result is a cool, quiet, unassuming decorative scheme that passively follows the lead of the architecture. The forms at Gössweinstein are complex, their interrelations subtle. There is nothing bombastic about the building. Its quiet interior is understated rather than dramatic and overt. The architecture of this church does not overwhelm or provide a dazzling finale for the pilgrim; it is not a place of exuberance and spectacle, but one that requires introspection and silent contemplation. Within the context of the jubilant architecture of South Germany, this interior provided an unusual pilgrimage goal; its architect was an explorer never hesitant to go his own way.

Though designed later, the last two longitudinal buildings from these decades—the parish churches at Trier and Heusenstamm—may reasonably be introduced here. Both of them are later than Münsterschwarzach, smaller, simpler in concept, and less interesting.

St. Paulin at Trier

The design of St. Paulin at Trier can be attributed to Neumann only with certain reservations. On 28 July 1733, he stopped in Trier en route to Luxembourg. Later, while in Koblenz, he gave instructions for a new church to the Augustine monk Joseph Walter. The cornerstone was laid 26 March 1734. Shortly thereafter the French occupied Trier, remaining until 1737; no construction was undertaken during this time. The church finally was erected between 1738 and 1743.[20]

Trier stands on the foundations of a Romanesque predecessor. The odd proportions of the facade (Fig. 58), slender and attenuated, are exaggerated by a single tower that not only rises high above narrow wings at either side, but also pushes forward, emphasizing its slenderness in relation to height. Moreover, the wings curve sharply from where they are attached to the tower, as if they were thrust back with force. The wings and the exterior nave and choir elevations are reminiscent, in their articulation, of work by 16th-century Italian designers, such as Romano and Vignola (Fig. 59). Each window bay is marked by a single, slender pilaster. The wall plane is then cut away into a rectangular shape around the slit-like opening of the window, creating a framing effect. In the four nave bays, the window is located awkwardly within this rectangle; its top is thrust against the rectangle top, but the sill floats freely at considerable distance from the base of the rectangle. A very narrow, curved bay marks the transition to the narrower choir, where shorter windows are arranged more regularly within the rectangular fields. The roof rests on the walls like an unarticulated lid. All parts of the exterior—facade tower and wings, flanks, choir—are imbued with an abruptness and restless excess that might almost be called Mannerist.

The extremes of the exterior are not carried inside, where a few basic elements are employed with more usual proportioning. Nave and choir, distinguished from one another by shifts in height and width, form a hall of six bays. Saturated with light from many large windows, the interior is articulated in a forthright manner with a minimum of means.

A rectangular vestibule located beneath the single tower of the facade gives access to the four-bay nave (Figs. 60–62). These bays are defined by broad but shallow wall piers, each faced with a single composite pilaster. Crowning pier and pilaster is a tall, richly profiled, strongly projecting entablature, above which the vault springs from a stilting block. The vault is an undulating surface running continuously through four bays. No crossing arches span it,[21] and a soft curve makes the transition to the tall lunettes opening its flanks. This rounded surface contrasts with an angular and hard-edged elevation. Piers, wall strips, and windows have clean, unornamented edges. The elevation has become a "window-wall" framed by the "structural skeleton" of piers, thin wall strips, and largely open vault. This elementary system is well served by the ample, direct light, the elegant stucco on capitals and entablature, and Christian Thomas Scheffler's frescoes and painted framing which cover all vault surfaces.

The choir, though richer and more concentrated, is similar to the nave. Raised seven steps above nave level, the vault is also lower, the walls closer together. Transition to this smaller area is over a convex section of wall and vault, which curves in from the nave and is articulated by paired pilasters; the vault between the different heights of choir and nave is marked by a step of simple profile.

In the choir, the two bays remain similar to those in the nave, except that cross ribs span the vault. Beneath a domical vault, the circular apse is divided into three equal sections by pilasters and ribs. Ample windows open the two side sections, whereas the middle section is treated as a shallow niche before which the gold altar statue of St. Paulin stands. Pressing against the pilasters and arching deeply into the vault, the windows eliminate the wall in their sections and help dissolve the dome. Equal in size to the other choir windows and those in the nave, their effect is more dramatic. They fill out the area between pilasters more completely, and are put on display by being partially angled into the interior. In a similar spirit, the choir elevation, arranged about a smaller space, makes a more insistent impression, even though it repeats the nave articulation. Add the stucco and gilt of this area, the large, airy baldachin-like altar, and the wrought-iron gates and handsomely carved confessionals marking both sides of the stairs, and the choir appears richer and more dense architecturally than the nave.

The elevation of Trier is white, the stucco pastel, the vault frescoes a solid hue, too heavy for the interior; but it is difficult to determine whether the present tone is due to the passage of time or an initial miscalculation by the artist. Be this as it may, certainly the movement upward from plain white to a pageant of color constitutes an integral part of the original design. The essence of Trier is the evolution of the architecture within its own realm, distanced from the spectator. Walking into the nave, the spectator experiences a spacious, light-flooded vessel. The detailing is crisp and clean, the forms basic and clearly exposed. A filigree of ornament and projecting entablature mark the transition into the undulating surfaces of the vault. Splayed steeply outward, the entablature cornice catches and reflects the light, becoming a luminous band. The vault frescoes, well lit by large lunettes, arch decisively over the frame below. The choir offers a more insistent architectural presence, but this is only a matter of degree, not a fundamental shift of interpretation. In the choir, the walls are pulled closely together, the vault lowered; the architecture is now physically nearer and, because of the ribs, more sculptural. Set on high pedestals, the altar baldachin seems to float within this space; the slender columns and airy crown of four gilt ribs make it appear insubstantial, ethereal. It does not occupy or consume space; it appears suspended within the area. Later than the church in design and execution (1745–52), this altar appropriately concludes the hall, enlivening but scarcely displacing the space. With this delicate vision, Neumann concludes his most reserved architectural statement. He had never reduced architecture to such a minimum before. Only his later design for the Dominican church in Würzburg will demonstrate a similar austerity, though within a very different setting.

SS. Cecilia and Barbara at Heusenstamm

The second longitudinal building is the parish and mortuary church of SS. Cecilia and Barbara at Heusenstamm, begun early in 1739.[22] The Heusenstamm facade (Fig. 64) uses the same elements as that of Trier, but the forms are angular and the proportions less extreme. The square central tower stands somewhat in front of flat and wider wings; flat volutes, edges minimally curved, reach to the third story of the tower. The articulating elements on the facade—pilasters, bands, windows, door, and niche—are treated in simple and direct fashion. Only four modest pieces of sculpture animate the facade slightly. The flat, plain pilasters are continued along the flank and around the polygonal crossing arms and choir. Severe and pedestrian, the Heusenstamm exterior is an appropriate shell for the interior.

The plain nave (Figs. 65, 66) is divided into two bays by shallow wall piers, each faced with a single pilaster. Lunette edges spring from the piers, spanning the width of each bay and cutting into a flattened barrel vault. At the crossing, four corner piers are hollowed out to accommodate freestanding Tuscan columns. The columns support flattened crossing arches, from which a saucer dome rises on flat pendentives. Since the dome is much smaller in diameter than the crossing itself, the area between dome, pendentives, and crossing arches is filled with triangular vault segments. In the polygonal transept arms, pilasters support a dome-like vault that is sliced away by lunettes placed over three windows; the vault does not quite reach to the crossing arch. A higher-set segment of vault separates the two elements, arching over the ceiling as a continuous band. The choir apse is semicircular rather than polygonal, and the central lunettes spring from bosses instead of pilasters, but otherwise elevation and vaulting are like those of the transept arms. Narrower than the crossing, the chancel bay barrel vault is lower than the saucer dome, and the floor is raised two steps.

Plans S.E. 202, 203, and 204 are similar and agree with the executed church except for some details, notably the form of the crossing piers, the plan of the facade tower on the first two sheets, and the size of the apse. The Koblenz drawing shows three nave bays rather than two. But one other project for the church reveals a very different point of view. In S.E. 174, there are no transept arms (Fig. 67). Instead, a very shallow area between crossing arch and straight outer wall forms a spatial cushion for the crossing vault. To the east, the crossing piers jut into the interior with a strong concave curve, setting off the choir. This area is also different from that of the executed building, consisting of a self-contained chancel bay opening into a polygonal apse. The result is an interior utilizing three distinct units—nave, crossing, choir—each subscribing to a high degree of independence.[23] From this interpretation, the shift into the erected monument is unexpected. Neumann takes over the vaulting system of Gössweinstein, which was employed to distinguish elements within a continuity, but applies it to a highly unified interior. The distinctions created by the vaults now become minor modulations of a single space.

The depressed vaults and severe order of Heusenstamm have a crypt-like character appropriate to the church's function as a mausoleum.[24] But an irresolute quality also permeates the interior, inflicting it with a blandness and lack of tension.

The bulky columns do not contribute to a definition of the crossing, nor do they intensify its plasticity. Tucked away into the far corners of the square, they are embraced by the pier mass and shadow. They do not support a voluminous or solid vault, but a series of papery, tilting planes, which seem incongruously associated with their stolid shafts. The flat vaults are spread indifferently over the interior. In this generally open, horizontal space, no single element or interpretation clearly asserts itself. It is one of Neumann's most colorless interiors: no aesthetic decision is formulated with conviction and vigorously pursued.[25]

Two court churches from these decades remain to be considered, one for the Würzburg Residenz, the other for the palace at Werneck. In these designs, Neumann works with ovals as the generators of shapes and spaces. The ancillary areas in the Schönborn chapel were generally ovoid, but now the oval assumes primary importance. The results are more complex than either Trier or Heusenstamm; they are also interesting chronologically. The Residenz chapel, Neumann's greatest extant church from these decades, was designed over a year earlier than Trier, while Werneck is contemporary with Heusenstamm, a challenging sequence for those intent on imposing linear developments on Neumann's work.

The Palace Church at Würzburg

Planning for the palace church in the Residenz began between 1719 and 1721 with Maximilian von Welsch's project for an oval church in the north palace tract.[26] Two years later, Neumann brought back further suggestions from his trip to Paris. In these, de Cotte proposed placing the church in the north stair hall, a solution quickly rejected by the patron, Johann Philipp Franz von Schönborn. Boffrand, though accepting von Welsch's configuration, felt that it would be too small, so he added a rectangular nave to the southern flank of the oval.

During the early 1720s building proceeded around the church site; no decision was reached as to how the church itself should be realized. Then planning and construction of the entire Residenz were virtually halted during Bishop Hutten's tenure at Würzburg (1724–29). With the election of Friedrich Karl von Schönborn as Prince-Bishop in 1729, work was taken up once more at a brisk pace. Now the Viennese architect Lucas von Hildebrandt became actively involved in the designing. Neumann journeyed to Vienna in 1729 and again in September 1730, Hildebrandt to Würzburg in June 1731. Correspondence between Würzburg and Vienna was voluminous. But despite Hildebrandt's presence as an architectural authority with a European reputation, documentation consistently demonstrates that Neumann developed the basic design of the church.

On a plan of the site of the Residenz, signed and dated by Neumann on 11 January 1730 (S.E. 292), the church appeared for the first time in its present location, the southwest corner of the palace.[27] In later drawings by Hildebrandt, the rectangular shape of this tract determined the internal space (S.E. 301, 302, 303). This was not so for Neumann, who considered a longitudinal oval with rectangular vestibule and choir at the end (S.E. 313; Fig. 68). The design he submitted, signed and dated 26 January 1732 (Berlin, Hdz. 4687, 4688), established the basic system of ovals within rectangular outer walls seen in the completed church. Because later changes and additions to this design, primarily by Hildebrandt but by Neumann as well, tend to blur its clarity, analysis here will concentrate on these sheets. Significant changes from design to built structure will be considered at the conclusion of the discussion.

Neumann's 1732 project contains an undulating, openwork form placed within thick outer walls (Figs. 69, 70). The former consists of a longitudinal oval located between smaller cross ovals; it is realized as a framework of freestanding columns, pilasters, a balcony, and steeply springing vaults opened by lunettes. Seven vertical window rows cut away a considerable portion of the outer fabric. Each consists of three units: two similar tall elements separated by a squarish one. Internal form and outer wall, though distinct visually and physically, are locked tightly into a unified composition. Neumann achieves this tour de force with masterful ease.

Swelling vault shells entirely devoid of ornament or articulation establish the ovoid themes. The bottom sections of these semiellipsoids are opened by lunettes along their flanks and by torsion edges that bend across the church. The four triangular spaces between the vaults are covered by vault segments similar to those Neumann was to use later at Heusenstamm.

The torsion edges of the vaults are not arches or ribs, as in the built church, but literally the thickness of the vault shell on display. Here for the first time in his work, Neumann conceived of the vault as a shell, similar to his vaults in the later churches at Kitzingen and Forchheim, the 1744 project for Vierzehnheiligen, and at Neresheim and Vienna. At Vierzehnheiligen and Neresheim, as happened here, these edges were disguised in the built churches to resemble ribs by means of illusionistic painting and stucco.

The distinction between torsion edge and torsion rib is fundamental. The unit of rib and vertical support establishes a structural skeleton, and the vault is conceived as a skin stretched over it. The edge, however, reveals the vault as a shell propped up on point supports. Since the shape of the vault shell mirrors that of the plan below, the flat plane on which the visitor stands contrasts with the voluminous, space-filled zone above—a three-dimensional development of a two-dimensional geometry, in which space as form swells into shadow and light beyond.

An elegant and dramatically open armature supports the ellipsoids. Sculptured brackets beneath the springing points of the vault stand on baluster blocks in the balcony railing. Below these are sections of projecting entablature, columns, and pilasters.[28] Elevation and vault rise through the full four-story height of the palace, even though the width of the church is modest. Horizontal accents of balcony, a string course in the first story, the window grid, as well as the generous space between vertical elements, modify the upward thrust.

Following the base of the vault, the openwork form curves in and out from the outer wall. Starting at either side of the altar, and progressing symmetrically along both flanks to the entrance, the armature swings out to the first window axis, then back into the church. From here the movement passes over a convex-concave-convex section of balcony and into the space of the major oval, arching through this out to the wall and back in again. The movement curves into the next area between ovals, then sweeps deeply into the end oval. Though pressing against the outer wall at several points, this webwork always remains clearly distinct. The lunettes, for instance, are given a deep edge, clearly distinguishing the vault shell from the external fabric. On the other hand, the openwork is arranged like a series of framing units (order, balcony, and lunettes) around windows. And the inner form elicits a response from the outer fabric: molded according to the undulating movement of the armature, the masonry swells forward and curves back accordingly.

Set almost flush along the outer wall surface, the regular placement and profusion of windows creates a straight, transparent plane as the outer boundary of the church. From here, the window openings are splayed through the thick masonry to the curving inner wall surface (Pl. II).

Neumann's orchestration of all these elements establishes a complex interaction between them. Upon entering, one's glance is pulled upward by the insistent verticality of the interior to the pure, voluminous vault. Here both the dynamics of curving shapes informing the longitudinal space and the centralizing assertion within it are established. These tendencies inform the webwork as well, but due to its extreme openness, they are more of a suggestion than a decisive statement. Behind the webwork, the themes are transposed to the greater solidity and reserved movement of the undulating wall surface. This masonry is opened by generous windows, generating a wall of light which saturates the interior. This brilliance in turn tends to dematerialize the masonry and openwork form. The curving internal layers appear to be generated from, or to open out towards, a plane of light. Set into motion by the ovoid vaults, the spatial dynamics are intensified by the various perforated, light-saturated layers defining it.

This use of light determines three sides of the church—the two flanks and the entrance. Though one flank is embedded in the palace, it is conceptually—and even to a certain extent visually—effective as a light source, since its window openings are filled with mirrors. That Neumann also thought of the elevation as filled with light is demonstrated in S.E. LXVII, the engraving produced for the consecration publication: light is shown pouring into the church from this side.[29] The altar end alone is left without windows (Figs. 70, 71). Here Neumann forsakes his pyrotechnic display by offering a windowless backing for the altar ensemble. Rising from a slightly raised platform into balcony level, this area is distinguished by its more somber lighting.[30]

The 1732 design is a colossal performance, combining seemingly contradictory elements into a complex unity. Ovoid forms are placed within a rectangular box. These forms are established absolutely by the ellipsoid vaults, yet are almost entirely opened up to the exterior rectangle in elevation. The outer surface of the box consists of a glass plane, but masonry links that surface with the dynamically curvilinear interior. Light constitutes a major factor in the dematerialization of internal mass, while presenting the final outer boundary. The longitudinal axis of the interior, culminating in the more somber altar ensemble, produces a directional thrust which is as imperative as the centralizing effect of the oval shapes. In short, a series of interpretative paradoxes are resolved into a compelling aesthetic statement.

Several modifications of this design resulted in the church as it stands today (Figs. 74, 75). Within a month of producing his project, Neumann was hard at work reshaping it. The changes can be seen by comparing the plan Hdz. 4689 to the January 1732 design (Fig. 72). Unhappy with the width of the church, Neumann narrowed it by 2 *Schuhe* while stretching the length from seven to eight window axes.[31] Neumann explained the change as improving circulation in the adjoining corridor; in fact, he was recasting the space within the church. These new dimensions suggest heightened tensions between axis and centrality. The relations between ovals are altered as well, a change which carries greater meaning. Neumann shortened the central oval from three to two window bays, marked its cross axis by a strip of wall with paired engaged columns, and lengthened the end ovals. Paradoxically, by balancing the size of the three oval units more evenly, contrasts indicated within the earlier design were intensified. A series of centralizing elements replaced a major oval that had subordinate spaces bracketing its end. Though smaller, the middle unit was emphasized by a decisive cross axis. The organ balcony was pulled into the church through the entire entrance oval, and the level of the choir floor raised.[32] The new cross axis affirms the weight of the major unit, while balcony and altar area enrich the end ovals. In short, the centralizing and longitudinal qualities of the design are enhanced, creating a more insistent space.

Following this, on 10 March 1733, Friedrich Karl requested that Neumann replace the brackets at the vault springing points with *"termes und sonsten"* ("herms and such"). These changes are recorded in Hildebrandt drawings S.E. LXXI and S.E. LXXVIII, which correspond to the present interior (Fig. 74). The bottom halves of the lunettes recorded in the first design are replaced by stubby pilasters, which in turn stand on other abbreviated pilasters substituted for Neumann's brackets. Both units taper strongly and are sculptured with a profusion of ornate forms. The architectonic clarity of Neumann's solution is blurred by astructural decoration.

A third change, announced in a letter of 24 April 1734, and illustrated in S.E. LXVI, pulls the altar balcony farther into the church, in order to locate a second altar on the balcony (Figs. 70, 71, 73). The original choir ensemble, a single unit rising through the full height of the church, is replaced by an arrangement stressing the two-tiered division of the interior (S.E. LXXVIII). Later Hildebrandt inserted massive side altars into the central oval. Unresponsive to the architecture, their dense forms obscure the cross axis.

A final difference between Neumann's original project and the existing church is the presence of oratories flanking the second-story altar (Fig. 71), which were absent in the 1732 drawings. S.E. XXXXIII, signed and dated by Neumann on 9 October 1736, illustrates this unit as it is found in the church today.

The post-1732 alterations of Neumann's design represent encroachments which weaken the architecture of the Würzburg palace church. Hildebrandt is the key figure behind these, and they show him to have been either insensitive or unsympathetic to Neumann's intentions. He sacrificed Neumann's lucid articulation of forms and spaces to provide for his own decorative willfulness. The fundamental difference in attitude toward design between Neumann and Hildebrandt is strikingly revealed in the history of this building.

The Palace Church at Werneck

Both Neumann and Hildebrandt were involved with the design of the Werneck palace church as well (Figs. 77, 79).[33] Projects from 1731 and 1733 exist for the palace. Construction was begun in the spring of 1734. The wing housing the chapel, to the left upon entering the court, was up by the spring of 1737. The 1738 building report announced that the chapel was ready to be decorated in the manner of the Würzburg court church. The entire palace, including the two towers in the inner court, was completed by 1745. Documentation is insufficient to assign the chapel definitely to one architect or the other. But since the chapel is an abbreviated version of the Würzburg court church, and since its form and space are as alien to any work of Hildebrandt's as they are congenial to that of Neumann, the design may be attributed to him with reasonable certainty.

In 1853, King Maximilian II of Bavaria approved Werneck Palace for use as an insane asylum; differences between Neumann's project and the extant church may be the result of rebuilding necessitated by the conversion. There are major discrepancies between design and building: two bays to the right of the entrance do not correspond to the earlier design; the vaults beneath the organ balcony (Fig. 81) now blend with walls and supports, obscuring zones of juncture (in Neumann's original design, the organ balcony was treated as a detachable unit); the bottom row of the two tiers of windows that Neumann had wrapped around the whole building (Fig. 77) has been eliminated; and two side altars, apparently taken from another building, are jammed into ancillary spaces along the cross axis (Pl. X). Finally, many details are altered: some window jambs are angled differently, pilaster shapes have been changed, the columns framing the entrance are placed on axis, rather than shifted off slightly to either side. To appreciate Neumann's original design intentions, these changes must be borne in mind.

The area assigned the chapel was an irregular rectangle (Fig. 78). Within these walls, Neumann placed a regular ovoid shape defined by a close-set series of ten wall piers and ten shaft-like ancillary spaces (Fig. 79). His unusual treatment of these elements effectively masks the discrepancies caused by divergent outside walls, producing the impression of a uniform and consistent structure.

Decorative pilasters, which become broader as they rise, are set onto the pier faces (Fig. 80). They support a strongly projecting entablature which is stepped forward over each pilaster and curves back into the shaft-like spaces at either side. Because these spaces are narrow, the entablature creates a decisive horizontal accent. Above the entablature, ten small arches spring from pilaster to pilaster; uniform in size, they are seen with two profiles. Those to either side of the altar, as well as the three at the entrance end of the oval, are treated with a modestly elaborate edge; the edges of the remaining arches are hollowed out as concave bands. The oval central vault, somewhat flattened in profile, lifts smooth-surfaced from these arches.

Capped by the entablature and small half-domes, the outside wall of each ancillary space is opened (in the original design) by two windows, one placed above the other, except where this is not possible due to enclosing palace tracts. The large windows eliminate most of the wall area. These spaces establish several axes: entrance and altar, each contained within a shaft, are placed opposite one another; diagonal accents are created by an elaboration of those areas to the right and left of both entrance and altar. Each of these four spaces is divided down the middle by a wall spur (the corner of the outside rectangle), which is faced by a tapering pilaster similar to those on the ten piers; originally four windows were intended for each corner arrangement. Lastly, a broad cross axis is established by paired ancillary spaces: uniform in treatment and with the shallowest interior areas, they create, in double rhythm, a broad, open zone distinguished from the deep, complex diagonals and the altar-entrance axis. As in the Würzburg court church, this cross axis is marked by wall, not windows.

Entering the chapel, the visitor is struck by an open and lofty space (Fig. 77). Tall, generous ancillary shafts combined with the mass of piers and dome produce this impression. Directly opposite stands the altar. As one strides toward it, other impressions produce a greater awareness of the interior and its dynamics. Spatially more complex and richer in lighting (originally) than the other subsidiary spaces, the diagonals seduce the eye (Fig. 80). Deep and brilliant, the definition of these areas is not immediately clear. Then the double spaces along each side of the oval become more insistent. This shorter axis is noticeably flat, as the inside boundary curves close to the outside wall. (Presently the side altars obscure this dynamic.) By introducing these axial tensions into a contained form, Neumann capitalizes on the irregularities between oval and rectangle. The play between longitudinal and centralizing tendencies inherent in the oval is expanded (entrance-altar axis), contracted (double side spaces), and enriched (diagonal axis) by a multiplicity of pulls and thrusts.

A further dimension is added to Werneck by the manner in which Neumann interprets solids in the chapel. Fundamentally, wall no longer exists. In place of a solid, continuous container, only the structural bones of the piers remain (Figs. 77, 79, 80). The eye skips through spaces from one vertical support to the next. The ovoid shape is not so much specified by the continuity of masonry, as it is indicated by the rhythm of powerful verticals. Within the shaft-like ancillary spaces, the impression of a wall-less structure is no less vivid. Windows transform the outer shell to glass. Light floods directly into the narrow area, dematerializing what little masonry remains. In effect, each ancillary space is transformed into a shaft of light. As if generated out of these luminous columns, the piers thrust forward to define an open ovoid perimeter.

This light-saturated, open space is held together by the vault (Fig. 77). Though actually flattened in profile, the smooth surface appears to billow majestically upward from the rapid rhythm of ten small arches. Lit only from the fenestration of the ancillary spaces, the gathering shadow in the shell confirms its voluminous strength. Above the diffuse, tension-filled elevation, it unequivocally defines the oval figure of the interior, solidifying and containing with sovereign repose the ambitious vertical thrusts from below. In principle, the function and effect of the vault is similar to that of Holzkirchen. But not only are the formal elements here of another nature, the chapel is realized with a distinguishing conviction.

A recapitulation of themes and design strategies reviewed in the above churches also will introduce Neumann's projects of the 1740s. His interest focused primarily on the creation of open, light-saturated space articulated by freestanding units. Each building can be characterized as an individual experiment, as another and different means of pursuing this intention.

Plans present a first index of Neumann's approach. Centralized churches employ circles (Holzkirchen, Fig. 32; and Bamberg, Fig. 36), Greek crosses (Bamberg again and Bruchsal, Fig. 37), and ovals (the Schönborn chapel, Fig. 25; Würzburg court church, Fig. 72; and Bamberg), while a Latin cross provides the starting point for Münsterschwarzach (Fig. 46), Gössweinstein (Fig. 53), and Heusenstamm (Fig. 65). At Trier (Figs. 60, 62), nave and choir are joined without benefit of crossing or transept. But this listing remains minimally descriptive. Neumann enriched the implications of plan in elevation and vaulting. The tholos represented Neumann's contribution to the Schönborn chapel (Fig. 26). He returned to this form at Münsterschwarzach (Figs. 47–49) and Bamberg (Fig. 36). Yet the context of each effort remains distinct. Undulating walls and bracketing ovoid spaces provide the setting in the Schönborn chapel; at Bamberg the tholos is contained within four rectangular arms; at Münsterschwarzach it becomes the crossing. The tholos idea is discernible at Holzkirchen (Fig. 34), though the interlocking of window frames, walls, and order, as well as the different radii determining the placement of order, entablature, and dome base demonstrate the dominance of other intentions. This elevation is assembled from discrete components, an approach also employed in three longitudinal interiors: Münsterschwarzach, Gössweinstein, Trier. The monumental, decisively rhythmic wall piers at Münsterschwarzach (Fig. 49) contrast with the "spatial wall" of the Gössweinstein nave (Fig. 54), and both of these elaborate interpretations contrast with the minimal though effective "skeleton" at Trier (Fig. 62). For the Heusenstamm interior, wall piers were used in a conventional and bland manner (Fig. 65). In the Würzburg (Fig. 72) and Werneck (Fig. 79) palace churches, Neumann placed openwork ovals within extensively perforated rectangles. Unlike the tholoi, these forms cannot be rotated on their axis. Conceptually, this reduces their independence within the interior, a fact Neumann recognized by establishing give and take between inner forms and outer wall. Some comparisons are revealing at this point. Though Werneck can legitimately be considered a condensed version of Würzburg, the oval cage is established by piers rather than freestanding columns. The plan of the Schönborn chapel (Fig. 25), on the other hand, appears to prefigure Würzburg (Fig. 72): three circular spaces arranged in a row and largely open to each other. However, the notion of an independent tholos located within an undulating space represents a different interpretation from three tangent oval units locked into a larger rectangle but determining the interior. Distinctions of this nature are elementary, but they do indicate the diversity of Neumann's approach to design.

The plan of Bruchsal is a Greek cross (Fig. 37), and stands isolated within the group. The paper-thin quality of the continuous walls, the flatly beveled corners of the crossing, and the floating dome are unique interpretations within Neumann's architecture, both as vocabulary and as syntax.

The vaulting systems in these churches draw the elevations together, mirroring in volumetric form the two-dimensional figure of the plan. The hemispherical dome on pendentives of the Schönborn chapel, capped by a substantial lantern, represents a conventional solution (Figs. 22, 23), as does the hemispherical Holzkirchen dome (Fig. 34), although Neumann's intentions for the lantern remain unclear. From this point on, Neumann's interpretations become more demanding and less usual. The steep profile, huge windows, and large lantern of the Münsterschwarzach dome (Fig. 47) create a monumentality matched by the massive, sculptural barrel vaults spanning nave and choir. At Würzburg (Fig. 75) and Werneck (Fig. 77), the smooth surfaces of the ovoid vaults emphasize deep spatial volumes that surge into them. Utterly different are the saucer domes set within triangular vault sections that mark the crossings at Gössweinstein (Pl. VI) and Heusenstamm (Fig. 66), and, in the former, the layering and multiplicity of its nave, transept, and choir vaults. The highly successful Gössweinstein crossing is integrated into the interior and at the same time distinguished from it; thus the crossing underlines the purpose of the church. At Heusenstamm, a similar unit is employed in a colorless and undifferentiated manner. The undulating barrel vault at Trier (Fig. 63), simple yet unique, concludes this catalogue.

The diverse design strategies utilized by Neumann are resolute and compelling. In each structure his prime purpose remains sovereign—the creation of dynamic, controlling, responsive space. We must now consider the instrumentation of these designs.

Light is of fundamental importance. At the Schönborn

chapel (Fig. 26), von Welsch had cast the die, forcing Neumann to work with his fenestration. The large, evenly displayed windows which open the Holzkirchen fabric suggest a greater awareness of light. Presumably Münsterschwarzach offered a decisive interpretation (Fig. 47): the external fabric was almost dissolved about the entire building, resulting in a strong and constant light throughout, projecting the wall-pier shell into a deep, luminous relief. At Trier (Fig. 63) and Heusenstamm (Fig. 66), the openness, expansiveness, and clarity of articulation are in large part due to the generous and consistent fenestration. An even more ambitious dissolution of the fabric occurs in Würzburg (Fig. 69) and Werneck (Fig. 77), where it becomes intrinsic to their light-saturated, transparent spaces. The illumination of Gössweinstein (Fig. 55), on the other hand, changes from area to area, accenting and differentiating various parts of the interior, with a subtle increase in intensity from nave to crossing and choir. In no building does Neumann utilize decisive dark/light oppositions such as that between the subdued bottom section of Bernini's S. Andrea and its light-flooded dome. In Neumann's churches, light intensifies light. The interiors begin brightly and within this context a yet greater brilliance determines accentuation.

In highly conscious fashion, Neumann asserts place and orchestrates procession within his interiors. In the Schönborn chapel, movement and location are pitted against one another and simultaneously harmonized in a tour de force. The axes enriching the circular shape of the Holzkirchen and Werneck ovals are composed in a different manner, yet their drama is felt vividly, generating oppositions that enliven ostensibly contained or nondirectional forms. As processional and centralizing devices, the axes of Münsterschwarzach and Gössweinstein, Würzburg and Trier and Bruchsal are fundamental to the unfolding, explication, and significance of space. Neumann's unequivocal handling of these elements demonstrates again his mastery of orchestrating the architectural experience.

IV.
The Forties and Early Fifties

The decade of the forties was Neumann's most prolific time, the period of his best known, most sophisticated, and mature work. Since many of these churches overlap in their creation and construction, they are discussed here not in chronological order but, instead, according to plan type: Greek cross, longitudinal, and the combination of central and longitudinal emphasis. These categories are not absolute; they serve merely to organize a rich body of material more comprehensively. The difficulty in neatly fitting category with building serves as a gentle reminder of Neumann's rich, disparate approach to design.

The Holy Cross Church at Kitzingen

One of three Greek cross churches designed in the forties, the Holy Cross church at Kitzingen-Etwashausen stands at the beginning of the decade.[1] In this building, Neumann began with a modified Greek cross plan, then lengthened it to a Latin cross while maintaining a centralizing intent in the interior.

The Kitzingen facade is one of Neumann's most sophisticated efforts (Pl. V, Figs. 84, 85). Its various parts are locked into a vigorous, three-dimensional composition in which entrance bay, facade wall, and tower are related to and played off against one another, while yet remaining independent and distinct.

The three-story tower appears to be both assertively pushed out before the church and securely pulled into it. Wings capped by tall volutes curve back vigorously from the tower to a set of pilasters and buttresses. These in turn are stepped one behind the other, continuing the movement away from the tower. On the other hand, the large, steep, solid forms of the roof slide forward so that the tower seems to rise out of the roof. The feeling that the tower is detached from the wall of the facade—two-story entrance and single-story wings—is established by the treatment of the central bay of the facade, which is framed by broad pilasters, capped by a pediment, and clearly narrower and separate from the bulk of the tower. The top story of the tower also is distinguished from the facade below by strongly beveled corners and a strong cornice, which create an appropriate base for its steep, energetically profiled roof dome.

In contrast to the complex composition of the facade and tower, the rest of the exterior is very simple. Below the large roof forms, the walls of nave, transept, and choir are flat and plain. Corners are marked by unembellished strips of pilasters and window frames. Behind the richly composed facade stands the plain exterior.

Consideration of the Kitzingen interior is best divided into three stages: the preliminary design of S.E. 208; the final design of S.E. 206, 207, 209, LXXXVIII–LXXXXI, LXXXXIII, and LXXXXIV; and the executed monument. After a discussion of the basic differences and similarities of these stages, the design will be considered as a whole.

Neumann's first plan was a Greek cross with a longitudinal accent (Fig. 84). Rather than terminate the entrance-altar arms with the straight end of their north-south counterparts, he added a curving wall to each, lengthening and differentiating them. These curving walls are set off by columns or piers placed before the apse and vestibule respectively. In spite of this longitudinal emphasis, it is the crossing which dominates the interior. The corners of the crossing are cut away to a 45° angle, expanding the size of the area considerably, and drawing the arms into more intimate contact with it. Placed several feet in front of each of these corners, a pair of columns, sharing a single pedestal, supports a section of entablature, which in turn is surmounted by a pendentive dome of flattened profile. The entrance-choir arms [2] are covered by barrel vaults and—over the curved ends—tripartite groin vaults. Each cross arm is covered by a vault of three curved planes that rises from the rectangular arrangement of walls. Though the vault of each of the four arms is marked by an arch near the crossing, the vault surface continues beyond the arch, dips slightly, then meets the crossing dome. A triangular vault segment fills the gap between arm and crossing vaults, dropping down from its apex to the width of the small barrel vault between crossing corners and paired columns.

In his final design (Figs. 85, 86), Neumann modified this project by adding a bay to the entrance arm, creating a Latin cross interior with a monumental crossing and stubby nave. The crossing is still dominant, but the longitudinal axis has become a decisive counterpoint.

In the executed church, the height and width of the crossing have been reduced. Instead of billowing upward, the dome scarcely rises above the height of the arm vaults; instead of sweeping out to them, the dome is sliced out deeply by the vaults. In plan, the dome has come to resemble a cross rather than a circle, minimizing the counterpoint between the center and the longitudinal axis. The existing documents do not reveal the circumstances surrounding this change to a more unified but less dynamic longitudinal interpretation.[3]

The entrance into Kitzingen is direct, open, and undramatic (Figs. 87, 88). The neutral quality of the nave does not demand the visitor's attention, which is immediately drawn to the freestanding columns and voluminous dome of the crossing, and to the column-framed altar beyond. The engravings suggest a far more powerful arrangement, although the present modified crossing evokes something of this effect.

The two bays of the nave are defined simply by single pilasters placed on low pedestals and supporting a modest entablature. The only other element in each bay is a centrally located, tall, round-headed window, the splayed jambs, base, and head of which are cut into the masonry to make a much larger frame in the interior than appears in the exterior. Rococo cartouches crown each window, rising through the entablature to the circular barrel vault, which is spanned by flat ribs springing from the pilasters.

The plan for Neumann's Bamberg church (Fig. 36) interpreted the crossing as a freestanding tholos. The torsion arches of the Schönborn chapel (Fig. 26) demonstrated one approach to the design of such a unit; the engravings for Kitzingen show another. To distinguish the crossing unit, Neumann has clearly separated it from surrounding walls and vaults. The freestanding paired columns are placed well before the wall, while the dome is divorced from adjoining vaults in two ways: its edge is lower, and it is separated from the small barrel vaults between crossing columns and outer wall by sickle-shaped vault segments that are higher than the vaults of nave, choir, and arms respectively. Disrupting the continuity of these surfaces, the segments function as shadow joints, preventing the other areas from abutting against or fusing with the dome.

One passes rapidly through the nave to the crossing, which is the central focus of the church. While this independent, sheltering canopy opens to all parts of the interior, the voluminous dome creates a distinct core. The cross axis of the transept arms also halts forward motion, but one is not lured into the broad, shallow arms, which nestle close to the tholos rather than pull away from it. In front of the visitor stands the altar, which cannot be approached, since the communion rail, raised on a step, swings out from the foremost pilaster of the choir into the crossing area. With forward motion halted by crossing and transept axis and barred by the communion rail, one is suddenly located in a central position within this longitudinal church. From here the entire interior is visible, with everything focused toward the tholos, and nothing leading out of it. This idea underlay Neumann's first, modified Greek cross project for Kitzingen. By expanding the western arm into a nave, and including the communion rail (not present in S.E. 207 or 208), he intensified the impact of his interpretation significantly. Kitzingen probably represents Neumann's finest resolution of the longitudinal-centralized problem in a building of moderate size.

The choir consists of chancel bay and apse (Fig. 88). The former mirrors the second nave bay in creating a plain, unassertive background for an altar tableau placed in the apse. The altar itself is raised on a platform between two columns which are connected by arches to form a small arcade—a counterpoint to the pier arcade at the entrance. A life-size crucifix hangs on the back wall behind the altar. The space between column and flanking wall to either side of the altar is filled by doors leading into the apse. Standing on top of these carved door frames are larger-than-life-size statues of saints.[4]

Here Neumann combines altar, sculpture, and architecture into a unified and dramatic deep relief (Pl. IV). The columns, arches, and curving apse wall create the architectural frame for a monumental, trapezoidal composition, which rises from the altar to the statues, and back to the crucifix. Tightly enclosed by the columns, the block-like altar and life-size crucifix are a severe statement of the purpose and dedication of the church. Beneath the outside arches, daringly perched upon the rococo framework of the wooden doorways, the two larger-than-life figures turn with brisk emotion, the one towards heaven, the other to the altar. The strict geometrical composition, the severity of the central axis, the dramatic pose of the saints and their contrast with the center, charge the tableau with an austere yet passionate intensity.

These dual qualities—severity and passion—constitute the leitmotives of the interior. Friedrich Karl, the building's patron, specified that the church should be realized without ornament or paintings.[5] Neumann complied with this in the stringent elevations of nave, choir, and arms, in which the Tuscan order is used throughout. Yet an emotional impact vitalizes this Spartan regime. What is seen from the entrance as a unity of crossing and altar, which then separates into two distinct units as it is approached, is certainly one aspect of this. The remarkable centralizing force created within a basically longitudinal form is another. Both include the third element: the lighting. In keeping with the absence of ornamentation and painting, the entire interior is white, with the result that a cool, clear light is evenly distributed. Neumann has set windows around the entire fabric with regularity, illuminating each area uniformly, with the exception of the crossing corners. In both the first and final projects, Neumann opened these beveled surfaces with windows,[6] which are not present in the engravings or in the executed building.[7] Sources of light closest to the crossing now occur in nave and transept arms. As a result, the dome, low hanging and high rising, lifts into deep shadow in striking contrast to the rest of the interior. This is true today even though the dome has been opened to the surrounding areas. This is the final distinguishing characteristic of the crossing tholos, a shadowy counterpoint to the otherwise luminous interior, the last of those basic emotional tensions with which Neumann imbued his otherwise severe interior.

The Käppele at Würzburg
(the later project)

Though separated by seven years, Neumann's two projects for the Würzburg pilgrimage church, known as the Käppele, are so different, it hardly seems possible that the same architect could have conceived of them for the same church.[8] The earlier design is a Latin cross which embraces two independent, curving units; the later is a modified Greek cross. Neumann's personal stamp marks the earlier project, while the executed building has a pronounced

Roman character. Because of this dissimilarity, only the executed design is appropriate here; the 1740 project is discussed within a different context.

Although not large, the church is distinguished in the landscape by towers, a broad facade, and undulating roofs (Fig. 89). The octagonal, three-story towers are vigorously pulled out from the corners of the facade and capped by elaborate, steeple-like roofs. The tall lantern perched above the crossing is cylindrical, but its articulation and roof are a variation of the towers. This animated set of spires complements a roof that is curved, peaked, molded, belted in, and flared out as it is drawn over the building in a curvilinear counterpoint to the angularity of the facade and towers. Towers and roofs together effectively signal the Käppele as a pilgrimage goal from the distance; the more sober elevation is characteristic of Neumann's general reserve in the design of church exteriors.

As in the preliminary project for Kitzingen, the east-west arms of the Käppele are longer than their north-south counterparts (Fig. 90). The entrance arm is filled mostly by an organ balcony supported on six columns (Fig. 91). The flanks of both arms are each opened by a large window. Above them ample clearstory windows cut into the circular barrel vault. Each cross arm consists of a half-ellipse covered by a dome that continues the curve of the wall. One large window opens the middle of the arm, a second above it the dome base. The crossing is a perfect square with its corners beveled at a 45° angle, against which a pair of engaged columns is placed. Above their entablature, a hemispherical pendentive dome springs from stilting. The dome apex is marked by a tall lantern.

Regularity and consistency are hallmarks of the interior (Fig. 92). The wall forms a continuous surface encasing the church. Crossing columns and the pilasters articulating the arm walls are of a uniform height, form, and coloring. The entablature, with *ressauts* over each pilaster and column pair, is wrapped about the entire church.

In contrast, crossing and arm vaults are discontinuous. A step cut into the masonry between them eliminates their possible line of juncture. Without being specifically developed as such, this treatment suggests a freestanding crossing tholos by creating the illusion that the crossing dome is a thick shell placed beside the arm vaults. In this way, the entire crossing unit—from paired columns, projecting entablature, and stilting, to the pendentive dome—is given a degree of independence within an otherwise highly homogeneous fabric.

As at Kitzingen, there is an inexplicable discrepancy between the surviving projects for the Käppele and the existing building. The projects are recorded in the ground plans S.E. 45, 46, 47, 48, and 52, and in the sections S.E. 49, 59, and 52.[9] These drawings depict two variations, which can be summed up here by reference to S.E. 48 and S.E. 51, both of which show the church largely as it stands, but in each case with several significant changes. Four differences mark S.E. 48 (Fig. 93). Firstly, entrance and choir arms are clearly distinguished from one another; the west arm is treated as a rectangle set at cross axis to the church, but a half-circle determines the choir. Secondly, the cross arms are dissolved by windows; in place of the single central window of the executed building, five large units replace most of the walls. Thirdly, the crossing is marked by arches rather than the executed step in the vault. And lastly, the paired columns of the crossing are engaged with the beveled corners; they carry a large dome which swings out into the arms, slicing through the crossing arches and into the arm vaults.[10]

S.E. 51 shows a less dramatic rendering of the church (Fig. 94). In the cross arms, the fenestration has been reduced to two units. An oculus opens the arm vaults; whether this was intended for S.E. 48 is, of course, impossible to say, since there is no elevation for this plan. The dome size also has been reduced; treated here as a pendentive dome, it is carried on torsion arches that swing in slightly, preserving the arm vaults intact. The crossing arches of S.E. 48 have disappeared.

Each of these interpretations, the first more adventurous than the second, reveals a church more striking than the standing building. In the present structure the entrance and choir arms are similar to one another; with the independent character of the former largely reduced, the latter is lengthened. Entrance-choir arms and north-south arms now mirror one another over the crossing, rather than generating movement between them. The dome, no longer carried on torsion arches, has largely lost its kinetic force. These changes conventionalize the interior, dissipating axial and spatial tensions. A greater stolidness pervades; mass is continuous and imbued with a sense of weight, space consists of static volumes without dynamic quality.

The lighting of the interior further emphasizes this ponderous sense. The fenestration is not as abundant as in most

Neumann churches; light entering from a limited number of sources spreads blandly through the interior. Even on a bright day, little more than an even glow is present. As a result, the light neither dramatizes nor dematerializes. It is merely the illumination of the interior, not a creative element of the internal space.

The heavy treatment of mass and elevation, as well as the somber lighting,[11] imbues the church with the character of 17th-century Roman architecture, though without reference to any specific monument. The static quality and reserved plasticity of the interior appear as a faint remembrance of Italian 16th-century work.[12]

Neumann's initial project for this church was adventurous and original. In contrast, the executed building has an eclectic character. The two projects—1740 as opposed to 1747–49—make strange bedfellows. Yet in view of Neumann's general design approach, the dichotomy is not surprising.

St. Katherine
at Forchheim

Very soon after designing the Käppele, Neumann tackled the hospital church of St. Katherine at Forchheim (Fig. 95).[13] A single sheet, dated 12 March 1748, with plan, cross section, and facade elevation, remains as a record of his intentions. Several unresolved points appear in the design which would have to have been adjusted before the church could have been built; thus it would seem that this was not a final project. Despite these difficulties, the drawing is sufficiently detailed to enable closer consideration.

Neumann envisaged the Forchheim facade as a wide central area with narrower wings. Corners are marked by pilasters, but most of the wall is penetrated by huge windows, an arrangement that continues along the sides of the church and around the choir. On the facade, large volutes connect the wings to a pedimented third story, where the wall is largely replaced by panels, pilasters, banding, a niche, and sculpture; the forms and proportions of this area relate awkwardly to the extensive fenestration below.

The plan of Forchheim is a modified and expanded Greek cross church. The crossing, slightly wider than it is deep, is surmounted by a hemispherical pendentive dome. Neumann achieves this relation between circle and rectangle with unorthodox elements: between the crossing arches and the dome itself he introduces crescent-shaped segments of vaulting that flare out from the arches and slice into the bottom section of the dome. Wider along the longitudinal than the cross axis, the crescent-like zones regularize the crossing, enabling it to be covered by the hemisphere. Each of the four arms joins the crossing piers as a slightly abbreviated half-circle, with the north-south arms of course wider than their counterparts. Covered by half-domes, the arm walls are richly fenestrated: a bottom band of squarish windows abuts tall vertical windows placed directly above, which in turn rise to the dome base. Each window is marked by a narrow, plain frame; jambs, base, and modestly curved head splay out through the thickness of the masonry. Each set of tall and squarish windows is set off as a vertical unit by a bordering line etched into the wall.

This Greek cross does not constitute the whole church. The entire western half merges with a rectangular unit made up of one bay accompanied by aisles at either side. The western cross arm is indicated only by a railing which curves into this bay. The western parts of the cross arms are similarly defined by railings where they merge with the aisles. Since the cross section on S.E. 215 shows only the eastern half of the church, none of the wall articulations or vaulting to the west can be determined. Particularly unclear is how Neumann would have solved the problem of merging the aisle vaults with the half-spheres of the arms.[14]

Forchheim exemplifies once again Neumann's attempt to combine the centralizing tendencies of a Greek cross church with the additional space and circulatory advantages of a longitudinal building. The two sections are locked together in a direct, almost abrupt manner, but the result would not have been simplistic. Had the church been built, the visitor upon entering would have been struck by its sense of openness, the result of the broad, rectangular entrance area, the extensive fenestration of the arms, and the generous opening of the two spaces into one another. Passing forward into the crossing, he would have discovered its symmetry and focal concentration.

Neumann's richly shaded drawing further specifies his intentions. Outer walls are largely replaced by windows and the voluminous internal space is interrupted only by the western crossing piers, yet the plasticity of mass is everywhere evident. The wash ranges from a light-saturated white to near black. It is employed to emphasize the double window framing, showing the thickness of masonry sliced away for the large openings. It underlines the rounded volumes of the arms, as well as the sculptural quality of the framing piers. Different tonalities distinguish pilaster from pier, stressing mass and projections from that mass. In the vaults a chiaroscuro of washes produces a vivid three-dimensional impression of curving, molded masonry. The vaulting is on the whole darker than the elevation and the very manner in which it is rendered in the drawing reveals its major purpose: to serve as a continuous, voluminous form, emphasized through shadow, which gathers together the energies of the elevation and defines the basic form of the plan. The cross-arm vaults range from velvety black to dark gray, in sharp contrast to the eastern arm vault, with its bright light and light-filled shadow. A broad spectrum of shading—from black to light—flows over the pendentive dome and vault crescents. In this way, Neumann stresses not only the continuous, voluminous surface of the vault, but also its plastic richness, set apart from the pendentive dome, the half-spheres of the arms, the crescent-shaped cuts into it, and the projecting crossing arches. The thick masonry of wall and piers climaxes in an elaborate sculptural interpretation in the vaults.

None of these Greek cross churches is of the "classic," centralized type, such as Sta. Maria della Carceri in Prato, or Sta. Maria della Consolazione in Todi. Instead, the arms at Kitzingen (Fig. 85) and Forchheim (Fig. 95) form major and minor axes placed in dynamic relation to one another; in the Käppele (Fig. 90) arms of dissimilar size result in a largely static interior. Neumann accents every crossing by a dome, the standard form marking the center of Greek cross churches. But each version is different: the more conventional pendentive dome with lantern at the Käppele (Fig. 92), the unorthodox arrangement of elements which supports the spherical dome at Forchheim (Fig. 95), the bold circular vault on columns at Kitzingen (Fig. 86). Elevations and lighting are treated with similar variety, as Neumann ranges from the plastic accentuating shadows of Forchheim (Fig. 95), to the combination of neutral walls and freestanding, open units in Kitzingen (Fig. 88), where internal spaces are accented by window placement, to the Roman massiveness and direct illumination of the Käppele (Fig. 92).

We now turn to a group of generally larger, more elaborate commissions. All are longitudinal churches that share one or more characteristic: Latin cross plan, wall piers, tholos-like crossing. Gaibach and the 1740 Käppele project contain all three hallmarks; the Würzburg Dominican church, Langheim, Mainz, and Maria-Limbach contain one or another.

On 5 August 1740, Neumann wrote to Friedrich Karl that

The Holy Trinity Church at Gaibach

he had prepared a design for the parish church of the Holy Trinity at Gaibach, to be located across the street from the Schönborn Residenz in that town.[15] Construction was begun in 1742, the consecration held 1745. No drawings survive for the church, but Neumann's authorship is indicated in two ways. First, statements in a number of letters associate him with the building, even though they never explicitly confirm him as architect. Second, the style of the church seems to reveal his hand. Neither index provides an iron-clad attribution, but together they make it so difficult to doubt Neumann's involvement with the design, that no scholar has ever challenged the assumption.

As at Münsterschwarzach, Neumann clips a single tower to the choir exterior (Fig. 97). The tower is rectangular in plan, but its third story, which rises above the roof of the church, is octagonal with a richer articulation than the first two stories; it is capped by a steep, domed roof. Elevation, transitions, and proportions are convincing. The facade, on the other hand, is strangely awkward: treated like a flat wall, it is tall and narrow, with large volutes over the wings and a thin, stubby middle section between them. The central pilasters of both stories are twisted inward so that an abrupt angularity disrupts the flat wall plane. Isolated within the facade, these angular forms carry little aesthetic weight; they amplify the awkward nature of this wall, which shields an interior of unusual curved spaces.

The plan (Fig. 96) of Gaibach consists of a two-bay nave attached by a transitional bay to an eastern section containing oval crossing, transept arms, and choir. Behind the facade, at either side of it, spiral stairs encased in masonry lead to the organ balcony. A vestibule zone splays out from portal to nave bordered by softly undulating walls. Inserted into this space, the organ balcony swings forward from it into the first nave bay. Supported there by two columns, it provides a low, canopied extension of the vestibule into the church proper.

Four elements constitute the two-bay nave: outer wall, wall piers, pilasters surmounted by cross ribs, and groin vault (Figs. 97, 98, Pl. VII). Each bay is defined by piers faced with a pilaster, from which broad cross ribs spring; groin vaults are located between them. The pier flanks bend back to the wall over a concave surface which continues vertically and without interruption into concave arches. In this way, the flanks of two piers and their common arch form a distinct unit between the piers. A tall window with round head, placed concentrically to the concave arch above, generously opens the plain exterior wall.

The nave elements are treated as distinct and independent units. Each is separated from a stepped edge which functions like a shadow joint, outlining the form. Devoid of all surface ornament, and painted a uniform off-white, the interior has a mass and plasticity in which no boundaries are slurred, no elements kneaded together: all is exact, distinct, and lucid.

The eastern half of the church consists of four ovoid units: the large crossing, the choir, and the smaller transept arms. Over the crossing (Fig. 99), four square piers support a pendentive dome of slightly flattened profile. The oval cylindrical walls of choir and arms (Fig. 100) continue into ovoid domes without a mark to indicate where one begins and the other ends. A single, tall, round-headed window opens the center of each arm wall, while two brighten the apse, one at either end of the oval. The only articulation of the completely smooth dome and wall surfaces are two pilasters set within each space. They support torsion ribs which bend up over the vault to the crossing dome. The joining of rib and crossing dome at the true center of each oval affirms the ovals' unity of form, even if they are cut away by the crossing vault.

Aside from small rococo cartouche or medallion figures which lighten the elementary entablature, the architecture of Gaibach is devoid of all decoration, be it stucco, painting, or sculpture. Only the three altars and a pulpit provide decorative accents. But ornament is unnecessary in this space, because the interior itself is austerely sculptural. The crossing strikes a dominant chord due to its substantial, sharp-edged, independent elements. The piers are distinguished on the one hand by their off-center relationship to the wall spur behind them, and on the other by their continuity with the dome. Pier-face and dome are treated as a single surface, and the pier flanks become the dome edge, separated from the vault surfaces of the adjoining ovals by an incised step. Independent from its surroundings, the solid dome rests on the four blocky piers with all the strength and permanence of a Romanesque vault—a quality intensified by the static nature of the unit, which is locked into place by the surrounding ovals and firmly anchored to the torsion ribs.

Connecting the rectangular nave to the curvilinear east end of the church is a remarkable area, a singular configuration within Neumann's oeuvre (Figs. 96, 99). Essentially it is a fragment of an oval similar to arm or choir units. However, the two articulating pilasters are pushed apart, with no wall connecting them, since here the unit is open to the nave. Torsion ribs twist from these pilasters over the vault to merge with the crossing dome. But this oval fragment also is joined to the nave. Its pilasters half bury those on the eastern wall piers of the nave. The cross rib that springs from the pilasters has no eastern edge; instead, it becomes the vault segment over the oval. Thus pilaster and rib are, respectively, partially covered by, and part of, the oval fragment. The connection of one space to the other is irrevocable.

The angular western half of the church is different from the curvilinear eastern half, but all parts—including the oval fragment—are united by a congruency of formal interpretation. In both halves, the wall and vault surfaces are without decoration, curving elements are paired with straight-edged units, parts are clearly distinguishable, and coloring is consistent. The whole is decidedly plastic in character.

Neumann's church at Gaibach is full of contrasts. He employs a curvilinear east end joined to a rectangular nave. The crossing is designed as a detached, self-contained unit, as were the Schönborn chapel and Münsterschwarzach, but instead of the round, open, dynamic space of these churches, the fabric is neither open nor treated as a series of layers or plastic frames; instead, the full imperious density of the masonry wall makes a continuous enclosure. Neumann's effortless combination of detachable elements within this impenetrable fabric is remarkable. Yet the interior is neither sparse and uncomfortably severe nor overwhelmingly monumental. The bright tonality and sculptural quality of forms blend with ample light from large, evenly distributed windows of modest size to create an inviting, human interior of quiet dignity and peaceful reserve.

Scholars have tended to consider Gaibach as the first introduction of a curvilinear crossing into a Latin cross basilica.[16] However, the crossing of Münsterschwarzach is earlier, while buildings such as the Schönborn chapel and Kitzingen—the first earlier, the second contemporary with Gaibach—display variations on the curvilinear theme. More importantly, it is the unique interpretation at Gaibach that determines the church's character and significance.

The Käppele at Würzburg
(the earlier project)

Neumann's 1740 project for the Käppele illustrates a bold interpretation (Fig. 101) that was in no way incorporated into the church as built (previously discussed).[17] The basic parts of this design, presented with great consistency in the various drawings, are a single-bay nave attached to a large, circular crossing; partially circular transept arms; and choir. Freestanding units are placed within this fabric. A flat, oval vault is supported by four columns within the nave, and a shallow pendentive dome with circular base, raised on four pairs of columns, occupies the crossing. Oval and circular forms are set within nave rectangle and crossing circle with a layer of space separating them entirely from all outer walls.

This insulating spatial layer is easily achieved in the nave. The columns that support the oval vault are placed directly before the engaged column that marks each of the four corners of the nave. The rectangle is expanded along the facade and north and south walls by shallow rectangular areas covered by barrel vault strips. Although the oval vault curves slightly into these areas, it remains detached from the walls. This snug fit, and the common use of columns, closely associates oval and rectangle, even if they are not physically joined at any point.

Placed within the undulating walls of transept arms and choir, the crossing is made independent within a more complex space. To the west, the crossing vault curves toward the nave oval, but the two never quite touch. In the other directions, it swings out over torsion arches into the flattened, partial domes that crown arms and choir. These arches actually cut into the neighboring domes only after they have risen a short distance, producing small, triangular sections filled by recessed vault segments between the different parts; thus, the separation of crossing and surrounding vaults is made explicit. Behind the four pairs of freestanding columns, Neumann curves back the external wall according to the perimeter of a circle drawn concentrically around the circle of the crossing. Paired, engaged columns, placed against this wall, are connected to the crossing order by means of shared pedestals and entablatures—the only elements of junction between inner and outer forms. The paired columns and tall torsion arches open the crossing unit to the other internal spaces. But its articulation and surrounding spatial zone ensure the crossing an independent existence greater than that of any comparable tholos discussed above (such as at Münsterschwarzach or the Schönborn chapel).

The spatial layering becomes more complex where it separates nave oval and crossing circle, distinguishing the units from the wall and from one another as well. Between the two forms the outer wall projects into the church, providing a thickening of mass behind the engaged columns of nave and choir. But the wall is carved away between the columns by a deep concavity that thrusts up through the entablature to a spherical vault segment which arches across the church and passes between the torsion arches of nave and crossing vaults, establishing a buffer between them. This confluence of parts charges the spatial layer at this point with its richest form and greatest movement. The tensions generated by the curved forms of both outer and inner wall are recorded in the active space separating them.

A combination of freestanding and engaged columns, used singly and in pairs, as well as the introduction of pilasters, unifies the interior while accenting distinctive parts of the space. Columns and pilasters are all the same size, capped by a common capital type, and they support the same strongly projecting entablature, which wraps around the entire church. A minor-key accompaniment to the horizontal entablature is a string course set at the springing point of the window arches.

Upon entering the spectator first would have passed into the nave oval set at cross axis to the church. This oval pushes off to the sides, where double windows open north and south walls. Their brightness would have accented the cross-axial placement of the unit and its independence from the outer walls. The circular crossing beyond was to be larger and less bright. Arms and choir each contain two windows the size of those in the nave, but they are located to the sides of each area, so that light would have entered obliquely into the crossing. In addition, the total space lit by these six windows is easily twice as large as that of the four-window nave, and the crossing dome is greater in size and height than its nave counterpart. The richer shading accents this more voluminous space, which would have swelled away from the visitor to the sides and above.

This analysis is of necessity based on plans and sections alone. Though only a project on paper, the 1740 version of the Käppele appears to be one of Neumann's outstanding designs. Working with a rich variety of forms and rhythms, he imposes a complex and sophisticated space within a sovereign unity.

On 19 February 1741 Neumann drew up plans for a new Dominican church in Würzburg to occupy the site of the order's mid-13th-century building, and construction began that year.[18] Neumann built nave and aisles for the church anew, constructing walls and a facade that encase those of the older structure (Fig. 102). The old choir and two small, rectangular spaces at the juncture of nave and choir were retained basically intact, but a slightly lower barrel vault was fitted into this area below the original vault. Pointed lunettes over the clearstory windows in the choir rise to the vault crown, where their points touch; these windows and those in the wall were enlarged in the rebuilding.

The new nave (Figs. 103, 104) is divided into four bays by blocky piers faced with pilasters in low relief. Strong arcade arches open to the groin-vaulted aisles. A round-headed window opens the outer wall of each bay, which is otherwise unarticulated. Above the nave entablature, a barrel vault rises with a modestly steep profile. Large round-headed lunettes are cut into the vault above the clearstory windows set one to a bay.

Even when festooned by the stucco, paintings, and furniture (all destroyed in World War II), the interior had a blocky, massive quality. Though Neumann built most of the structure anew, the impression of a baroque-ized medieval monument remained. Hauttmann [19] considered this the result of a conscious decision: to create the illusion of an old building which had been fixed up in the style of the times. This phenomenon was by no means confined to architecture: a number of sculptures survive, such as the Rottenbuch Pietà (Fig. 105),[20] which attempt precisely the same thing. It is not clear if an overriding persuasion lies behind these efforts, or whether each is a separate and isolated incident. Certainly no source explains the attitude in Neumann's work. He built on old sites on several occasions but reacted to each situation differently. At Bruchsal he employed the old choir of a longitudinal church as one transept arm in a new Greek cross building. Part of the flank foundations of Maria-Limbach's predecessor, discussed below, was employed for that church's facade. The foundations of a Romanesque church support the present-day St. Paulin, Trier. In each instance, old masonry appears to have been used as a matter of convenience. For the Dominican church, however, the old nave was razed and a new, slightly larger one erected just outside those foundations, yet in a style that alludes to the earlier structure.

Scholars have looked at Bruchsal as a Gothicizing interpretation. Bachmann [21] suggested the Trier Liebfrankirche as a reference, and Hauttmann [22] supposed that the Gothic qualities of the building were produced in response to major programmatic considerations: the church was to serve as a mausoleum for the bishops of Speyer. Another tradition, however, maintained that St. Peter at Bruchsal was designed in emulation of St. Peter's (Bramante-Michelangelo's) in Rome.[23] Neumann's efforts at Bruchsal and the Würzburg Dominican church could have been spurred on by a medievalizing ideology (the late-18th-century artificial ruins in England, such as those at Hagley Park, come to mind), but no evidence for this has come to light.[24] Be this as it may, the Dominican church reveals Neumann in yet another light: the fecund creator of forms and spaces designed a building to appear as if he had not designed it at all.

SS. Mary, John the Evangelist, Nicolaus at Langheim

Neumann's project for the Cistercian monastery church at Langheim, begun the year after his project for the Dominicans, remained unbuilt.[25] Drawings for it depict a structure of immense size, interestingly organized inside, although some problems remained unresolved. Had the Langheim church been constructed, Neumann may have ironed out these difficulties; during construction at Vierzehnheiligen and Neresheim, for example, problems were eliminated as the architect developed his design strategies.

Four sheets illustrate Neumann's Langheim project.[26] They depict a church with a vestibule slotted between the two towers of the facade, a four-bay nave and two aisles, an ovoid, domed crossing flanked by rectangular transept arms, and a choir consisting of a rectangular chancel bay and a semicircular, raised apse. There is only one exterior view, a grandiose facade elevation (Fig. 106): bordered by narrower, one-story wings, two tall, richly articulated roofed towers rise to either side of a double-storied, three-bay central section. The towers are pulled forward slightly, columns frame the entrance, and over-life-size statues are set around the upper levels. The numerous facade windows are framed elaborately, enriching the existing collection of pilasters, panels, entablatures, and bands. The freestanding portions of the towers are articulated with engaged columns, segmental pediments, and steep domed roofs capped by tall, slender lanterns. The huge lantern rising above the crossing dome is framed by the facade towers, and the dome is, in turn, flanked by four smaller towers, two on each transept. Neumann conceived the Langheim exterior in the grand tradition of the seven-towered basilica, and he elaborated the elevation accordingly.

The interior measurements on the drawings indicate both the immense size and the interrelated dimensions of the whole (Figs. 107–112). The total length of the church is 240 *Schuhe,* which has been divided into a nave of 120 *Schuhe* and a crossing and choir that together measure 120. From crossing to dome apex is 120 *Schuhe,* while the transept is 120 *Schuhe* wide. Nave width (including the width of the arcade arch) is 60 *Schuhe,* each aisle 12. The order, including the pedestal, rises to one-third the height of the dome and one-half the nave height.

Sheer size is dramatized by Neumann's handling of the fabric (Figs. 108, 109). Tall, wide lunettes help to dissolve the nave vault, which is given a delicate air by vault cross ribs that are set high on stilting and treated as narrow bands. Pairs of columns arranged at right angles to nave length make tall arcades; single columns engaged to the outer wall of the aisles are set on axis with them.[27] This unorthodox configuration creates aisles that are reminiscent of a Greek temple peristyle. The sculptural elements are complemented by broad arcade arches and groin vaults—an assemblage of solids that contrasts with the aerial spaces of the nave.

Contrasts are intensified within the crossing (Figs. 108, 110). Four massive piers encase an oval cylinder. The piers contain the ends of the oval but not its flanks. Consequently, the crossing arches to the east and west are straight, while those to the north and south are torsion arches which bend slightly into the transept arms.

The crossing is realized as two cylinders. The first is established by paired engaged columns, entablature, and colossal brackets; the second, by the concave faces of the piers that continue into pendentives rising straight up (in contrast to the standard pendentive shape of an inward-bending spherical triangle). Physically joined, the two cylinders are distinct: the sculptural and structural skeleton of the inner layer and the outer solid plane. Above, the dome draws the crossing together under a thick shell with all the weight of a solid, Roman vault. But its steep profile, commonly associated with lighter structures, is cut away by a cincture of deeply set windows below and a mammoth lantern above, again creating intriguing contrasts.

Although the crossing is impressive, ambiguities and unresolved elements mitigate its effectiveness. In separating the cylinder into two layers, Neumann has left several points unclear. Firstly, the relation of the dome to the layers below is undefined, both in position and form. Due to the projecting ring at the base of the dome, it is impossible to determine visually if the dome continues either the inner or outer cylinder layer. Secondly, the definition of the solid shell is inconclusive. In both longitudinal and cross sections, the pendentives are shown to have an edge of some thickness, which runs parallel to the north-south crossing arches or curves out to the arches in the east and west. But as the pendentive drops to the pier, this edge is lost behind the entablature zone; toward the arms, it could be imagined buried behind columns and pilasters, but it disappears into the inner faces of the piers.

Perhaps less crucial, but also aesthetically unresolved, is the relation of the cylinder as a whole to the crossing piers and surrounding areas. It would seem that the idea behind the heavy piers was to provide sufficient mass to contain the form. This is the case to the east and west; but the piers are not wide enough to absorb the form along its north and south flanks. Thus the need for torsion arches, which swing beyond the piers and into the transept arms. The upshot is a form which remains clearly independent of nave and choir but bulges out into the transept arms. This divergent relation of the crossing to other spaces in the church exposes a slackness of interpretation.

Unhappily fragmented and disparate within themselves, the transept arms relate unconvincingly to the rest of the interior as well. The spaces are unfortunate in that one-story intrusions break up the area below, and the crossing dome slices into the vault above. The encasing fabric does not fare much better. The end walls are treated as decorative reliefs, with flat pilasters incorporated into shallow framing, and stucco and curved moldings foaming between the windows and above the panels (Fig. 108). On the other hand, the walls along the cross axis are largely consumed by windows, and allude to a muscular, sculptural framework in the use of paired orders and broad crossing ribs (Fig. 112). The reserved plasticity of these elements, however, contains none of the power displayed in nave and crossing, and remains foreign to the impressive, densely sculptural handling of the choir with its full range of pilasters and columns.

In the choir, space contracts, the sources of light are restricted, and the wall is charged with a sculptural dynamism (Figs. 108, 111). It is the narrowest area of the interior, yet the corner columns, backed by pilasters, push even farther into these limits. Above the columns rise statues or strongly projecting, profiled cross ribs. Complementing this richness, the recessed areas around door and loggia in the side walls are encrusted with stucco decoration. In the small apse, the elevation bristles with pilasters; depth is created here by lunettes that cut into the thickness of the vault. With only two clearstory windows lighting the chancel bay, as opposed to a wreath of openings in the apse, a concentrated but limited light is shown in the drawings to produce deep areas of shadow that further enhance the plasticity of walls and vaults.

The Langheim drawings are sufficiently detailed to convey an impression of intended effects. From the long, richly contrasted and cavernous nave and crossing, the visitor would have stepped abruptly into a more intimate, more solidly plastic and somber space—an area conducive to reflection, with the altar, raised before a semicircle of windows, as its focus. After the expansive drama of nave and crossing—at the far end of this long axis—the visitor would have been brought close to the altar, contained within a space of relatively small dimensions. The festive nature of this area is marked by the sculptural elaboration, its solemnity by the restricted light. This "festive solemnity" is the finale of a creation flawed in several details yet masterful as a whole.

St. Ignatius at Mainz

Begun in 1742 at the same time as Langheim, Neumann's Jesuit church at Mainz survives today in only a handful of documents.[28] Aside from some minor uncertainties, the interior can be reconstructed from these papers: no exterior presentations exist. Six drawings are in the Eckard Collection (S.E. 238–43), and two further partial renderings were discovered recently at Marburg (Staatsarchiv, Kartenrepositur, C187 M, Sheets 1 and 2). The stonemason's contract in Darmstadt provides information about the crossing.

Distilling Neumann's design for Mainz from these items is an involved process. They apparently contain a number of projects and/or variations by at least two architects. It will be argued here that J. V. Thoman first submitted designs for the church (S.E. 242 and the gray plan on S.E. 241), which Neumann then corrected, arriving at a preliminary project (S.E. 238 and 243). From these corrections Neumann developed a final and quite different version (S.E. 239, 240, red plan on 241), which was executed with one important change in the crossing.

Two plans, one rendered in red and superimposed upon a plan realized in gray, are shown on S.E. 241 (Figs. 113, 114). Döbler has attributed convincingly the gray plan to J. V. Thoman. It is related to one of the two plans shown on S.E. 242. The other plan on S.E. 242, drawn over that of Thoman, is a variation of his design. To this variant plan belong the sections of S.E. 239 and 240 (Figs. 115, 116). The plan and longitudinal section on S.E. 243 are related to the Thoman gray plan of S.E. 241: similarities are apparent in choir, crossing, nave, and, to a degree, in the vestibule. This plan agrees with one of the two plans on S.E. 238, where again one plan is superimposed upon a second that is stylistically unrelated to Neumann's work, though it is connected to the Thoman projects on S.E. 242 and 241. The association between S.E. 243 and Neumann's plan on S.E. 241 is established by the similarity of spaces placed around the outside of the choir, and which are absent in Thoman's projects.[29]

The following conclusions can be drawn from these overlappings and interconnections: Thoman offered the Jesuits a project (S.E. 238) and variations (S.E. 242). Neumann corrected this project (superimposed plan on S.E. 238) and had this design, though not completely thought out, drawn up by an office hand (S.E. 243).[30] At perhaps the same time, Neumann transformed Thoman's other project (S.E. 242, 241). It was this second, thoroughly conceived project that is presented in S.E. 239 and 240.

This explanation raises questions about the two recently identified Marburg drawings: a partial section and plan related to Neumann's project (Figs. 117, 118). Because the plan, in contrast to S.E. 241, 239, 240, shows freestanding, paired columns in the crossing, and the Mainz stonemason's contract calls specifically for eight freestanding columns, it has been assumed that these poorly preserved sheets were working drawings, representing the final modifications for the executed church. But the sheets themselves make such an interpretation doubtful. Both section and plan offer several interpretations of the area depicted, instead of the straightforward, "structural" detailing characteristic of a working drawing. This is most obvious in the plan, where three different versions of the pier and its relation to the outer wall are suggested, plus several modifications of that wall.[31] One would hardly expect such experimentation in a working drawing; it is, however, very much part of the *pensieri* (idea sketches) that Juvarra, for example, employed so brilliantly. Indeed, it would appear that the most defensible, and also most productive, understanding of these renderings is as *pensieri,* albeit done with straightedge and compass. What is fascinating about the Marburg plan is that Neumann experiments with vividly opposed interpretations. At the one extreme, he ties a substantial crossing pier to the outer wall with richly articulated masonry, shutting the transept arms off from the aisle and treating them as independent spaces. At the other extreme, a freestanding pier on the crossing perimeter is honed away to a sparse minimum, and freestanding, paired columns are placed before it. Here mass is delicately poised within a continuous flow of space between crossing, nave aisles, and transept arms. Whether these sheets precede or follow the presentation project (S.E. 239, 240) is impossible, and certainly not important, to determine. What is significant is the nature of Neumann's wide-ranging variations: from plastic containment to airy openness.

The "final" project for Mainz (Figs. 114, 115, 116) shows a church with a four-bay nave and an aisle at either side; a circular, domed crossing located between shallow transept arms; and a two-bay choir terminated by an apse. A tripartite division of the elevation is of the "court chapel" type: simple ground level, major story above, and a clearstory as the third tier.

Neumann designed the nave as a self-contained unit within the church, yet one that was surprisingly open. The pedestals at either end are set at 45° angles, the columns on them support torsion arches, and the barrel vault between is dropped slightly. Having thus bracketed the nave, Neumann reduced the elevation to a slender grid standing before the largely dematerialized outer boundary of plain wall that frames large areas of glass.

The crossing is divided into three zones horizontally— pedestals, columns, and dome—and vertically into two domed cylindrical units, one slotted into the other. Pedestals, columns, entablature, stilted elements, and the dome define the inner unit, while the flanks of piers, the pilasters and entablature, lower torsion arches, and the crescent-shaped elements of the dome establish the outer shell. The impression that inner cylinder and dome form a distinct unit which can be rotated on its axis is presented with conviction: a circular tholos has been placed snugly within a cylindrical shell.

The transept arms, mostly solid wall and articulated differently, are distinct from the skeletal crossing and its voluminous cylinder of space. But like the nave, they are extensively open to the crossing, and locked into the outer cylinder by means of the crossing pier flanks and torsion arches.

Space contracts in the choir: it is narrower, the aisles are omitted, the floor raised. The absence of ground-story windows results in a concentration of masonry around the altar. The sense of a voluminous, open space is limited, drawing the dynamics of the church to a close about the altar. By designing a standard choir, Neumann did not maintain the intensity of formal description he presented in the rest of the church. With no centralizing emphasis, the choir is less clearly defined than are nave, crossing, and arms, and therefore it stands as a disparate area within the interior—more a thing apart than a distinctive part within the whole.

The visitor would have entered a tall, half-cylindrical unit of considerable severity, mostly unarticulated masonry, which opened broadly into an expansive, richly defined nave—a longitudinal area containing the suggestion of centralization. A plastic skeleton of pedestals, orders, ribs, and arches or balconies framed the nave yet permitted it to flow openly into generous bordering spaces (aisles and balconies). After the nave, the tall crossing tholos would have stopped the spectator's forward movement beneath a mammoth lantern. Distinctive transept arms established a bold cross axis. Following this pause, the visitor would have stepped into the first choir bay, beyond which was a space that could not be entered, where the mass of the church was drawn in about the altar. Procession from entrance to altar was measured and rhythmic; though the raised altar would have been clearly visible from the moment one entered, the interior would have unfolded with a calculated awareness of movement, with each unit demanding its own attention.

Unlike other "court chapel" interiors, the ground and second stories at Mainz were treated not as two distinct levels, but as one. The pedestal and order became a continuous vertical shaft, so that the order was not merely the distinctive articulation of the second story; instead, it was raised by its support high above the spectator's head, forcefully monumentalizing the interior.[32] Yet the unit was not insistently massive; on the contrary, it was distinguished by a slender elegance which complemented the open skeleton of piers and arches against which it was set.

An impressive lighting scheme further intensified the internal spaces. From floor to vault crown, the exterior skin of the nave was broadly glazed. Bright exterior light would have dematerialized the nave skeleton, outer wall, and clearstory, daringly and dramatically reinforcing the expansive nature of this area, to which the crossing arms, largely masonry, offered a bold counterpoint. The crossing dome, bathed in a flood of light from above, was distinguished from the other vaults, which were illuminated only from the sides or below. In the choir, light entered from the second-story clearstory only, emphasizing the more closed space, the more insistent mass, particularly at the lower level around the altar. The open, expansive space of nave and crossing was tempered here by a concentrated, inward focus.

St. Ignatius at Mainz was to have been a large church, given a strong unity by the use of stories, articulating elements, window forms, and by spaces that flowed freely into one another. Sheer size was made monumental by the orders. Within this entity Neumann incorporated a rich counterpoint of distinct and disparate spaces, a sense of procession, and a controlled use of contrasting light. The surviving evidence, as understood here, indicates that the church represented one of his outstanding efforts.

Maria-Limbach

After this flurry of activity—five designs in less than two years—Neumann did not return to the longitudinal basilica type for almost a decade, and then the building was modest in size and effort. Begun in 1751, the fabric and vaulting for the pilgrimage and parish church of the Visitation of Mary, at Limbach am Main, known as Maria-Limbach, were complete by 1754, though the furniture, some of it modeled after Neumann's designs, was in place only by 1762.[33] Of the ten drawings associated with the church, one alone belongs to the project stage (S.E. 192, Fig. 123). The others appear to be presentation drawings for the executed building, views for publication (S.E. 193, Fig. 121; also S.E. 194, 195, and 196, Fig. 120), and completions (tower by Neumann's son, Franz Ignaz Michael, on S.E. 235; roof construction by Löffler, S.E. 413, 414) or variations by other hands (Georg Friedrich von Fackenhofen's lost rendering and the Bamberg sheet by Neumann's Würzburg pupil, Johann Michael Fischer).[34]

At Maria-Limbach—as at Gaibach—Neumann makes the facade a thin wall and locates a tower at the apse (Figs. 119, 120). Here, however, the tower is not clipped to the outer shell but is drawn into and placed above it, uniting the external mass into a more compact composition. The facade wall consists of a three-bay central section that is two stories high and capped by a pediment.

One-story wings are joined to this higher, central unit by simple volutes. The bays of the facade are separated by flat, very plain pilasters, and most of the wall is opened by windows. Along the flanks and choir, this austerity becomes unarticulated wall with unframed window openings punched into it at regular intervals. The rectangular tower is capped by a steep, domed roof, but otherwise its elevation is as plain as the rest of the exterior.

The three-bay nave of Maria-Limbach joins a narrower two-bay choir with semicircular apse (Figs. 120, 121). A webwork of flat supports, arches, and balconies, set close to the outer wall, wraps about the entire interior (Fig. 122). This reduced and simplified version of the Mainz church is illustrated in the presentation drawings, as well as in the left-hand side of the plan on S.E. 192 (Fig. 123). The right-hand side of this plan, however, shows an entirely different solution: a three-bay nave and two-bay choir with apse remain incorporated within an outer skin no different from that shown on the other sheets, but inside, bay sizes and articulation differ completely. In the nave of this version, two larger bays are separated by a narrower one, all with concave walls. Piers continue the wall curves, pointing into the interior at a 45° angle. Two sides of the resulting triangular form are faced with a pilaster. These presumably would support torsion ribs, which in turn would swing into the bay, producing vault divisions opposite those of the elevation. Neumann's plan is remarkably similar to Christoph Dientzenhofer's churches (Figs. 124, 125) at Obořiště (1702) and Eger (1707–11; also the city of Neumann's birth and early education).[35] Neumann departs from these prototypes in the choir. In contrast to the square choir of Obořiště, and the absence of a choir at Eger, at Maria-Limbach the nave's rich wall curvature continues into the choir, producing an undulating two-bay space terminated by a round apse. Like Maria-Limbach, both Dientzenhofer churches are of medium size. But the dynamics of sculpted walls and curved vaults at Maria-Limbach, the "syncopation" between elevation and vault sections, the richness of articulating parts, and the boldly activated space, create a sense of resonance and amplitude which visually expands the physical limitations of size. This is undoubtedly the underlying intention of S.E. 192-right: to aggrandize the visual perception of a small building.

Instead of this, the severely diminished version of Mainz was chosen for execution (Figs. 115, 117), a version in which austere and cool forms produce a space of brittle clarity. It is undoubtedly this quality of asceticism that has prompted some authors to see in the church a transition from rococo to neoclassicism, others to consider it the bloodless late work of an architect whose creative powers had been drained.[36] The existence of S.E. 192-right, however, demonstrates that neither explanation holds. While S.E. 192-right may derive from Obořiště and Eger, the details of the plan are personal to Neumann; certainly elevations and vaults would have been characteristic of the master as well. Why the simpler design was chosen for execution is not known; it may have been that the limited funds for the church were fixed by Friedrich Karl von Schönborn's will and Neumann took pains to remain within those restrictions.

A crystalline clarity and overriding sense of reduction distinguish the interior of Maria-Limbach (Fig. 120). Sharp, simple edges, surfaces that are plain and flat, and a sparse application of color and decoration produce a space of precise and severe definition. Nave and choir supports are merely shallow rectangles in plan; the flattened lower arches spring from a band wrapped around these piers. A delicate gray distinguishes this band and the fronting pilaster from the off-white support; a slightly darker tone sets off the straight balcony balustrade. Above, a sharp edge separates arcade arch and lunette. Quiet rocaille decoration within the arch and elsewhere was originally pale gold.[37] Vaults over aisles and balconies, as well as the transverse arches at both levels that connect the supports to the outer wall, are completely free of elaboration and precisely differentiated from one another. The outer wall itself is unarticulated. The barrel vault and lunettes of the nave are marked by a few thin bands and meager rocailles; these decorative elements are somewhat richer in the choir. Within this austere framework, the more fully decorated pulpit and side altars and the elaborate and colorful high altar, realized with an almost magical sense of gossamer lightness, stand forth as vivid displays of lighthearted decorative art.

Though far smaller and without crossing and transept, Maria-Limbach resembles Mainz (Fig. 115) in its use of a layered shell for the interior. In contrast to the richness and diversity of the larger church, the layering of Maria-Limbach is consistent throughout. "Wall" is separated into two sections, a plain outer skin perforated by windows, and a flat webwork of piers, pilasters, arches, and balustrades, which incorporates a spatial cushion. This flat, space-containing relief defines a primarily rectangular area; only the apse, from which the spectator is excluded by a confessional rail, curves outward. The quality of procession and spatial dynamics is dispelled; in its place, Neumann has substituted an inert interior. The brittle elements of the rectilinear shell enclose the space with dispassionate control.

The multiplicity of design strategies employed by Neumann in the six buildings just discussed becomes even more impressive when joined with the contemporary Greek cross churches and those in the following section. Before continuing, a brief recapitulation will draw some of these design themes together.

Four of the longitudinal churches contain detachable, domed crossing units. Gaibach (Fig. 96) and the 1740 Käppele project (Fig. 101) employ pendentive domes with shallow profiles. But whereas the Gaibach dome is ovoid and carried by square piers, the Käppele dome is circular and rests on freestanding, paired columns. Weight and mass complement the static nature of the former, while the latter is treated as open and light, and is distinguished from the external fabric by a spatial layer, conveying the impression that it could be rotated on its axis.

The steep profiles of the crossing domes of the other longitudinal churches culminate in immense lanterns. The domes are carried by paired columns: those at Langheim (Figs. 108, 112) are engaged, those at Mainz (Figs. 115, 116) freestanding. The order rests on pedestals of normal size in Langheim, and at Mainz is incorporated into a court chapel scheme. The oval Langheim dome springs from pendentives; Mainz employs a pendentive dome. The 1742 Langheim project, closely resembling the 1727 Münsterschwarzach design (Fig. 46), suffers from several ambiguities in articulation, from its hesitancies and experimental nature; it is contemporary with the mature and sophisticated Mainz crossing.

Equal to this diversity of crossing units is the variety of barrel vaults: the disparate groin vault sections at Gaibach (Pl. VII), the light, reduced unit at Langheim (Fig. 109), the centralizing interpretation at Mainz (Fig. 115). Maria-Limbach and the Dominican church in Würzburg have no crossings; their solid barrel vaults are conventional.

Neumann matches inventive elevations with this vaulting. At Gaibach (Fig. 96), he molds the wall piers to concave frames; in the Käppele project (Fig. 101) he combines wall piers with a freestanding oval unit in the nave; simple rectangular piers mark the Dominican church (Figs. 103, 104). Langheim (Fig. 108), Mainz (Fig. 115), and Maria-Limbach (Fig. 120) all contain nave webworks, though each remains an individual interpretation: paired columns and large lunettes at Langheim; a three-tiered system of piers, columns, arches, balconies, and lunettes at Mainz; flat piers, flat pilasters, shallow arches, and straight balconies at Maria-Limbach. The choir elevations of Mainz and Maria-Limbach continue those of the nave, while the Langheim choir is more closed and sculptural.

The lighting in all the churches is strong and lucid. At Maria-Limbach the fabric is opened regularly about the entire building, filling the interior with a uniform, bright illumination that accentuates the dispassionately clear articulation. The other churches contain window patterns that change from area to area, accenting and differentiating various parts of the interior. In none of the interiors are decisive dark-light oppositions brought into play. Within the context of an already bright interior a yet stronger light determines emphasis. This is the fact of the extant churches and it is the message of the projects, where shading consists of light-saturated washes of pastel hues and silver gray. Neumann utilizes light with an intensity equal to his dazzling internal spaces.

Of the three remaining churches to be considered, Vierzehn-heiligen and Neresheim have had extensive scholarly research lavished upon them, while the unbuilt court church for the Schön-born palace in Vienna—in certain respects more complex and ambitious than either—has received little attention. Each structure has an assertive centrality within a longitudinal interior, achieved by locating a dominating oval vault between smaller units set symmetrically at either end. But as usual in Neumann's work, the common denominator is less significant than an understanding of the variations within the basic theme.

Church of the Assumption of Mary at Vierzehnheiligen

It is frequently repeated that Vierzehnheiligen, Neumann's best-known creation, "one of the most ingenious pieces of architectural design ever conceived," was the product of happenstance.[38] As usually reported, his conventional 1742 design for the church was modified by the architect and construction supervisor, Gottfried Heinrich Krohne. Adding insult to injury, Krohne located the church farther east than Neumann had intended. This meant that the sacred area of the Fourteen Helper Saints (Nothelfer) whom the building was to commemorate, would end up in the nave rather than in the choir as planned. Upon discovering these errors, Neumann designed a new church, adding a grand, though highly unorthodox, crossing and nave to the extant portions of Krohne's choir. All of this is so, yet the information is incomplete and consequently misleading.

Neumann's 1742 designs for Vierzehnheiligen consist of two projects and a variation.[39] Recorded on S.E. 73-left, 76-right, and 79 (Fig. 126) is a longitudinal, Latin cross church with many similarities to Langheim. A two-tower facade fronts a three-bay nave. Single columns separate nave from aisles. Steep lunettes slice deeply into the barrel vault, producing large areas for generous clearstory windows. Though it is distinguished as a unit by coving to the east and west, the nave, as well as the aisles, opens broadly to the circular crossing, where a spherical dome, its mass dramatically reduced by wide, semicircular crossing arches, rests lightly on tall stilting that surmounts four pairs of freestanding columns. Semicircular crossing arms swing out to either side of the crossing. A rectangular chancel bay, articulated by engaged and freestanding columns and covered by a coved barrel vault, leads into a slightly lower apse. All of this is similar to Langheim in format, even though the design is plainer in parts and less imposing in size.

This project is varied on sheets S.E. 76-left, 77, 78, 80 (Fig. 127), 89, and 90. A balcony runs through the three nave bays to the crossing. It is supported by flat arches that spring from shallow pilasters, to which half-columns are engaged. A similar pilaster-arch arrangement frames the balcony opening above. Two tiers of windows above the balcony replace the single apertures of the aisle below. This arrangement continues in cross arms and apse. All sheets are signed,[40] with S.E. 78 and 89 dated "Wirtz-burg den 26 Julii 1742." Because of the date, the greater number of drawings with more specific details, and the presence of a pencil sketch of a longitudinal section on S.E. 73 showing a balcony added to the freestanding columnar arrangement, this variation is traditionally assumed to have been intended for execution.[41]

In addition to these variations, Neumann worked out for his personal satisfaction a separate project. Employing an outer shell similar to the variations above, the spatial concept of the interior is completely different. Already recorded on S.E. 73-right, 74, and 75 (Fig. 128), it is to these ideas that Neumann returned when he redesigned the church in 1744. Thus Vierzehnheiligen as it stands today is not simply the result of Krohne's interference. Instead, Neumann turned an unfortunate situation to his advantage by reaching back to an earlier interpretation which was a particular favorite.

Neumann's personal project, "composed by and for myself" ("selbst und vor [i.e., "für"] sich entworffen"), consists of a sequence of curved spaces. A rectangular vestibule, the only straight-walled unit,[42] opens into a longitudinal oval that fills the nave. Four curved niches billow out to accent the diagonal axes. A circular crossing meets curved transept arms to the north and south and to the east leads to an oval chancel bay placed at cross axis to a rounded apse.

All three plans include this layout. Analysis here will be based specifically on S.E. 75 (Fig. 128), since this appears to be the most thought-out version of the project, incorporating shifts in articulation from S.E. 73-right and 74, which clarify the spaces and their relationships to one another.[43]

No sections specify the design, but the basic concept is clearly revealed in plan. Eight columns support the oval, which swings out from the vestibule and pushes into the outer wall; its east end curves back into the interior and tangent to the crossing. Defined by four pairs of freestanding columns, the crossing is separated from the outer shell by broad passageways. Like a tholos, this unit appears as if it could be rotated on its axis, stressing its independence and self-containment. The transept arms offer modest variations of the circular form; realized as quarter-circles, each arm contains four evenly spaced, engaged columns. The transition to the sanctuary is made by a change in articulation: pilasters distinguish the cross axial oval of the chancel bay, which rests solidly in the external masonry. Finally, the quarter-circle apse is adorned with engaged columns and pilasters. Nave, transept arms, and chancel bay all join the crossing by means of torsion arches. Segmental vaults cover the passageways around the crossing.[44]

Teufel criticizes this design for its disharmonious rhythm. Three curvilinear units are arranged down the length of the church and three across. Within this system, he finds the nave oval disproportionately large, while the crossing, as the designer's fulcrum, does not possess the aesthetic weight that it should. From the point of view of the strident rhythms and powerful centralization of ovals and circles in the 1744 design, this criticism is understandable, but to consider the earlier project merely a preliminary exploration perfected in the later one is to impoverish both.

Peculiar to the earlier design is the manner in which Neumann specifies each area within the processional system with an individual, curvilinear unit. The longitudinal placement of the first oval directs the visitor down the nave. At the same time, this forward motion is modified by the inherent centralization of this oval due to the diagonal accents created by the niches. The centralizing theme becomes paramount within the circular crossing. But the crossing is in turn broadened into a cross axial arrangement by the transept arms. From the crossing the interior contracts into the oval of the chancel bay. Set at cross axis to the church, embedded within masonry walls, employing pilasters rather than columns, the open architecture of the interior is contained and concentrated. Finally, the circular apse, distinguished by three-quarter engaged columns supporting a torsion arch, and smaller still than the chancel bay, closes off the interior.

The placement of these forms also is different from the 1744 design. The sense of procession inherent within them recognizes the longitudinal basilical framework, so that one basic assumption informs both inner and outer layers. Both designs have in common an external fabric of oval and circular units. Freestanding at places, the internal forms open out to, nestle within, and at times mold the outer wall, acknowledging that boundary and working with it. In these qualities lies the generative power of the earlier interpretation for the later project. In short, the earlier project contains characteristics of its own as well as significant affinities with the later one.

Neumann's 1744 design is variously recorded: in plans (S.E. 83, 87, Fig. 129; also S.E. 91 and 92 by his son, F.I.M.N., dated 1753 and 1754 respectively); in a section (S.E. 86, Fig. 131); in exterior views (S.E. 81, 84, 85, 88); and in two models (one by Neumann housed in the Historischer Verein, Bamberg, Fig. 132, and a second, cruder affair which is owned by an inn in Schwürbitz über Lichtenfels/Ofr.). There are differences in detail within this documentation, but basically it records the church as built.

Inside the Latin cross shell of the 1742 projects (extended, however, to a four-bay nave), three ovals—a large unit between similar smaller ones—are placed longitudinally, filling the church from west to east. In addition, small ovals mark the junction of two of the major units, while spacious circular forms serve a similar purpose in the transept. The three ovals are skeleton cages in elevation, consisting of engaged columns, pilasters, piers, flat arches, and balconies. Large windows puncture the outer fabric regularly, producing three tiers of fenestration, one below the balcony, one above, one in the clearstory. Boldly opened by steep lunettes, the swelling shells and torsion arches of the vaults vigorously define the basic geometric figures outlined in plan and elevation.

Section and model contain one important discrepancy in the vaulting. Teufel considers the former, illustrating balloon-like shells without lunettes around the clearstory windows, to be the fantasy of an office draftsman. Suspicion is justifiably aroused by the crudeness of the rendering, which includes windows depicted in the curving vaults as if they were set into a straight wall. Dimensions and curvature as such, however, cannot be dismissed so easily, even if they appear unbuildable at first glance. Neumann had designed deep, voluminous vaults on other occasions, and had even erected an "unbuildable" vault over the Residenz stairhall at Würzburg. For that matter, model and church both contain an approximately five-to-four relation between elevation and vault—the same as in the section. The section looks so different because the lunettes are omitted, the shell profile is rounder, and the meeting point between center and end oval is lower. Most questionable of all is the curvature of the two end vaults, which flatten toward the center unit. Warped shells of this nature destroy the relation between plan, elevation, and vault and are therefore alien to Neumann's architecture.

This discussion of the Vierzehnheiligen drawings was undertaken to clarify the early history of the church, to introduce the basic parts of the building, and to suggest Neumann's compositional intentions. From the outside, the issues Neumann confronted in these projects are scarcely apparent. Vierzehnheiligen looks like a conventional basilica with two-towered facade, nave and side aisles, transept, and polygonal choir (Fig. 133). Its sandstone shell is articulated in an unassuming fashion by single pilasters. The most elaborate treatment of the exterior is the top story of each tower, where engaged columns, broken, segmental pediments, and domed roofs create a rich play of forms (Fig. 134). Yet two unconventional characteristics are expressed on the exterior. The shell is in large part dissolved by windows: whether on facade, flanks, or choir, whether low down or high up, closely packed rows of windows are everywhere—an unexpected distinction in a conventional basilica, which pricks one's curiosity. Also uncommon is the manner in which the central portion of the facade bulges forward. This is the western oval of the interior pushing out against the shell; from the outside, however, the curvature is unexpected within an otherwise rectangular, planar arrangement of walls. In short, the conventionality of the basilica format is put into question by the number of windows, their placement, and the treatment of the facade. Inside, these questions are resolved by Neumann's dramatic and unorthodox interpretation of space and light.

Like Neumann's personal 1742 project, and contrary to the commonly published opinion, Vierzehnheiligen's internal curving spaces do not create an independent world, separate from and unconnected to the rectangular perimeter. Inner and outer layers engage one another, separate, and create contrasts in a variety of ways (Fig. 129, Pl. XI). Decisively pushing out the facade, the western oval cuts back through the masonry of the towers to swing into the nave, removed from the outer fabric by aisle and balcony. Joining this oval and yet almost entirely freestanding, the smaller flanking ovals sweep into the external fabric with their outer flanks. Reduced in this area to a narrow passageway, the balcony presses against the wall, leaving it clearly apparent. This minor cross axis announces the major oval by creating a pause in the longitudinal arrangement of the interior. At the same time, it is in balance with the larger cylindrical space to the east, which establishes a major cross axis before the choir. The impressive openwork of the central oval curves majestically through the nave. The transept arms, realized as cylinders capped by spherical domes, nestle deeply in the outer wall. Also largely contained by external masonry, the choir oval curves back between sacristies in a final boundary.

Whether close or distant, interior and exterior remain distinct and visually effective. If internal forms directly engage the perimeter, their elevations are marked by pilasters to slender, vertical sections of vaulting between lunettes. The freestanding portions employ the richer articulation of columns, balconies, and arches. In both mass is minimal: the skeletal inner layer opens to a highly perforated outer wall. The pilasters, or the columns and lunettes, frame vertical bands of three windows. This system is interrupted only by the facade towers to the west and the sacristy buildings flanking the choir. Oval and circular forms produce a compelling dynamic in their interaction with one another and with the outer wall, heightening the dramatic integration of a longitudinal and centralized interior.

Altars play a major role in this drama. The altars in the oval units are set on platforms and decisively pulled away from the outer walls into their oval areas; they are distinct elements arranged within the space, but they also repeat the shape of the space, generating exciting interactions as they are experienced in time. The heart-shaped Shrine of the Fourteen Helper Saints by J. J. M. Küchel is even more spectacular. It creates an emphatic presence, because it occupies the center of the church along the entrance-choir axis and contains a solid lower zone. Wherever the spectator moves within the building, this structure must be acknowledged—its rich variety of forms, the views seen through it, its dramatic character. Vibrant and alive, it intensifies the space, expanding an already demanding multiplicity of readings.

The diaphanous nature of the spaces indicates the fundamental importance of light within (Figs. 129, 131, 134). The interior is everywhere open to light, which floods in, reducing the substance of the openwork along its edges, emphasizing its delicate appearance. Complementing this brilliant illumination is the treatment of surface: gilt, silver, and pastel, placed with reserve within the all-pervasive white interior, augment the froth and spangle of ornament. Though realized only after Neumann's death, these elements are an integral part of the whole, magnificently completing his architecture.

Vierzehnheiligen confronts the spectator with ebullient and

bewildering complexity. Overwhelming one at first with a vast, undulating area, the differing oval and circular units gradually become apparent. But internal space expands beyond these forms, and a new, ordered complexity—open yet defined—begins to emerge. Movement permeates the whole: each new position taken by the spectator presents new challenges of view. The church as a performance is as imaginative and varied as its architecture.

The Hofburg Church at Vienna

Neumann's 1746–47 project for the Imperial Palace in Vienna, the Hofburg, floundered because the War of the Austrian Succession prevented its realization. Recorded in several projects, Neumann's vision of the palace as a whole, and in particular its colossal staircase, has benefited from much scholarly analysis; his equally magnificent church, part and parcel of these designs, inexplicably has been neglected.

Three versions of the church are recorded in the drawings, a "small" project (Hdz. 4734, Fig. 135), a "middle" project (Hdz. 4729, Fig. 137), and a "large" project (Hdz. 4728, Fig. 138).[45] Discussion here focuses on the plan and section of the "large" project, by far the grandest, most thoroughly conceived, and best-recorded church in the Hofburg material. In it, a large oval opens to a similar rectangular unit at either end. Within this simple configuration, Neumann creates an interior that is both monumental and complex.

As with no other building or project in his oeuvre, each of the three basic areas is defined by a triple layer in elevation (Fig. 136). In the oval, four pairs of free-standing columns support an ellipsoid pendentive dome. Behind them stands a second, elaborate layer. Sections of wall with pilasters frame a two-story unit that curves around the oval ends. Below, piers with connecting arches support a balcony, which in turn supports columns and joining arches. The width of a passageway separates this layer from an outer wall articulated by pilasters and perforated with windows at three levels.

A similar system informs the rectangular units to either side. Their circular pendentive domes are carried on piers faced by pilasters. Large columns that match those of the crossing mark east and west ends. In elevation, the second layer of piers, columns, and balcony, and the outer wall and windows are similar to their counterparts in the central oval.

These elements are made effective by changing emphases and formal variations. The symmetrical placement of oval and rectangles, for example, also must be understood in a time sequence.

Entering a rectangular area, the visitor passes along the short axis of the central oval to reach the rectangular choir. The two inner layers of the entrance rectangle define the smallest internal area with the deepest passageways. By being thrust toward the spectator, these inner boundaries are emphasized while the outer fabric is excluded. Expanding broadly beyond the limits of this space, the oval becomes a decisive cross axis. Movement through the vestibule toward the altar is brought to a temporary rest here, as the vault lifts majestically overhead and the curving openwork sides accent the longitudinal axis of the oval. Beyond lies the choir rectangle, which is distinguished within the symmetrical unity of the church. It is wider and deeper than its vestibule counterpart and contains broader flank arches; it closes in a shallow apse set into the masonry of the eastern wall.

This movement is accomplished by the contrast of angular with curved units, opposing the static quality of vestibule and choir to the expansive crescents of the oval. Yet circularity is not entirely foreign to entrance and choir elevations, since balconies in both curve forward, while a rounded apse terminates the choir.

The elevations of the Vienna project may be Neumann's most sophisticated. Like the Jesuit church at Mainz, they combine a monumental order with a two-tiered division. But unlike Mainz, these elements are arranged in rich counterpoint. The freestanding columns and pilasters supporting the oval and spherical vaults are monumental. They stand on uniformly high pedestals and employ similar capitals. The vaults spring from a stilting which completes the sense of imposing and lofty dignity distinguishing the order. Pilasters and columns of the two-storied second layer are proportioned in relation to one another, not according to the colossal order. Moreover, the curving sections of wall supported by the balcony columns are kept distinct from the vaults; only the cornice and stilting zone are common to both. Drawn together at this point, the different vertical rhythms are succeeded by distinct and separate vaulting units. Finally, the outer wall becomes a foil to both inner layers: the lower band of windows begins exactly at the top of the pedestal of the monumental order; in all other respects the window patterns and their framing pilasters are related to the second-layer openings.

Interior space is defined by several distinct layers arranged concentrically in depth. Though all subscribe to the same unifying configuration, they remain separate and distinct within it. This is revealed most clearly in the oval; its vault is supported by freestanding columns, a tholos-like form. The walls enveloping this tholos are set around it and clearly distinct from it, but they have been opened in the crescents and broken away entirely toward the rectangular vestibule and choir. The outer perimeter is separated from this intermediary wall by a passageway. Perforated by large windows, it also is characterized by a strong sense of openness. The importance of light in differentiating the internal layers is vividly recorded in the luminous shading of the section. The dematerializing effect of light on the internal openwork may be understood as analogous to the Residenz church or Vierzehnheiligen. The spectator looks toward the light through the openness of one layer to the next; distinct in placement, each layer is informed with a distinctive rhythm as well. Yet in their articulation, these layers complement one another, so that a decisive definition of interior space is established by open borders. Neumann's ability to resolve conflict and paradox in a seemingly effortless manner is demonstrated again in this church. The creation of spaces within space, the drama of movement within symmetry, the complexity of elevations, and the brilliance of light are combined at Vienna in one of Neumann's most spectacular performances. When we recognize that this church was only part of an equally imposing palace complex, his Promethean vision is magnificently revealed.

The Holy Cross Church at Neresheim

Neumann began the designing of Neresheim by returning to his work for Langheim.[46] The three plan variations on S.E. 111 (Fig. 139) reveal all the components of Langheim, including the use of paired, freestanding columns set along the cross axes of the nave. A plan with left and right alternatives is shown on S.E. 109 (Fig. 140). The left half repeats one of the S.E. 111 variations. Over an erased right half, however, a new plan type is introduced, with single freestanding columns making narrow aisles which run continuously through nave, transept, and choir. A wall treated as a double-layered space container has supplanted the wide aisles.

In all of the five options on these sheets, Neumann doggedly pursued a Latin cross basilica format, even though this created unresolvable dilemmas. The cause of these difficulties lay in two conditions stipulated by Abbot Aurelius from the outset: his insistence that the old tower of the Romanesque church be kept and incorporated into the new building, and that the two monastery hallways, located to the east and west of the major court, both lead into the church. In his experiments with the Latin cross, Neumann attempted to locate the church between the Romanesque tower to the west (which he incorporated into the facade) and the walled-off eastern border of the site. Consequently, numerous difficulties arose. The transept arm jutted irregularly into the monastery court, and the two paths of circulation from the monastery could not be led successfully into the church. Aligning the eastern passageway with the center of the transept arm inevitably brought its western counterpart into the nave asymmetrically and uncomfortably far toward the west.

The decisive resolution of these problems occurs on two additional sheets, S.E. 110 and 112 (Fig. 141, Pl. I). The first, in pencil and with parts cut out and pasted over, records the process of experimentation. The second—containing plan, longitudinal and cross sections, and facade elevation, and finished with ink and color washes—surely was intended for presentation. In both, Neumann pushed the crossing into the center of the church, creating nave and choir of equal length. The transept arm now stands centered on the monastery court, and the two hallways lock into the church symmetrically at either side. In both drawings, a second major decision also was made: the crossing oval vault is no longer supported directly by the crossing piers; these are, instead, pushed out and joined to the external fabric with four pairs of columns standing before them. This preserves the notion of double layering suggested in S.E. 109-right (Fig. 140), and also pulls the massive crossing piers out of the space, opening and freeing it. But this decision was not yet clearly realized. On S.E. 112 (Pl. I) the piers still block the aisles. And in both sheets, the entranceways not only remain cluttered with columns, but are confusingly complex; anyone stepping into the church would be disoriented. If the two alternatives are similar in these points, a significant difference in vaulting distinguishes them: whereas S.E. 112 pursues the Langheim notion of combining a barrel vault in nave and choir with an oval crossing, creating difficult, even forced, zones of juncture, S.E. 110 (Fig. 141) suggests the use of domical units in the nave; freestanding, independent, circular elements are placed here one after the other.

These strategies are pursued in S.E. 113 (Fig. 142) and 114, two very similar plans which include three new ideas. The ends of the transept arms are squared rather than convex; the aisles are reduced to narrow passageways, returning to the notion of a double-layered wall in S.E. 109-right (Fig. 140); and the two-tower facade, with a new north tower balancing the Romanesque southern one, is abandoned. Instead, massive corner piers incorporating staircases flank the great swing of the facade; the western end is pulled out before the Romanesque tower and realized without deference to it. This interpretation is shown in elevation on S.E. 115.

On 8 October 1748, Leonard Stahl, construction supervisor at Neresheim, sent Neumann a plan indicating problems of construction. It is preserved on S.E. 117 (Fig. 143) and shows the church as it was envisioned when construction began (S.E. 116, 118, and Rep. XIV oben III are similar). In it, the problems revealed in the preceding material have been confronted, and the Neresheim concept has crystallized in a striking manner. A generous oval crossing, supported on four paired columns, dominates the interior. Oval transept arms flank this space. Two cross-axial ovals, set tangent to one another, constitute the nave, and are balanced in the choir by two circular units. The wall is treated as a double-layered plane. Despite the conviction of this design, the crossing piers remain awkward; their stiff, long curve introduces too much solid, oddly articulated wall into the interior. They continue to plug the passageways between wall layers, preventing an effective juncture of crossing with nave and choir, and restricting the entry from monastery to church. Changes in pencil on this plan propose the basic, final solution. The transept arms are made rectangular once again, and part of the pier is cut away by a circle, introducing a cylinder of space before the monastery entranceways and emphasizing these areas within the spatial sequence. Nave and choir passageways also are opened up, so that they join easily with the crossing.

Minor refinements are contained in the remaining Neresheim material, with the exception of four points. The first concerns the small columns flanking the piers at balcony level which lighten the mass of the pier in this zone. The issue is raised on S.E. 121, where for one pier two small column variations are shown, in both cases freestanding, but once with a pilaster backing on the pier, once without. Where the small columns appear on other drawings (on S.E. 122; for only one bay on S.E. 123 and 124; on F.I.M.N.'s S.E. 129, Wallerstein I, and Nicolai, Fig. 144), they are all shown freestanding and with pilasters. Suddenly on Wallerstein II they are shown engaged with the pier as they appear in the building today. Presumably the same conservative attitude prevailed here that spoke for lowering the vault height and constructing it of wood. Binding the small columns into the pier is more conservative from a structural point of view, but it also has aesthetic consequences. The solid mass of the pier is now more assertive. The freestanding, small columns would have emphasized the transparency of this zone, especially with light from the large windows visually dissolving the borders of this solid mass.

A second important change occurred during construction in the transept arms (Figs. 145–147), which Neumann had opened with five rows of windows—three in the broad end, one in each of the short sides. Those in the sides were filled up when built, introducing a larger area of solid wall and further reducing internal transparency.[47]

In a third change, the choir width was adjusted, making this area narrower and further distinguishing it from the nave. As a final alteration, secondary pilasters were introduced behind the primary units—as can be seen in the nave of the built structure—thereby adding plastic emphasis to the openwork (Figs. 148, 149). These changes modify the aesthetics of Neresheim. Neumann's intentions, as revealed on paper, must be remembered in considering the interior as built.

Opening the nave wall are three vertical bands of windows framed by two freestanding units (Figs. 145, 149). Arranged on a cross oval plan, they are placed tangent to one another within the nave, with segmental spaces slotted between them. Established in elevation by pilasters placed diagonally against piers, the oval configurations are delineated above the entablature by torsion edges which circumscribe ovoid vaults (Fig. 150). Deep lunettes open to clearstory windows in both vaults and the segmental vaults between. Originally, the ovals were connected to the outer wall only by the bridge-like entablature with flat supporting arch, creating a passageway at clearstory level. In the executed church, the entablature is supported by small columns standing on a low-set balcony, which produces a second walkway and a second tie to the outer wall.[48]

A narrower bay makes the transition to the crossing. Stepped out slightly beyond the nave walls, it contains a niche directed toward the crossing, as well as a section of the passageway that separates the crossing unit from surrounding areas.

The crossing consists of four pairs of columns and a steeply profiled pendentive dome (Pl. VIII). A large oval cylinder placed lengthwise in the church, its capping dome is distinguished by torsion edges from tangent vaults in the cardinal directions. Wide passageways further separate it from the outer wall behind the paired order. The crossing is flanked by small longitudinal ovals placed within rectangular exterior walls.

Similar to its nave counterpart, a transitional eastern bay leads into a three-bay choir (Fig. 148). Narrower than the nave, it originally contained two freestanding circular units. In elevation, vaults, and relation to the outer wall, the units were similar to the oval nave units. The choir ended in a plain wall before which the altar was to be placed.

Though basically symmetrical in format, the spatial relationships of Neresheim must be experienced as a processional sequence in order to be understood. A cavernous affair, the interior contains a series of monumental tholoi, each freestanding and open, each demanding individual attention from the spectator. These tholos units temper progress toward the altar. The visitor is drawn through these zones not so much by the attraction of a distant altar as by the unfolding vision of the immense crossing dome with its imposing columns. The unexecuted, deeper dome with lantern can be imagined as particularly effective. A cross axis is vigorously established by the transept arms when the wall participates in the heightened drama of this area: unarticulated and straight in the nave, here it is transformed into an undulating surface studded with pilasters. The crossing creates an appropriate caesura, since the deep choir of the monastery church is reserved for the monks. A confessional rail and rise in floor level, located just beyond the crossing, confirm on the spectator's level the break between crossing and choir.[49]

Though its vertical thrust and outward extension into the transepts are dramatic and compelling, the fact that the crossing oval is placed lengthwise in a longitudinal interior asserts itself gradually. The spectator cannot advance physically, but attention is drawn to the choir, where, as conceived by Neumann, two circular units present an area of containment. The width is narrowed; the altar is placed back toward the concave east wall;[50] the rhythmic movement through the interior is brought to rest.

More than in any other Neumann church, the outer wall serves as a neutral background for immense windows (Pl. IX). In both nave and choir, the plain surface is uninterrupted by orders, panels, or frames. Only three horizontal bands mark the wall in relation to the pedestals of the order. Around crossing and transept arms the external fabric flourishes with pilasters. But at this decisive cross axis, the eye is attracted to the sides, where regularly placed tall windows and generous clearstory openings eliminate substantial areas of masonry. As in the churches discussed above, this wall of light is fundamental to the transparency of the interior.

Because Neresheim is partially absorbed by monastic buildings, its facade and tower (Fig. 151) are its most important external elements; flanks and choir are left as plain, stucco walls. Again, as at Gaibach, Neumann clips a tower onto the choir, but it remains lower than the lantern crowning the crossing dome, and consequently is effective only when seen from the monks' cemetery located behind the choir. On the other hand, Neumann has added a new top story and domed roof to the Romanesque tower, making it the hallmark of the church when seen from afar. Largely embedded in the monastic buildings and distinct from the facade, this tower is not experienced as an integral part of the church as one enters; at this point the facade alone is effective.

The facade is two-storied (Fig. 152). Solid, pier-like units enriched by clusters of pilasters frame a three-bay unit that swings forward, is capped by a substantial pediment and opened by six large windows. Pilasters, panels, sculpture, and framing further enliven this area. Neumann's intentions for the facade are shown in several drawings, most clearly in S.E. 115, 126, 127. The present state of facade and tower derives from 1789–93, when the tower was made higher and the facade topped by an additional frontispiece.

Neresheim commonly has been evaluated as a dispassionate and cool space.[51] Some have considered these qualities nascently neoclassic.[52] And with this, Neresheim is presented as a grandiose finale to Neumann's oeuvre: a magnificent church summarizing his art, but revealing as well sentiments of a new age. This view, stressing certain characteristics at the expense of others, leads to inaccurate conclusions.

Without doubt, Neresheim is a serene, proud, and lofty space. The monumental dimensions of the interior immediately evoke awe. Almost 13 feet high, the pedestals of the order tower above the spectator (Fig. 153). The crossing alone is more than 65 feet long. On this scale, the symmetry of the church produces an impression of powerful but reserved formality. The dominant white tonality and minimum amount of decoration reinforce this severe elegance.

But these qualities must be seen in the perspective of the aesthetic considerations just discussed and of history. The symmetry does not create a static balance; movement is vital to the interior, and it is realized both by the spectator experiencing the architecture and by the architecture itself—in the relation of the internal units to the wall, in the sinuous curves of the torsion arches (Figs. 149, 150).

The stern impression would have been tempered in other ways as well. A dramatic contrast would have been created between the immense crossing dome and the other vaults, developing an emotional pull between them. Furthermore, Neumann envisioned decorations on the articulating members as well as ample stucco ornament generally.[53]

The completion of the interior derives from the last decades of the 18th century. Martin Knoller painted the vault frescoes between 1770–75; the stucco was undertaken between 1776–78 by Thomas Scheithauf, who then created the altars from 1778 to 1792. The organ was installed by Johann Nepomuk Holzhay, 1792–97. The character of this work is different from that which Neumann would have commissioned for Neresheim a generation earlier, yet it is of the highest quality and is effectively integrated with the architecture. The recently completed restoration of the interior brings this home vividly.

The churches discussed in this section consist of longitudinal, symmetrically arranged interiors with a dominant centralizing oval. At Vierzehnheiligen (Fig. 128) and Neresheim (Fig. 145), the oval is placed lengthwise within the building; at Vienna (Fig. 136) it follows the cross axis. Accompanying the oval are rectangular units (Vienna), cross ovals (Neresheim), longitudinal ovals (Vierzehnheiligen), and circles (Neresheim). Segmental spaces separating these major forms are employed at Neresheim, and developed into ovals and circles at Vierzehnheiligen. In all, the elevations are skeletal frameworks which open to an exterior wall of light. Vierzehnheiligen (Figs. 131, 132) and Neresheim (Figs. 144, 145) have contrasting inner and outer shells; Vienna has three layers. The inner shell hollows out and is at points engaged to the external masonry at Vierzehnheiligen, while at Vienna and Neresheim inner and outer elements are kept physically separate. Pilasters and window framing articulate the perimeter throughout at Vierzehnheiligen, but pilasters alone are employed in the crossings of Vienna and Neresheim, the walls otherwise remaining plain. All depend on solid shell vaults with torsion arches or edges to define the internal spatial units. At Vierzehnheiligen the central oval is only slightly higher than the vaults to either side; the difference is more pronounced at Vienna; at Neresheim it is decisive. Intrinsic to each of these churches are the dynamics of the forms themselves, the organization of procession, and the dominance of light-saturated, transparent spaces.

V.
Pedigree,
Theory,
Symbol

Neumann's ability to express vividly a range of architectural intentions has been explored. A basic omission from this review must now be considered: the background of these ideas and their significance. Both tasks offer problems. Previous scholars have searched for the sources of Neumann's projects, but most of what they provide is not very informative, much less convincing. There are two reasons for this. Formally, the relationship between suggested inspirations and resultant products is so generalized that the connection is rarely persuasive. Moreover, no scholar has been able to unearth hard and fast evidence that documents a particular point of presumptive contact. If the search for sources has, so far, been unproductive, the second problem has not been touched at all. Reflections about the meaning of Neumann's architecture are nonexistent; this aspect of his work simply has been ignored. To cope with this double-edged dilemma, the known range of Neumann's architectural experiences, his contacts with various personalities and places, and the nature of his involvement with architectural theory will be considered.

Neumann's travels indicate how extensive was his personal acquaintance with several theaters of architectural activity in Europe. In Chapter I, it was noted that his trips with Greising would have familiarized him as intimately with Franconian work in general as he already was with Petrini's in Würzburg itself. Next door to Franconia, Bohemia provided a second large area of significant contact. Until the 1730s, if not longer, Neumann kept in touch with his home town of Eger in western Bohemia. At least twice he had occasion to travel through Bohemia—as early as 1717 due to the Belgrade campaign with Prince Eugene, and more definitely in 1729, the date of his consultation with Hildebrandt in Vienna. Moreover, at least one member of the Dientzenhofer dynasty of designers from Bohemia, Johann, figured directly in his life.[1]

One relation between Neumann's work and earlier Bohemian architecture is evident in the vaulting systems: smooth vault shells, with torsion ribs and vault edges as definers of space. Christoph Dientzenhofer's church in Eger is an exemplary instance of this.[2] St. Clara (1707–11, Fig. 156) consists of a rectangular nave containing two generally oval units set at right angles to the main longitudinal axis of the church. To articulate the interior, Dientzenhofer used piers that jut diagonally into the main spatial area and support three-dimensional ribs. The walls between the central piers are perforated by door and window. The walls of the ovoid units are completely smooth and unarticulated; they are treated like an elastic skin ballooned out by the spatial content. The slender structural system stands like a wicket within this dominant spatial entity. The vaults are canopied over the enclosed space, and the papery walls bend out around it.

Since this building was completed the year Neumann left Eger, he may have retained memories of it. Certain unusual aspects of the church can be compared to his later works. For example, the internal forms are not isolated within the rectangular shell but interact with it, cutting into the wall mass or pushing out from it. Neumann would similarly orchestrate the interaction of inner and outer forms in many of his buildings.

Secondly, the vaults at Eger are smooth shells; and though the tangent vault borders are treated as ribs, the outer ones are not. What at first appears to be a rib is in fact the edge of the vault shell. Neumann would treat vault edges in precisely this manner. The edge itself curves three-dimensionally; it is not a rib or arch supporting the vault. This interpretation of the vault as a shell, with the thickness of the edge clearly displayed, is not found elsewhere in Europe during the period.

Bohemian architects, however, inevitably used piers to support the vaults, while Neumann was fascinated by vaults rising from freestanding columns, a notion that, as we shall see, he derived from France. Moreover, the exact correspondence between vault, elevation, and plan that characterizes Neumann's interiors is not pursued in Bohemian work. Common to both is the oval vault as a collector of internal space, but this form was widespread in Europe by this time. Furthermore, the oval in Bohemian architecture is commonly placed at right angles to the length of the church, its ends anchored to the outer wall, in contrast to Neumann's longitudinal sequence of freestanding ovals.

Neumann's familiarity with Viennese architecture was also extensive. After the siege of Belgrade he returned to Vienna, where he was already sufficiently recognized by local authorities to be offered an officer's commission. He doubtless visited the capital's architectural landmarks. Hildebrandt, in turn, visited Würzburg in 1719. The Viennese architect was consulted for the designs of the Residenz and the Schönborn chapel. Following Friedrich Karl's election as Prince-Bishop of Würzburg in 1729, the professional lives of the two men became interwoven.

Hildebrandt was trained by Carlo Fontana in Rome, as well as in northern Italy, and his secular and sacred architecture, from the Schwarzenberg palace to the upper Belvedere, from the Piarist church to the abbey of Göttweig, retained a sense of that Roman severity that originated with Bramante (Fig. 157). Yet he also absorbed qualities of the *bizzarria* found in the work of Borromini and Guarini. He employed these in a pronounced decorative manner, which loosens and lightens his designs considerably. Only once, in the church at Gabel (1699–1711),[3] did Hildebrandt address an architectural matter in a manner similar to Neumann. For the Gabel interior (Fig. 158), he employed torsion arches under the central dome and hollowed out its supporting piers. The torsion arches, however, are contained within the crossing square, which, in turn, is separated from the oval ancillary spaces by a second set of arches. Hildebrandt did not turn to torsion arches at Gabel in order to define one spatial configuration in relation to others. And he did not pursue even this approach in other buildings, where he maintained his allegiance to Roman design traditions.

Neumann reacted to Austrian architecture generally, and to Hildebrandt's work specifically, by avoiding references to both.[4] He identified neither with the realization of space in Austrian buildings, nor with the treatment of the elevation, nor, finally, with that type of decorative ensemble. The bitter rivalry between Neumann and Hildebrandt may partially explain this. While the

Schönborn revered Hildebrandt's advice and accepted him as an equal, they considered Neumann merely an employee. Just the same, the authority of Neumann's designs inevitably won the day in any confrontation between the two; the history of the Hofkirche demonstrates this decisively. Aside from this specific antagonism, however, Austrian work generally would not have interested Neumann; its more mural and massive character was foreign to his own architectural attitudes.

Roman persuasions also determined the efforts of Lothar Franz's chief architect, Maximilian von Welsch, whose designs evoke memories of solid, decorated, late-16th-century Roman work. Even as late as 1742, in his competition design for Vierzehnheiligen (Fig. 159), he illustrates a stern building of the Gesù type (begun by Vignola in 1568).[5] Employing a conservative architectural vocabulary, von Welsch treats heavy, massive walls, piers, and vaults with unrelieved seriousness. He and Neumann both were connected with the designing of the Schönborn chapel, as well as with the early planning of the Würzburg Residenz. Yet from the outset, Neumann's work reveals no trace of von Welsch's influence. That the two architects were diametrically opposed in their approach is revealed in Neumann's fundamental transformation of von Welsch's intentions for the Schönborn chapel: from space imprisoned within continuous walls, to space defined by a freestanding tholos (Figs. 24, 25).

Neumann had other contacts with Italy as well. Johann Philipp Franz, his first patron, was an Italophile. He had traveled extensively in Italy, had studied and made social contacts there, and was influenced by the architecture of Italy. The Schönborn chapel was a direct result of his interest in certain Italian building programs. Johann Philipp Franz supported Neumann at the start of his career, but primarily for work on the Residenz and in the administration of building activity within the bishopric of Würzburg. He had been dead for several years when Neumann received his first independent church commissions in the late 1720s. Consequently, the influence he may have had on Neumann's ecclesiastical work remains remote and elusive.

The same must be said for Neumann's 1718 sojourn in Milan.[6] Although it is reasonable to suppose that he would have familiarized himself with the architecture of that vicinity, the major arena of the new architecture in Italy was not Milan, but Turin. And though Guarini's buildings were up by 1718, the bulk of 18th-century building associated with the "Piedmontese School" was not yet under way. But these observations suffer from the paucity of specific knowledge available about Neumann's Italian trip. Only one document has come to light revealing his stay in Milan; exactly what he did there, where he went, and with whom he had contact is not known.

The last major area of significance to Neumann's background is Paris and its environs, such as Versailles and Marly, with which his contact was at first vicarious. In 1721 he visited the fabulously rich libraries of the Uffenbach brothers in Frankfurt.[7] Open to the public, the Uffenbach collections were almost a tourist attraction in their time. The guest book for 1711–33 contains the signatures of 846 visitors from all over Europe; Neumann's signature appears on 23 April 1721.

The three Uffenbachs had assembled three distinct collections. Zacharias Conrad von Uffenbach's library contained, among many other items, books on military architecture, mathematics, geometry, and fireworks. His brother Johann Friedrich Armand von Uffenbach was an art lover. Owner of a world-famous collection of art publications, his holdings included about 30,000 drawings and prints.

Probably most significant for Neumann was the library of the third brother, Johann Friedrich von Uffenbach. His collection of 1,822 volumes comprised almost every work of architecture published by 1721. In addition, large numbers of *vedute* from France, Holland, England, and Italy were included. Significantly, French architecture interested him particularly. During his travels, he made drawings of innumerable French monuments, concentrating on detail. His long stay in Paris, 11 September 1715 to 11 April 1716, was devoted to an exhaustive study of French architecture. He had absorbed Brice's guide from cover to cover and was personally acquainted with the author. He met Oppenord over afternoon coffee. For Neumann, Johann Friedrich's collection provided an excellent orientation for his own Parisian visit.

Such a visit occurred in 1723, when Neumann journeyed to Paris to consult with de Cotte and Boffrand on the Residenz plans.[8] He passed through Mannheim, Bruchsal, Strasbourg, and Nancy, and returned via Brussels, Frankfurt, Kassel, and Fulda. In Paris he had several conferences with both de Cotte and Boffrand, diplomatically avoiding mention to either one of his consultations with the other. Boffrand visited Würzburg the next year, and in 1745 published his designs for the Residenz as one of his major executed works.

The architecture in France that presumably would have interested Neumann had been designed by masters of an earlier generation, Perrault and J. H. Mansart. The Louvre staircase, the Versailles chapel (Fig. 160), and Ste. Geneviève were each based on a skeletal cage of columns. By his own admission, Neumann was interested in the freestanding column, and his designs demonstrate time and again the crucial role of the columnar cage to his spatial interpretations. But the work of his contemporaries with whom he had direct or indirect contact—de Cotte and Boffrand on the one hand, Oppenord on the other—contained little of significance to his efforts. The evolving polemic which led from Perrault to rich realizations of columnar open architecture—Laugier's masterful theoretical summary of 1753 and the building it directly inspired, Soufflot's Ste. Geneviève—was only in its earliest stages at the time of Neumann's visit to Paris.[9] We have no indication that he was familiar with the then new and crucial texts by Fréart de Chambray and Cordemoy that explored these concerns. In short, we can propose that Neumann was exposed in Paris to an architectural potential, which, together with a variety of other persuasions, he later pursued in independent fashion—just as different French designers were to pursue it in their own manner during the same decades.

These background suggestions may be augmented by considering prevalent architectural theory of the time. The connection is tangential at best, since neither Neumann nor anyone closely associated with him wrote or commented on theoretical problems. He did offer instruction on military and civil architecture at the university in Würzburg from 1731 on, but no specifics survive concerning the material he covered. Presumably it entailed the subject matters Müller had taught him: surveying, mathematics, and geometry. These were practical disciplines directed toward the technicalities of construction, be it fortification or chapel. Ideological considerations were foreign to such deliberations.

On the other hand, we do have an indication of the contents of Neumann's library, and we can reconstruct something of the intellectual climate in which such texts were produced, read, and used. Neumann's reading material [10] ranged broadly beyond architectural matters, reflecting the interests of a "universal man." Main areas of concentration include dictionaries and grammars, poetry and fiction, theology, law, medicine, natural science, philosophy, history, geographies and maps, mathematics, optics, perspective, considerations of painting, sculpture, drawing, and engraving, publications about functional structures, especially waterworks, and material on the science and history of war, fortifications, and artillery science. Almost sixty architectural treatises are listed, representing major names in Italy, France, England, and Germany. A complete list of these is given in Appendix IV. It contains such diverse items as the Palladian "line" of Palladio–Scamozzi–*Vitruvius Britannicus,* Paul Decker's *Fürstlicher Baumeister* with its colossally scaled and bombastic projects, J.–F. Blondel's elegant publication on country houses, Wilhelm's manual for roof construction, volumes by Le Pautre and Schübler on decoration, and Daviler's dictionary of architectural terms.

Instead of discussing specific items, we can more profitably understand the significance of this material by considering it within the context of contemporary German publishing on architecture. The prevalent architectural literature of the 17th and 18th centuries in Germany may be divided into three basic categories: foreign material—direct imports, translations, German versions of outside writings—and indigenous publications of two kinds: those pursuing the pragmatic, and those celebrating the spectacular. Neumann's holdings included a representative amount of all of these.

Notable among the Italian material in Neumann's collection was a large number of "classical" writings. He owned two of Rivius's *Vitruvius,* and two Vignolas in translation by Fäsch. In addition, Serlio's books 3, 4 (Venice 1540), and 5 (Venice 1551), as well as the first German translation of the whole treatise (Basel 1609), were included. There were three copies of Palladio: a 1642 Venetian edition, a French edition (Muet's *Traité* of 1646), and a German translation by Böckler (1698). Related to these are two editions of Scamozzi's *Idea,*[11] the Italian 1615 edition and a 1678 German translation. On the other hand, particularly "Baroque" publications from Italy included Pozzo in German translations of 1711 and 1719, and the 1740 G. G. Bibiena, *Architetture, e Prospettive.*

French work is represented by a number of volumes from the 1720s and before, and a second group published only during the last ten years of Neumann's life. The first category includes Leonard Dientzenhofer's 1697 translation of Dieussart, *Theatrum Architecturae Civilis,* notable primarily for its comparative presentation of the orders according to Palladio, Cataneo, Vignola, Serlio, Scamozzi, and Branca, and a 1719–20 translation of J. B. Toro's book on the orders. Marot's *Recueil* dates from the early twenties, and Jambert's *Architecture Moderne* from later in that decade. Of the second group, J.−F. Blondel's *Distribution plaissance* was published in the late 1730s, the others all after 1743: Briseux, Boffrand, Le Pautre. Only one publication represents England, but it is major, a 1717 edition of C. Campbell's *Vitruvius Britannicus*.

Closely connected to Italian treatises on the orders, be they Serlio, Vignola, or Palladio, are large numbers of similar efforts by German authors. These began with Blum in 1550 [12] and were still being written two centuries later.[13] In terms of sheer number, they were the most popular of any genre in Germany.[14] Though at times the visual interpretation of the orders was extraordinary, as in Dietterlin's *Architectura,* the format of presentation and the effort to establish a system of proportions remain closely related to Italian biases. Neumann owned several of these books, one by Indau, one by Nonnenmacher, two by Erasmus.

In contrast to this material, two literary genres existed which were more particular to the German scene. One attempts to record all building types in word and illustration, imposing a simple, unified system of proportions. Free in large part from stylistic demands, the text is primarily descriptive. Stress is laid on mechanical considerations (how foundations are properly put in or the pieces of a door assembled) and on functional demands (circulation, ventilation, lighting, heating, and so on). From an aesthetic viewpoint, the designs in such texts are often pedantic to the point of distraction. Major efforts in this direction began early with Furttenbach's works (Fig. 161), and were continued by Goldmann and Sturm. Of these, Neumann owned two of Furttenbach's volumes and five by Sturm, including his volume on church architecture.[15]

More striking is the second group of indigenous publications, which capitalizes dramatically on visual presentation. These volumes do not illustrate what their author had built, seen, or esteemed; they do not record theories of architecture; instead, those projects which the architect felt to be valid and worth imitating are displayed. The visual material is of prime importance; it was intended to "sell" the ideas of the creator, if not to serve as an apotheosis. "It is obvious," wrote Paul Decker in the Foreword to his *Fürstlicher Baumeister,* a prime example of this genre, "that these are not the uninteresting, common inventions seen everywhere; instead they are such, in which the rules of symmetry as well as of decorative variation have been taken into consideration; so that those who wish to make use of this work may always find sufficient help and considerable easing of their task." These publications present the most spellbinding creations of a particular architect, and also the most spectacular of what was generally available in South Germany. The beginnings of the genre extend back into the 17th century with Abraham Leuthner's *Gründtliche Darstellung der Fünff Seullen* of 1677. His first pages on the orders are copied lock, stock, and barrel from Blum. But the remaining, larger part of the treatise consists of plate after plate of projects for portals, niches, baldachins, tombs, churches, palaces, altars, fountains, and so on, all without an accompanying word. The classic statement in this genre is Decker's 1711–16 work, a handsome folio production with lush engravings of a brilliant architecture (Fig. 162).

Fischer von Erlach's *Entwurff einer historischen Architektur,* significant because it marks a first attempt to write comparative architectural history, is also essentially of the same type. As he says in the book, he intends "to please the eye of the amateur by some examples of different ways of building and to inspire the artists to inventions rather than to inform the erudite." The visual emphasis of these works is brought home in a volume by P. J. Sänger published in 1730. The title of this book indicates a staid Vitruvian approach, *Vorstellung einiger Modernen Gebäude zum Pracht, zur Zierde und zur Bequemlichkeit eingerichtet (Presentation of Several Modern Buildings, Designed According to Beauty, Firmness and Utility);* the work contains only projects, however, and is without text. The viability of the genre until well toward the close of the 18th century is demonstrated by a publication such as J. D. Steingruber's *Architectonisches Alphabet* in 1773. Similar volumes in Neumann's library included Decker and Fischer, in addition to two less elaborate publications: Fäsche and Schüber.

The nature of this material confirms the picture of Neumann's background suggested by his travels and contacts. It reflects the diversity of architectural literature found in Germany in the 17th and 18th centuries. Visually no one-to-one relation can be established between any publication and Neumann's designs.[16]

In sum, we have seen that Neumann was extraordinarily well versed in a broad range of European architecture as a result of his travels, his contacts with other designers, the enthusiasms of his patrons, his extensive reading. We noted the absence of obvious prototypes in his buildings and analyzed his disparate approach to the creation of form and space. Finally, we recognized that Neumann was not merely a Schönborn architect, but an organizer with numerous responsibilities: bridges, waterworks, fortifications, construction supervision. In view of this situation, a fundamental conclusion appears inescapable: that Neumann plunged into each individual project with a sense of practical responsibility and aesthetic freedom; and that he did not subscribe to any overriding theoretical persuasions. The result is the rich, synthesized, personal architecture so enthusiastically supported in the 18th century and still compelling today. Neumann's life was packed with work. His keen sense of service drove him from one obligation to the next with energetic efficiency. His correspondence expresses an extraordinary conscientiousness toward his work, and the number of projects he undertook reveals explosive vitality. The mixture in one person of scrupulous civil servant and creative powerhouse is not easily reconciled with our expectations. Yet we cannot answer otherwise to the evidence. When the court church in Würzburg was dedicated in 1744, Neumann referred to himself as the "tool" for a project initiated by a movement of Friedrich Karl's finger. Clearly Friedrich Karl saw Neumann in this role. Neumann was the Prince-Bishop's chief consultant in matters dealing with architecture, streets, waterworks, military matters, and industrial undertakings.[17] The Prince conferred with the aristocrat architect Hildebrandt as an equal, but spoke to Neumann with the familiar form of address.

Does this mean that Neumann's work remains a collection of individual performances with no developmental or theoretical consistency to integrate one with the other, that it must be released from all ideological significance, that it represents nothing but formal interest? I think not. But the content of this architecture is not to be found in a coherent derivation from prototype, or in an adherence to theoretical principle. Secular patrons did not express symbolism in churches they commissioned, and the Church made explicit reference only to meanings contained in the representational art in its buildings. But Neumann's church designs do have meaning when considered in relation to the character of religious purpose alive in many strata of society at that time.

Religious persuasion informed, in a profound and fundamental way, large social groups within South Germany (Fig. 163).[18] This was expressed in an outpouring of devotional tracts, in great masses of people moved to follow the pilgrimage, in extraordinary enthusiasm for religious festivals, in the ever more splendidly arranged practice of Catholic ritual. A neoscholasticism, originating in Spain, became very popular in Germany, and theology emerged as the highest intellectual pursuit. This body of thought was built on an acceptance of dogma, and did not demand that conclusions be based on scientific reasoning. It was deeply felt that philosophy could not contradict theology. A worldly leader was not considered the ideal type, as was the churchman who was prince—such as the many Schönborn who were Prince-Bishops. Dynamic and polemical theology spilled from the universities. God was characterized as the "highest good." The goal of belief was a quest for the unity of *unio mystica*. Leibnitz's *Theodicée* of 1710, commissioned as an answer to Pierre Bayle's skeptical *Dictionnaire historique et critique,* drew together the optimistic, unifying sensibilities inherent in these beliefs. The thinking of the religious mystic Jakob Böhme is revealingly characteristic. God was seen by him as an absolute, archetypal power, the world as a manifestation of His continual creating. The act of creation was not a single, historic gesture, but a continual upheaval out of a godly center, "an eternal speaking, the breathing out from His own being." [19] Consequently, change was the manifestation of life, whose very form is change. Curiously, this religious fervor did not submerge the ego. We are continually confronted with assertive individuality, with a passionate belief in self. Time and again we find it is God who is called down to the individual, who is even found dependent on the human being. This is expressed in hymns ("O Saviour, rip open heaven and plunge down quickly to earth" [20]) and in the work of theologians such as Angelus Silesius ("I know that God cannot live at all without me, if I am destroyed, it will be necessary for Him to die" [21]).

These elements suggest the significance of Neumann's religious buildings. Their collective impression of variety, exuberance, and individuality records and expresses the religious sensibility that inspired them. The totality of each building reveals the unity of *unio mystica*. Their meaning is an emotional one, not an intellectual construct. Like his architectural contemporaries, there was no need for Neumann to argue the purpose of something universally understood. As for his peers, to pursue the polemics of theory was unnecessary, because these did not relate to the meaningful architectural issues. Finally, these facts of his time indicate why each building remains primarily an individual performance (the change of constantly creating), and why his churches were so extraordinarily popular (expressions of religious fervor).

Neumann's recognition at death equaled the enthusiasm and respect accorded his work during his life.[22] Only sixty-six years old, he died shortly after seven o'clock on the morning of 19 August 1753. Three days later he was buried in the Marienkapelle in Würzburg. A battalion of soldiers preceded his bier through the streets. Pulled by four horses draped with black cloth, it was followed by two cannon. As the coffin was lowered, the battalion fired a volley. From the Marienburg castle on the hill, three cannon fired three times. This event was movingly recorded by observers, who were struck by the fact that streets and houses along the funeral route were overflowing with mourners.

Appendices

APPENDIX I: The Parish Churches

Many parish or country churches were designed in Neumann's office from the 1730s on. These are plain, undemanding, small structures containing little of architectural interest. Before listing the commissions, a few summary observations may be made.

The schema of the country church is highly consistent. The nave contains two bays, wall piers, and no aisles. A narrower one-bay choir is terminated by a polygonal apse. Interior space is covered by a barrel vault with lunettes, though on occasion groin vaults (e.g., Retzbach, Hofheim) or coved ceilings (e.g., Ingolstadt) are used. Exterior walls are treated simply. The facade usually remains a plain wall topped by a pendentive. Some of the larger undertakings present a square tower sporting an onion-shaped roof. The tower is three-fourths embedded in the facade (and opened inside as choir and organ balcony). Construction reveals degrees of crudeness foreign to the workmanship of Neumann's larger churches. Yet the different parts of each building (piers, vaults, pilasters, tower, and so forth) are treated as cleanly defined, sharp-edged units. Coloring is white, decoration minimal when present.

In a few instances, parallels exist between the formal qualities in a country church and a larger commission: the Dittigheim plan is similar to one for Heusenstamm (S.E. 173 compared to S.E. 174), the treatment of wall piers and wall at Euerbach resembles the Gaibach nave elevation, Grafenrheinfeld contains a reduced version of the openwork at Maria-Limbach. As a group, however, the country churches subscribe to a single type which does not relate to Neumann's more ambitious efforts.

Amorbach. Parish church St. Mary (formerly Benedictine abbey church). 1741–47.
Arnstein. Parish church St. Nicolaus. 1732–34.
Bad Kissingen. Cemetery church St. Burcardus. Begun 1726.
Burgebrach. Parish church St. Veit. 1730–31. S.E. 133 (burned); Würzburg, Universitäts Bibliothek, Delin I/1, 73, 74.
Dirmstein. Undenominational church St. Lawrence. Designed 1740; built 1742–46. Speyer, Staatsarchiv, Karten und Pläne, Nr. 1116 (four sheets).
Distelhausen. Parish church St. Mark. 1730–38.
Dittigheim. Parish church St. Vitus. First design 1739; second design 1744; built 1748–52. For the 1744 design: S.E. 166–73 (burned), Koblenz, Abt. 702, Nr. 3865.
Euerbach. Parish church St. Michael. 1738–46. S.E. 145, 146.

Geisfeld. Parish church SS. Mary and Mark. Nave rebuilt 1753–54. Koblenz, Staatsarchiv, Abt. 702, Nr. 315, 316.

Gemeinfeld. Parish church. Project 1737. S.E. 134 (burned).

Glosberg. Parish church of the Nativity (formerly a pilgrimage church). 1728–35.

Grafenrheinfeld. Parish church of the Finding of the Cross. Designed 1748. First project S.E. 151, 152 (both burned); second project S.E. 181–83 (burned).

Grosswenkheim. Parish church of the Assumption of Mary. Designed 1740–49.

Hofheim im Ried. Parish church of St. Michael. First project 1743; second project 1747; consecrated 1750.

Höpfingen. Parish church St. Aegidius. First project 1738; second project 1742; built 1753 in reduced form. S.E. 161, 162 (both burned).

Ingolstadt. Parish church of the Immaculate Conception. 1751–53.

Kleinrinderfeld. Parish church St. Martin. Designed 1740.

Krensheim. Parish church St. Aegidius. Two projects 1740.

Leiwen. Parish church St. Steven. Project 1752.

Merkershausen. Parish church St. Martin. Neumann's project 1737; reworked by Johann Michael Schmitt and built; consecration 1743. S.E. 130–32 (burned) are Schmitt's reworkings of Neumann's project.

Michelau. Filial church SS. Michael and George. 1736–42. S.E. 141, 142, 159 (all burned).

Project for a church. S.E. 147 (burned).

Retzbach. Parish church St. Lawrence. 1736–40. S.E. 163, 164 (both burned).

Röthlein. Parish church St. Jacob the Older. 1729–41. S.E. 153–57 (burned).

Saffig. Parish church St. Cecilia. 1738–42.

Schnackenwerth. Parish church St. Andreas. Project 1744. S.E. 143 (burned).

Schonungen. Parish church St. George. Begun 1740. S.E. 136 (burned).

Schraudenbach. Filial church St. Jacob the Older. Begun 1752. S.E. 148 (burned).

Unterwittighausen. All Saints parish church. 1738–41.

Zell. Residence church.

Zeuzleben. Parish church St. Bartholomew. 1753–55.

APPENDIX II: Miscellaneous Ecclesiastical Designs

Included in this listing are three projects peripherally related to Neumann's ecclesiastical work.

Bonn-Poppelsdorf. The Holy Cross pilgrimage church was built on the Kreuzberg 1627–28. Badly ruined during the French siege of Bonn, 1689, the structure was renewed 1746–51. At this time, holy stairs were set onto the hillside leading up to the choir of the church. Their design is supposedly based on a Neumann project. Surviving documentation does not reveal the nature or extent of Neumann's involvement. S.E. 227, an anonymous project, is related to Neumann's design. See H. Reuther, *Kirchenbauten,* pp. 47–48; and P. W. Schulten, *Wallfahrtskirche auf dem Kreuzberg* (Rhein. Kunststätten, N.F. 1960), Neuss, 1960.

Bruchsal. Neumann designed the tower of the palace church in 1738. It was built by 1740, and resembles Neumann's usual single towers for church facades or choirs. See H. Reuther, *Kirchenbauten,* pp. 50–51.

Project: Würzburg, Universitätsbibliothek, Delin. II/82. A house chapel is located on the ground floor of the three-story house tract shown in this drawing. An oval set along the entrance-altar axis dominates the space. Vestibule and apse are realized as three-quarter cross ovals, while the large transept arms are rectangular and opened along their flanks by three windows. Over the oval a flattened pendentive dome is supported by four piers. Fragments of similar vaults cover the transept arms. Torsion ribs define all three units, which are placed tangent to one another, with segmental areas filling the four resulting gaps. The oval and transept arms create a unit similar to the crossing shown on S.E. 110 for Neresheim. For this reason, G. Neumann in his book on Neresheim suggests that Delin. II/82 is a Neumann design and is contemporary with the Neresheim drawing. See H. Reuther, *Kirchenbauten,* p. 111.

APPENDIX III: Excluded Churches

Several buildings mentioned on occasion in the literature on Neumann are not considered in this study. They are listed in alphabetical order.

Bamberg, hospital church St. Katherina. No visual documentation survives for this destroyed church. Parts of the walls and roof support are still incorporated within the hospital buildings, but they convey only the most general idea of the original structure, a circular space of about 46 feet, apse, rectangular vestibule, and flat niches marking the transverse axis. See H. Mayer, *Bamberger Residenzen,* Bamberg, 1951, p. 106.

Bayreuth, Catholic parish church. On 27 December 1744 Neumann mentioned two designs for an oval church with a vault supported by eight free-standing columns. A building may have been put up by Joseph Saint-Pierre (Merten makes no mention of it), and been extensively rebuilt during the first half of the 19th century. Other evidence is lost or indecisive. S.E. 234, a plan and view of the church and surrounding construction, was burned in 1945 and no photograph or illustration of this sheet remains. Two other drawings are uninformative: Bamberg, Erzbischöfl. Archiv, Pfarrakt B4 FII/6; Bayreuth, Domkap. A.B., sheet 46 (signed "Balthasar Neumann,

Obrister, den 26Xbr 1744"). See Walther Brandmüller, "Die Baupläne für das katholische Oratorium in Bayreuth" in *Fränkisches Land, Beilage zum Neuen Volksblatt Bamberg,* 8, 1961, Nr. 17; and Klaus Merten, *Der Bayreuther Hofarchitekt Joseph Saint-Pierre (1708/9–1754),* Diss., Frankfurt am Main, 1964.

Dettelbach, parish church. A few months before his death, Neumann designed a larger building for this town. On S.E. 184 was a plan, longitudinal section, two cross sections, and a view of the exterior flank. The sheet was signed "Wirtzburg den 6. Martii 1753 Balthasar Neumann Obrister." This drawing, burned in 1945, was not reproduced anywhere, and the one photograph of the sheet could not be located at the Kunsthistorisches Institut of Würzburg University, where it supposedly is housed. Consequently, there is no surviving evidence for the design. Since S.E. 184 had not attracted any attention before the war, one suspects the design was not compelling.

Karlsruhe, church in the margrave's palace. The church as such was never designed. In Neumann's projects for the palace (Karlsruhe-Baden, Generallandesarchiv, Baupläne Nr. 41–57), the location of the church is indicated only as a rectangular area; no articulation has been included. This would certainly have been seen so, had Neumann been selected to erect the palace. Instead, Albrecht Friedrich von Kesslau reworked Neumann's third project and undertook the building. See J. Durm, "Zur Baugeschichte des Residenzschlosses in Karlsruhe" in *Festgabe zum Jubiläum der 40 jährigen Regierung S. K. H. des Grossherzogs Friedrich von Baden,* Karlsruhe, 1892; and E. Gutmann, *Das Grossherzogliche Residenzschloss zu Karlsruhe,* Beiheft 5 zur *Zeitschrift für Geschichte der Architektur,* Heidelberg, 1911.

Schwarzenberg, Franciscan-Minorite cloister church of the Birth of Mary. Neumann was apparently only consulted about the project by an anonymous designer; he was in no way connected with the construction of the church. The plain, four-bay hall reveals no Neumann features in wall piers, windows, walls, vaulting, altar, organ balcony, or facade. Reuther suggests that the structure came from Neumann's office, but stylistically even this seems improbable. See H. Reuther, *Kirchenbauten,* pp. 86–87.

Stuttgart, church in the ducal palace. Neumann's projects for the palace represent modifications of Leopold Retti's designs, which were already in construction. Neumann accepts unchanged the position and form of Retti's church in his projects. See L. Andersen, *Studien zu Profanbauformen Balthasar Neumanns, Die grossen Residenzprojekte für Wien, Stuttgart und Karlsruhe,* Diss., Munich, 1966; and L. Schurenberg, "Balthasar Neumanns Stuttgarter Residenzpläne" in *Zeitschrift des Deutschen Vereins für Kunst-*

wissenschaft, vol. 3, 1936, pp. 303–325.

Wiesentheid, parish church St. Moritz. Neumann's authorship of this church traditionally has been advanced with reserve, since the relation of choir to hall, as well as the character of the orders and windows are all utterly different from anything else he ever did. Now documentation has made it almost completely certain that he did not design the structure. See J. Hotz, "Beiträge zur Kirchenbaukunst Balthasar Neumanns" in *Das Münster,* vol. 14, 1961, pp. 305–321.

Würzburg, Jesuit church St. Michael. Surviving documentation does not enable a reconstruction of Neumann's project. S.E. 237, 244, 245, 246 record site plan, longitudinal section of the nave, and two facade elevations. The incomplete section does not show the crossing, dome, or choir. See M. H. von Freeden, *Balthasar Neumann als Stadtbaumeister,* Berlin, 1937, fig. 13; and K. Lohmeyer, *Die Baumeister des Rheinisch-Fränkischen Barock,* Vienna/ Augsburg, 1931, fig. 88 for S.E. 237 and 245. S.E. 244 and 246 are not published. The original drawings were destroyed in 1945. A negative of the former survives in the Kunsthistorisches Institut der Universität, Würzburg, one of the latter in the Mainfränkisches Museum, Würzburg.

APPENDIX IV: Architectural Treastises in Neumann's Library

Only architectural treatises in a strict sense are listed by full title. Numbers at the end of each entry refer to the inventory designation in the *Verzeichniss der Bücher . . . .* of 1804. Listings follow the *Verzeichniss* except for necessary additions, which are included in brackets.

This catalogue should be considered together with related publications of architectural ornament, views and guides, mathematics and geometry, the art and science of rendering, and military architecture. Among the great number of works on decoration, for example, are numerous pieces by Berain (476, 477, 595, 607), Cuvilliés (600, 601, 625–30), Decker (440, 446, 716), Le Pautre (438, 594, 686, 758), Pineau (593), Schübler (713, 715, 720), and Toro (727). Impressions of European architecture are revealed in views and guides from Austria, England, France, Germany, Hungary, Italy, the Low Countries, Russia, Spain, Switzerland, and Turkey. This material includes important basic items such as Brice (296) and Marot (793, 794), Falda and Specchi (695, 768). Volumes on statics (mathematics and geometry), architectural rendering, and military architecture further complement these sources.

Aviler, Augustin Charles d', *Dictionnaire d'architecture par raport à l'art de bâtir,* Paris, 1693. (790)

Aviler, Augustin Charles d', *Explication des termes d'architecture,* Paris,

1691. (789)

Blondel, Jacques François, *De la distribution des maisons de plaisance, et de la decoration des édifices en général,* 2 vols., Paris, Jombert, 1737–38. (786)

Boffrand, Germain, *Livre d'architecture,* Paris, Cavelier, 1745. (591)

[Briseux, Charles Etienne or Tiercelet, Gilles]. *Architecture moderne, ou L'art de bien bâtir pour toutes sortes de personnes . . . ,* Paris, Jombert, 1728. (779)

Briseux, Charles Etienne, *Manière de bien bastir pour toute forte de personne,* Paris, Muet, 1663. (680)

Briseux, Charles Etienne, *L'art de bâtir des maisons de campagne,* 2 vols., Paris, Prault, 1743. (787)

Briseux, Charles Etienne, *Traité du beau essentiel dans les arts appliqué particulierement à l'architecture, et démontré phisiquement et par l'expérience,* 2 vols., Paris, Chereau, 1752. (597)

Campbell, Colin, *Vitruvius Britannicus; or, The British architect, containing the plans, elevations, and sections of the regular buildings both publick and private in Great Britain, with variety of new designs,* 2 vols., London, the author, 1715–. (770)

Decker, Paul, *Ausführliche Anleitung zur Civilbau-Kunst,* 3 vols., Nuremberg, Weigel, n.d. (606, 662)

Decker, Paul, *Fürstlicher Baumeister,* 3 vols., Augsburg, Wolff, 1711–16. (581)

Dieussart, Carlo Philippo, *Theatrum Architecturae Civilis . . . ,* translated by Leonhard Dientzenhofer, Bamberg, Immel, 1697. (618)

Erassmus, Joh. Ge., *Bericht von den fünf Säulen,* Nuremberg. (653)

(Same as (?): Erasmus, Georg Casper, *Seülen-Buch, oder Gründlicher Bericht von den Fünf Ordnungen der Architectur-Kunst . . . ,* Nuremberg, Hoffmann, 1667.)

Fäsch, Johann Rudolf, *Joh: Rudolph Fäsches . . . anderer Versuch seiner architect: Werke,* 5 parts, Nuremberg, Weigel, 1722–29. (661)

Fäsch, Johann Rudolf, *Architektonischer Werke 2ter Versuch,* 5 vols., Nuremberg. (621)

Fischer von Erlach, Johann Bernhard, *Entwurff einer historischen architectur, in abbildung unterschiedener berühmten gebäude . . . ,* 5 vols., Vienna, 1721. (623)

Flachner, Johann Adam, *Arithmetisch- und architectonisches Stiegenbaubüchlein,* 3 vols., Fulda, 1732. (802)

Galli da Bibiena, Giuseppe, *Architettura, e prospettive . . . ,* 5 parts, Augsburg, Pfeffel, 1740. (587)

Homann, Johann Baptist, *Fünf Säulenordnungen.* (261)

Indau, Johann, *Wienerisches Architectur- Kunst und Säulen-Buch,* Augsburg, Wolff, [1686]. (649)

Labacco, Antonio, *Libro d'Antonio Labacco appartenente a l'architettura nel qual si figurano alcune notabili antiquita di Roma,* n.d. (some editions: 1552, 1557, 1559, 1576, 16–). (579)

Labacco, Antonio (?), *Nouveau livres des cinque ordres d'architecture, enrichi de differens cartels, portails, fontaines, baldachins,* Paris, n.d. (580)

Nette, Johann Friedrich, *Land- und Lusthäuser,* Augsburg, Wolff, n.d. (660)

Nonnenmacher, Marci, *Architektonischer Tischler oder Pragerisches Säulenbuch,* Nuremberg, 1710. (650, 739[?])

Palladio, Andrea, *L'architettura di Andrea Palladio, diuisa in quattro libri . . . ,* Venice, Brogiollo, 1642. (684)

Palladio, Andrea, *Traicté des cinq ordres d'architecture desquels se sont seruy les anciens.* Augmenté de nouvelles inuentions pour l'art de bien bastir, Amsterdam, Wetstein (?), 1646. (782)

Palladio, Andrea, *Zwey Bücher von der Baukunst,* translated by Georg Andreas Böckler, Nuremberg, 1698. (685)

Pozzo, Andrea, *Mahler- und Baumeister-Perspective,* 2 vols., translated by Ge. Conz. Bodenehr, Augsburg, 1711. (690)

Pozzo, Andrea, *Mahler- und Bildhauer-Perspective,* 2 vols., translated by Johann Boxbarth, Augsburg, 1719. (691)

Ryff, Walther Hermann (Rivius, Gualterus Hermannus), *Bawkunst zu rechten Verstandt der Lehr Vitruvii,* 2 vols., Basel, 1582. (706)

Ryff, Walther Hermann (Rivius, Gualterus Hermannus), *Vitruvius teutsch . . . ,* [Nuremberg, Petreius, 1548]. (769)

Scamozzi, Vincenzo, *L'idea della architettura universale,* 2 vols., Venice, author, 1615. (709)

Scamozzi, Vincenzo, *Grundregeln der Baukunst,* Sulzbach, 1678. (710) [Same as (?): *Grundregeln der bau-Kunst; oder, Klärliche beschreibung der fünff säulen ordnungē und der gantzen architectur des berühmten baumeisters Vincent Scamozzi,* Nuremberg, Hofmanns, 1678.]

Serlio, Sebastiano, *Architettura,* books 3 and 4, Venice, 1540; book 5, Venice, 1551. (735, 737)

Serlio, Sebastiano, *Architettura,* German translation, Basel, 1609. (736)

Sturm, Leonhard Christoph, *Architectura civili-militaris,* Augsburg, Wolffens, 1719. (745)

Sturm, Leonhard Christoph, *Vollständige Anweisung alle Arten von Kirchen wohl anzugeben,* Augsburg, Wolffens, 1718. (744)

Toro, J. Bernard, *Unterricht von der Säulenordnung,* 2 vols., translated by ?, Nuremberg, 1719–20. (728)

Vignola, Giacomo Barozzio, called, *Grundregeln uber die fünf Säulen,* translated by Johann Rudolf Fäsch. Nuremberg, n.d. (Two copies, 780, 781)

Vignola, Giacomo Barozzio, called, *Regola delli cinque ordini d'architettura,*

[Roma, Rossi, 1620 (?)]. (578)

Wilhelms, Johann, *Architectura civilis, d.i. Beschreibung und Vorreissung vornehmer Dach- und anderer Werke*, 2 vols., Frankfurt, 1705. (775)

Notes

Introduction

1. See pp. 123–129.
2. Heinz Kähler, *Hagia Sophia,* with a chapter on the mosaics by Cyril Mango (trans. by Ellyn Childs), New York, Praeger, 1967, is an excellent recent text on the church. Richard Krautheimer, *Early Christian and Byzantine Architecture,* Baltimore, Md., Penguin, 1965 (Pelican History of Art, Z24), is an outstanding review of Byzantine architecture generally, with several pages devoted to Hagia Sophia.
3. From the vast literature on Gothic architecture, these titles offer informative surveys; each contains further and often extensive bibliographies:

Robert Branner, *Gothic Architecture,* New York, Braziller, 1961.

Paul Frankl, *Gothic Architecture,* Baltimore, Md., Penguin, 1962 (Pelican History of Art, Z19).

Hans Jantzen, *High Gothic: The Classic Cathedrals of Chartres, Reims, Amiens* (trans. by James Palmes), New York, Minerva, 1962.

Otto Georg von Simson, *The Gothic Cathedral: Origins of Gothic Architecture and the Medieval Concept of Order,* 2d rev. ed., New York, Pantheon, 1962.

4. H. Jantzen, *High Gothic,* coined the term, "diaphanous wall" to refer to this phenomenon of a dematerialized screen containing its own space and light.
5. Elizabeth Gilmore Holt, *A Documentary History of Art,* 2d ed., Garden City, N.Y., Doubleday, 1957–58, p. 44.
6. Allen Braham and Peter Smith, *François Mansart,* London, Zwemmer, 1973, with an extensive bibliography of older literature.

Paolo Portoghesi, *Borromini* (trans. by Barbara La Penta), London, Thames and Hudson, 1968.

Heinrich Thelen, ed. and critical commentary, *Die Handzeichnungen Borrominis,* Graz, Akademische Druck- und Verlagsanstalt, 1967–.

Rudolf Wittkower, *Art and Architecture in Italy, 1600 to 1750,* 2d rev. ed., Baltimore, Md., Penguin, 1965 (Pelican History of Art, Z16), pp. 130–151.
7. Richard Pommer, *Eighteenth-Century Architecture in Piedmont. The Open Structure of Juvarra, Alfieri, and Vittone,* New York, New York University Press, 1967, p. 8. For Guarini, see also:

Albert Erich Brinckmann, *Theatrum novum Pedemontii: Ideen, Entwürfe und Bauten von Guarini, Juvarra, Vittone wie anderen bedeuten Architeckten des piemontosischen Hochbarocks,* Düsseldorf, Schwann, 1931.

Guarino Guarini e l'internazionalita del Barocco, Atti del convegno internazionale promosso dall'Accademia delle scienze de Torino, 30 September to 5 October 1968, Turin, Accademia delle scienze, 1970, 2 vols.

R. Wittkower, *Art and Architecture,* pp. 268–275.

Chapter I

1. The most useful sources for Neumann's biography are:

Walter Boll, *Die Schönbornkapelle am Würzburger Dom,* Munich, Müller, 1925.

Max H. von Freeden, *Balthasar Neumann als Stadtbaumeister,* Berlin, Deutscher Kunstverlag, 1937.

M. H. von Freeden, *Balthasar Neumann, Leben und Werk,* 2d expanded ed. Munich, Deutscher Kunstverlag, 1963.

Joseph Keller, *Balthasar Neumann,* Würzburg, Bauer, 1896.

Karl Lohmeyer, ed., *Die Briefe Balthasar Neumanns an Friedrich Karl von Schönborn, Furstbischof von Würzburg und Bamberg, und Dokumente aus den ersten Baujahren der Würzburger Residenz,* Saarbrücken, Hofer, 1921.

K. Lohmeyer, *Die Briefe Balthasar Neumanns von seiner Pariser Studienreise 1723,* Düsseldorf, Schwann, 1911.

Quellen zur Geschichte des Barocks in Franken unter dem Einfluss des Hauses Schönborn. Part I: *Die Zeit des Erzbischofs Lothar Franz und des Bischofs Johann Philipp Franz von Schönborn, 1693–1729,* vol. 1: Augsburg, Filser, 1931, vol. 2: Würzburg Schöningh, 1950, editors: Anton Chroust, P. Hugo Hantsch, Andreas Scherf, Max Hermann von Freeden.

2. M. H. von Freeden, *Balthasar Neumann,* p. 9.

3. For example, both von Welsch and Hildebrandt were officers in the engineer corps.

4. See documents two and eight in Michael Renner, "Unbekannte Briefe und Quellen zum Wirken Balthasar Neumanns 1728–1753" in *Mainfränkisches Jahrbuch für Geschichte und Kunst,* 13, 1961, pp. 129–46 (*Archiv des historischen Vereins für Unterfranken und Aschaffenburg,* 84).

5. A brief review of Petrini's work is included in *750 Jahr Pfarrei Stift Haug Würzburg, Festschrift zum Jubeljahr 1965/66,* Würzburg, Pfarrmt Stift Haug, n.d.; see also: Albrecht Braum, *Antonio Petrini, der Würzburger Baumeister des Barock und sein Werk,* Diss. Würzburg, 1934.

6. Walter Jürgen Hofmann, *Der Neue Bau von Kloster Ebach,* Neustadt a.d. Aisch, Degener, 1971, offers a detailed summary of work on Greising.

7. Neumann's activity at Ebrach has been speculated upon often since documentation of his work there remains vague. Most opinions now favor the present interpretation. Cf. W. J. Hofmann, *Ebrach,* pp. 192–96, with a review of the literature on the problem.

8. See Peter Hirschfeld, *Mäzene, Die Rolle des Auftraggebers in der Kunst,* Berlin/Munich, Deutscher Kunstverlag, 1968, p. 199 for a sampler.

9. Otto Meyer, *Kürfurst Lothar Franz von Schönborn,* Bamberg, 1957, pp. 22–24, contains an excellent bibliography of literature on the Schönborn. See also: Josef Friedrich Abert, *Vom Mäzenatentum der Schönborn,* Mainfränk-ische Hefte, 8, 1950 (Freunde Mainfränkischer Kunst und Geschichte, E.V., Würzburg).

Hugo Hantsch, *Reichsvizekanzler Friedrich Karl Graf von Schönborn (1674–1746), Einige Kapitel zur politischen Geschichte Kaiser Josefs I. und Karls VI.,* Augsburg, Filser, 1924 (Salzburger Abhandlungen und Texte aus Wissenschaft und Kunst, Band II).

Pater Konstantin Hohenlohe, *Friedrich Karl Graf Schönborn, Reichsvizekanzler und Bischof am Bamberg und Würzburg, 1674–1746. Eine biographische Skizze,* Vienna, 1906 (Oesterreichische Leo-Gesellschaft. Vorträge und Abhandlungen. No. 26).

Andreas Scherf, *Johann Philipp Franz von Schönborn, Bischof von Würzburg (1719–1724), der Erbauer der Residenz,* Munich, 1930 (Schriftenreihe zur bayerischen Landesgeschichte, vol. 4).

Karl Wilhelm Wild, *Staat und Wirtschaft in den Bistümern Würzburg und Bamberg. Eine Untersuchung über die organisatorische Tätigkeit des Bischofs Friedrich Karl von Schönborn, 1729–1746,* Heidelberg, 1906 (Heidelberger Abhandlungen zur mittleren und neueren Geschichte, Heft 15).

10. Heinrich Kreisel, *Das Schloss zu Pommersfelden,* Munich, Hirmer, 1953, pp. 25–30.

11. W. Boll, *Schönbornkapelle,* pp. 16, 18.

12. Baron Ludwig Döry, "Balthasar Neumann und die Brüder von Uffenbach" in *Stifter-Jahrbuch,* VII, 1962, pp. 247–256.

13. *Quellen zur Geschichte des Barocks in Franken,* Nr. 1143.

14. On a conference in Würzburg, 19–24 February 1720, see *Quellen zur Geschichte des Barocks in Franken,* Nrs. 720–728, 733.

15. H. Kreisel, *Pommersfelden,* p. 12, notes that when Boffrand visited Pommersfelden, Lothar Franz explained to him that as far as the exterior of the building went, he let his architect Jo-

hann Dientzenhofer do what he wished.

16. For Lothar Franz's inability to cope with the stair at Pommersfelden, see H. Kreisel, *Pommersfelden*, pp. 25–30.

17. *Quellen zur Geschichte des Barocks in Franken*, Nr. 1065.

18. W. Boll, *Schönbornkapelle*, pp. 4, 5, 32, 115–116.

19. An alternative to this tradition did exist—the centralized court church. One thinks of Charlemagne's chapel at Aachen for origins, and of more recent examples such as de l'Orme's Anet, Frisoni's Ludwigsburg, and Mansart's design for Blois. Neumann acknowledged this tradition in his Bamberg Residenz project.

20. Hans Reuther, "Die mainfränkische Barockarchitektur. Der gegenwärtige Stand der Forschung" in *Zeitschrift für Kunstgeschichte*, 22, 1959, pp. 283, 285.

21. Michael Renner, "Ein Unbekannter Brief Balthasar Neumanns" in *Mainfränkisches Jahrbuch für Geschichte und Kunst*, 12, 1960, p. 221 (*Archiv des Historischen Vereins für Unterfranken und Aschaffenburg*, 83).

22. I explored this issue personally and together with several historians of theology. A telling example can be found in Erich Bachmann, "Zur Symbolik der Johannes von Nepomuk-kirchen" in *Johannes von Nepomuk,* exhibition catalogue, 1971, Passau, pp. 88–96. Bachmann demonstrates that the "Nepomuk-kirchen" have no common characteristics. The dedication is revealed in painted and sculptural programs, not in characteristic architectural forms or plans. Some buildings are made intentionally symbolic, such as Der Grüne Berg bei Saar, others follow the formulas for parish churches, others are centralized in one way or another. But no single symbolic Nepomuk form for churches exists. On the liturgy in the west, including post-Tridentine severity and 18th-century theatricality, see: Josef A. Jungmann, *Missarum Sollemnia,* 5th ed. Vienna, 1962.

Chapter II

1. See Wolf Casper von Klengel's sketchbook: Eberhard Hempel, "Unbekannte Skizzen von Wolf Casper von Klengel (1630–91), dem Begründer des sächsischen Barock" in *Abhandlungen der sächsischen Akademie der Wissenschaften zu Leipzig,* Berlin, Akademie-Verlag, 1958, pp. 3–16.

2. See the material in Werner Oechslin, ed., *Die Vorarlberger Barockbaumeister,* exhibition in Einsiedeln and Bregenz, May–September 1973, Einsiedeln, Benziger, 1973.

3. A similar predilection for working first and foremost with plans can be seen in the work of the Vorarlberg architect, Caspar Moosbrugger. See W. Oechslin, *Vorarlberger Barockbaumeister,* p. 29.

4. Fritz Hirsch, *Das sogenannte Skizzenbuch Balthasar Neumanns, Ein Beitrag zur Charakteristik des Meisters und zur Philosophie der Baukunst,* Heidelberg, Winter 1912 (*Zeitschrift für Geschichte der Architektur,* Beiheft 8), concluded that Neumann could not draw. This position was never accepted by others, and ample evidence demonstrates the opposite: Neumann specifically notes on many sheets that he drew them, his correspondence contains frequent reference to his having drawn up this or that, and a consistency of style informs many of these renderings.

5. Neumann's signature alone on a sheet does not necessarily prove his authorship; often this indicated only that the design concept was his.

6. *Plan und Bauwerk, Entwürfe aus fünf Jahrhunderten,* exhibition catalogue, Bayerische Akademie der Schönen Künste, Zentralinstitut für Kunstgeschichte in München, 30 May to 31 July 1952, Hirmer, 1952.

7. Concerning the distinction between "oval" and "ellipse," see Edgar Lehmann, "Balthasar Neumann und Kloster Langheim" in *Zeitschrift für Kunstgeschichte* 25, 1962, p. 242.

8. Richard Teufel, *Vierzehnheiligen,* 2d. ed., Lichtenfels, Schulze, 1957, and R. Teufel, "Der geometrische Aufbau der Pläne der Wallfahrtskirche Vierzehnheiligen" in *Zeitschrift für Kunstgeschichte,* 19, 1941–42, pp. 163–187.

9. Gerhard Henkes, "Hilfslinien für die Proportionierung des Querschnitts der Jesuitenkirche" in *Mainzer Zeitschrift,* 54, 1959, p. 40.

10. This review of discussion procedure is derived from a detailed examination of the building histories of Neumann's churches.

11. See, for example, Joseph Furttenbach, *Architectura Civilis,* Ulm, Saurn, 1628, p. 8: "Die ursach unnd brunnenguel dieses unglücklichen fortgangs [rebuilding part of a structure] entspringet thails auss unerfahrenheit wann man den rechten stylum darinnen nicht waist: thails auss unachtsam: und saumlosigkeit: mehrsten thails aber (welches auch ein grobes Stuck der ungeschichligkeit oder vermessenheit ist) wann man vor fortsetzung dess Bawes die wolfundierte Grundriss und von Holtz gemachte verjüngte Modell, oder visierungen entweder unterlasset oder vol gar nit zustellen waist."

12. Helpful on this issue, in addition to the building histories of Neumann's churches, is Hans Reuther, "Balthasar Neumann und der Naturstein" in *Der Naturstein,* III, 1948, Nr. 2, pp. 20–22, Nr. 5, pp. 36–37.

13. This was not always the case; at Neresheim, the vaults were constructed first.

14. Presumably the lack of a standardized approach to roof construction, such as existed for walls and vaults, explains why it is discussed so much in the literature, while walls and vaults are not.

15. The standard brick size was 4.5/5 × 12/13 × 29/31 cm.

16. Exceptions are the Vierzehnheiligen vaults and the vaults intended for Neresheim, discussed below.

17. Both Vierzehnheiligen and Neresheim were vaulted long after Neumann's death, yet I believe this technique is his invention. The method is a dramatically new concept in one sense, in another it is only a one-step extension of tradition but one that results in a quantum leap. Traditional is the use of tuff blocks and mortar; new is clamping the blocks together with iron. A second fact speaks in favor of Neu-

mann's authorship: he used iron bands around vaults, such as at the Käppele, and he laid iron rods into the walls of Vierzehnheiligen to strengthen the wall over door and window openings. Such instances demonstrate a responsiveness to this material.

18. Carroll William Westfall, "Alberti and the Vatican Palace Type" in *Journal of the Society of Architectural Historians,* May 1974, vol. XXXIII, Nr. 2, p. 111, maintains that Alberti, elaborating on Vitruvius's comments, celebrated brick as the finest of building materials.

19. Leonhard Christoph Sturm, *Vollständige Anweisung Alle Arten Von Kirchen Wohl Anzugeben,* Augsburg, Wolffens, 1718, pp. 12–20, presents a particularly inventive range of solutions.

20. Some examples: Nuremberg, St. Lorenz; Munich, Frauenkirche; Würzburg, Cathedral. More immediate are Johann Dientzenhofer's cathedral at Fulda, begun 1704, and his Benedictine abbey church at Banz, begun 1710, which were vaulted in this manner.

21. An example, often cited in other literature of the time, and present in Neumann's library, is Johann Wilhelm, *Architectura civilis, d.i. Beschreibung und Vorreisuung vornehmer Dach– und anderer Werke,* 2 vols., Frankfurt, 1705 (first published 1649).

22. Sturm, *Kirchen,* p. 24.

23. Sturm, *Kirchen,* p. 12.

24. Some suggestive statements by Neumann are in: Joseph Keller, *Balthasar Neumann,* Würzburg, Bauer, 1896, p. 169; H. Reuther, "Franz Ignaz Michael Neumanns Konstruktionsriss für Neresheim" in *Zeitschrift für Kunstgeschichte,* 21, 1958, p. 43; R. Teufel, *Vierzehnheiligen,* p. 28, point 10.

25. European masters of modern architecture—among them, Loos, Oud, and Mies—advocated this position. American designers were involved in a similar debate about ornament and architecture in the period between the world wars. During the decades following World War II, it was *de rigueur* to build unornamented architecture. Frank Lloyd Wright was an important exception to this. His "In the Cause of Architecture"

in *The Architectural Record,* 23, March 1908, pp. 155–220, maintained that ornamentation should be constitutional, a matter of the nature of the structure beginning with the ground plan.

26. This is revealed in many ways, but two instances characterize the situation. Henry-Russell Hitchcock, *Rococo Architecture in Southern Germany,* New York, Phaidon, 1968, p. 209, points out that it was Neumann himself who brought the stucco decorator Antonio Bossi to Würzburg in 1733 so that he might undertake the ornament for several Schönborn projects. Neumann's sensitivity toward matters of decoration is borne out as well by observations of his such as, "I wish humbly to report to your Grace that at midday on the 24th, I inspected the church and painting at [the church in] Heusenstamm. The painting is certainly good and rather beautiful, but the painter is not [suited] for your Grace's Residenz." See K. Lohmeyer, *Neumanns an Friedrich Karl von Schönborn,* p. 129. The significance of "ornament" can even be gauged in purely monetary terms. According to P. Paulus Weissenberger, *Baugeschichte der Abtei Neresheim,* Kohlhammer, Stuttgart, 1934 (Darstellungen aus der Württembergischen Geschichte XXIV), fully half of the costs incurred at Neresheim were for completing—that is, decorating—the church.

27. F. Hirsch, *Skizzenbuch,* p. 44.

28. F. Hirsch, *Skizzenbuch,* p. 50.

29. S.E. 92, which shows the altar, is by Franz Ignaz Michael Neumann, and dates after Neumann's death.

30. This information is from Hans W. Hegemann, *Die Altarbaukunst Balthasar Neumanns,* Diss. Marburg, 1937, and from a close study of individual church histories. Several specialized studies are also generally informative about Neumann's approach to the design of altars: Fritz Arens, "Die Errichtung des Hochaltars im Wormser Dom" in *Der Wormsgau,* 6, 1963–1964, pp. 25–42; Joachim Hotz, "Balthasar Neumanns Hochaltar in Wormser Dom" in *Der Wormsgau,* 6, 1963–1964, pp. 9–25; Ursula Röhlig, "Ein Entwurf Balthasar Neumanns für den Hochaltar des Domes zu Worms" in *Münchener Jahrbuch der bildenden Kunst,* 3rd series, XIX, 1968, pp. 157–168; Rudolf Schreiber, "Ein neuentdeckter Altarentwurf Balthasar Neumanns für St. Klara in Altspeyer" in *Pfälzer Heimat,* 1, 1950, pp. 97–105.

31. This intimate integration did not always occur. At Worms, Neumann changed the Romanesque choir to accommodate the altar, albeit with such sensitivity that the alterations are discernible only after detailed scrutiny. Altspeyer was a project forced upon him and in which he was uninterested. Consequently he submitted a proposal without ever visiting the building.

Chapter III

1. The exterior of the Early Christian church, especially in the West, was often a simple brick shell, which contrasted with the rich materials and mosaics of the interior. In medieval church design, interior and exterior are treated more equally. Speyer and Amiens are indicative examples of buildings in which towers, special architectural features, and sculpture can be as dramatic outside as are the spaces, liturgical furniture, and stained glass windows inside. Concern with the interior increases again during the 15th century: Italian architects designed churches from the inside out, so that many buildings were left with unfinished rubble walls on the exterior.

2. Individual buildings are documented in the notes; only the problems of documentation and interpretation are included in the text. The note for each building consists of three parts: (1) Chronology of design, construction, and completion. (2) Bibliography. H. Reuther, *Die Kirchenbauten Balthasar Neumanns,* Berlin, Hessling, 1960, contains extensive bibliographic entries for each church. The relevant pages in Reuther are included at the beginning of each bibliographic section, supplemented only by material that he omits. (3) Illustrative material. A list of all

drawings, engravings, and other renderings pertinent to the documentation of each building. Drawings are by Neumann or from his office unless otherwise noted. An asterisk (*) indicates that a specific item is unpublished to date. "S.E." refers to material from the Sammlung Eckert, Mainfränkisches Museum, Würzburg. Roman numerals in an S.E. listing (e.g., S.E. XXVI) denote material from the so-called Balthasar Neumann sketchbook contained in the Sammlung Eckert. Since the Sammlung Eckert represents the most extensive collection of Neumann material, items from it begin each section. The notation "Burned 1945" refers to drawings destroyed in the 16 March 1945 bombing of Würzburg.

3. Maximilian von Welsch's so-called "Mainzer Projekt" for the chapel was produced in the winter of 1720–21. Neumann reworked this before 9 April 1721. Cornerstone laid on 4 June 1721. Fabric completed 1723. Work halted 1724 due to the death of Prince-Bishop Johann Philipp Franz von Schönborn. Work resumed 1729 with the election of Friedrich Karl von Schönborn as Prince-Bishop. Decoration completed and consecration 1736.

Bibliography:

H. Reuther, *Kirchenbauten*, pp. 106–108.

M. H. von Freeden, *Balthasar Neumann*, pp. 19–20, 66.

Eberhard Hempel, *Baroque Art and Architecture in Central Europe. Germany, Austria, Switzerland, Hungary, Czechoslovakia, Poland. Painting and Sculpture: Seventeenth and Eighteenth Centuries. Architecture: Sixteenth to Eighteenth Centuries*, Baltimore, Md., Penguin, 1965, pp. 31, 151.

H.-R. Hitchcock, *Rococo*, p. 219.

Illustrative material:
S.E. 21, facade and plan, Bayer, 1718.
S.E. 22, plan, Hennicke, 1718.
S.E. 23, facade, Hennicke, 1718.
S.E. 24, longitudinal and cross sections, Hennicke, 1718.
S.E. 25, facade, Von Welsch, 1720–21.
S.E. 26, longitudinal section, Von Welsch, 1720–21.
S.E. 27, plan.
S.E. 28, facade.
S.E. 29, facade.
*S.E. 30, east flank.
S.E. 31, east flank.
S.E. 32, cross section.
*S.E. 33, facade.
*S.E. 34, facade.
S.E. 35, elevation and plan of oval chapel.
*S.E. 36, elevation and plan of oval chapel.
*S.E. 37, elevation and plan of oval chapel.
S.E. 38, longitudinal section and half ground plan.
*S.E. 39, longitudinal section with marble veneer.
S.E. 40, cross section and half ground plan.
S.E. 41, plan and elevation of side altar area.
*S.E. 42, plan for altar placement and floor pattern.
*S.E. 43, plan. Burned 1945.
S.E. 44, half longitudinal section and half facade elevation. Burned 1945.
Altars and decoration for the chapel are shown on S.E. XXXXII, XXXXV, XXXXVII, XXXXIX, CV, CVI, CVII, CVIII, CIX, CX, CXI, CXIII, CXVI, CXVIII, CXXIIb.
Würzburg, Historisches Verein, XII B184, variation of S.E. 38. Burned 1945.
———, XII B188, floor pattern. Burned 1945.
Würzburg, Martin von Wagner Museum der Universität, Inv.-Nr. 471, early project by unknown hand.
———, Inv.-Nr. 5003, variation of S.E. 40.
Würzburg, Staatsarchiv, Repertorium der Risse und Pläne, Würzburger Serie Nr. II/34.
Würzburg, Universitäts-Bibliothek, Delin. III.

4. No standard term has entered the literature for this element. Werner Bartsch, *Balthasar Neumanns Entwurf*

zur Hofkirche der neuen Residenz zu Bamberg, Diss. Berlin, 1969, pp. 86–89, discusses E. W. Grashoff's term, "spherical arch," various phrases by J. Burckhardt, such as "an arch constructed over a segment of a circular plan" ("ein über einen Kurvensegment errichteter Gurtbogen"), G. Neumann's "curved arcade" ("Bogenarkade"), only to formulate his own terminology, a "free-standing or engaged curved arcade" ("gekurvten Frei- bzw. Wandarkade"). Anthony Blunt, Philibert de l'Orme, London, Zwemmer, 1958, pp. 39, 49, refers to arches with a three-dimensional twist or curve when discussing de l'Orme's Anet. Heinrich Gerhard Franz, Bauten und Baumeister der Barockzeit in Böhmen, Entstehung und Ausstrahlungen der bömischen Barockbaukunst, Leipzig, Seeman, 1962, pp. 57, 60, mentions convex arches in reference to Hildebrandt and Guarini, a phrase which seems to derive from plan descriptions and unfortunately minimizes the significant spatial implications of the form; in discussing Christoph Dientzenhofer's St. Clara in Eger, p. 61, the term is elaborated to "twisted-spherical" units ("windschiefsphärisch"), while a similar form in St. Niklas Kleinseite, p. 65, is termed a "spherical-curved" arch ("sphärisch-gekurvter Gurtbogen"). M. H. von Freeden, Balthasar Neumann, p. 53, mentions spherical or curved arches. E. Hempel, Baroque, p. 234, terms the form a "diadem arch," which implies that the element has a decorative quality and neglects its architectonic significance. Niklaus Pevsner, "The Three-Dimensional Arch from the 16th to the 18th Centuries" in Journal of the Society of Architectural Historians, X v II, No. 4, 1958, pp. 22–24, refers to "three-dimensional" arches. R. Pommer, Piedmont, p. 8, refers to "cylindrical" arches. R. Teufel, Vierzehnheiligen, p. 122, writes of arches that rise like screws ("steigen die Gurten schraubenförmig auf").

This selective survey reveals the absence of a common term in art historical literature that is compact and descriptive. "Torsion arch," with its suggestions of three-dimensionality and tensions inherent in the shift from plane to plane, is offered here as a solution to the problem.

5. The tholos is a freestanding cylindrical unit that consists of orders and dome arranged on a circular plan.

6. H. G. Franz, Böhmen, pp. 165–166, sees the space as a combination of Bohemian forms (torsion arches) and a "consequent French classical style" (dome, plan, stylistic features). Günter Neumann, Neresheim, Munich, Filser, 1947, p. 7, suggests as sources, the Cappella Lancelotti in S. Giovanni in Laterano, Rome, Prunner's Dreifaltigkeitskirche in Paura, and Guarini's S. Fillipo Neri in Casale.

7. Designed 1726, construction completed 1730, secularized 1803. Roof incorrectly replaced after a fire in the 19th century (see S.E. 199b). Restored 1908–1913. New consecration 1913. Restored 1956.

Bibliography:
H. Reuther, Kirchenbauten, pp. 64–65.
M. H. von Freeden, Balthasar Neumann, pp. 20–21, 67.
M. H. von Freeden, "Balthasar Neumann" in Encyclopedia of World Art, New York, McGraw-Hill, 1965, vol. X, cols. 612–613.
H.-R. Hitchcock, Rococo, pp. 209, 259.

Illustrative material:
*S.E. 198, plan. Burned 1945.
*S.E. 199a, plan. Burned 1945.
S.E. 199b, elevation of north front.
Würzburg, University Library, Delin. II/118, plan.
*Würzburg, Mainfränkisches Museum, Winterhelt Collection, plan.

8. Neumann's intentions for the lantern are not clear. Two exterior elevations—S.E. 199b (Fig. 33), and another from the Sammlung Winterhelt in the Mainfränkisches Museum, Würzburg—show unglazed lanterns. The latter contains a little pyramidal form that pokes into the lantern from below. If this was a small skylight, an inexpensive lantern

would have been provided for this smaller, modest church. The present lantern consists of eight slender colonnettes and domed roof. Inside, a circular recess in the dome appears to be the remnant of a lantern opening, but the top is closed off. Blind lanterns were employed by Lemercier and the Mansarts so that an external accent on the dome could be combined with a smooth inner surface for frescoes. Neumann proposed a similar strategy for an initial Neresheim project (S.E. 112, Pl. I), but here both the continuous surface and the light source are lost.

9. The case for Neumann's authorship of the Bamberg church is based on circumstantial evidence. The church plan illustrated here is shown on a plan of the Prince-Bishop's Residenz in Bamberg that can be dated June or August 1733 and is a copy of an original. No documentation has been discovered that unequivocally associates Neumann with this plan. However, on 17 December 1730 Neumann completed a masterplan for rebuilding the Residenz (this plan is lost, but the correspondence concerning it survives), and, together with his assistant, Johann Michael Küchel, he undertook substantial work on the Residenz from 1731 to 1733. These circumstances convincingly associate Neumann with the 1733 plan, and therefore with the church design on it.

Bibliography:
H. Reuther, *Kirchenbauten,* p. 46.

Werner Bartsch, *Balthasar Neumanns Entwurf zur Hofkirche der neuen Residenz zu Bamberg,* Diss. Berlin, 1969.

Illustrative material:
Bamberg, Stadtarchiv, plan of 1733, Project, copy of a Neumann original?

10. W. Bartsch, *Bamberg,* proposes a very specific elevation, illustrated on p. 133, derived from other Neumann designs and court churches by other designers, such as that at Blois and Ludwigsburg. Though a detailed effort at reconstruction, Bartsch's proposal re-

mains conjectural. Heinrich Mayer, *Bamberger Residenzen. Ein Kunstgeschichte der Alten Hofhaltung, des Schlosses Geyerswörth, der Neuen Hofhaltung und der Neuen Residenz zu Bamberg,* Munich, Kösel, 1951, p. 105, suggests balconies accessible from the palace, colossal columns and entablature, supporting a flat dome with lunettes. H. Reuther, *Kirchenbauten,* p. 46, postulates a pendentive dome which opens to barrel vaults over the ancillary spaces in the cardinal directions; no reasons for this inference are given.

11. The east arm of Neumann's church uses the choir fabric of the older building. It has been suggested that Bruchsal was built in the image of Bramante-Michelangelo's St. Peter's in Rome: conversation between Thyrry and Schönborn, reported in Hans Rott, *Die Kunstdenkmäler des Amtsbezirks Bruchsal (Kreis Karlsruhe),* from the series, *Die Kunstdenkmäler des Grossherzogtums Baden,* Tübingen, Mohr, 1913, p. 28.

The stucco work by an unknown master was complete by the summer of 1745. Johann Michael Feichtmayr the Younger designed and built the side altars 1754–55, and finished the pulpit in 1756. The tomb of Damian Hugo von Schönborn, carved by Ferdinand Tietz, was put up in the choir in 1758, and in 1773 its counterpart for Prince-Bishop Franz Christoph von Hutten was installed by Johann Stahl. The vault frescoes by Joseph Mariano Kitschker were only painted in 1907. During a "restoration" of 1900–09, the stucco was stripped from the exterior walls, exposing the rubble surface seen today.

Bibliography:
H. Reuther, *Kirchenbauten,* pp. 48–50.

M. H. von Freeden, *Balthasar Neumann,* pp. 46, 68.

J. Gamer, "Pfarrkirche St. Peter (Bruchsal)" in *Balthasar Neumann in Baden-Württemberg. Bruchsal-Karlsruhe-Stuttgart-Neresheim,* exhibition catalogue, Staatsgalerie Stuttgart, 28 September to 30 November 1975, pp. 31–37.

E. Hempel, *Baroque,* p. 158.

Illustrative material:

Berlin, Kunstbibliothek der Staatlichen Museen, Hdz. 6053, plan and elevation of north balcony by Leonhard Stahl, ca. 1745 (?).

Bruchsal, Aussenstelle des Staatlichen Hochbauamts I Karlsruhe, Mappe II. 2, plan.

———, .4, site plan.

Karlsruhe, Generallandesarchiv, G/ Bruchsal, Nr. 46, plan and elevation of facade.

———, Nr. 47, facade, different design.

———, Nr. 48, plan.

———, Nr. 60, legend on sheet by an anonymous hand: "Pianta della chiesa di S. Pietro fabricata di nuovo su il monte del borgo di Brucsal con il suo cemiterio circondato con un muro nuovo secondo la grandeza di prima con qualche chase del borgo e sue strade. Pianta della chiesa vechia come fu situata. Case del borgo di Brucsal. Strada per salire alla chiesa e simiterio venendo del borgo. Strada che si cunduce per il borgo dirito alla citta. Spiegatione della chiesa nuova: imo Facciata e porta principale che corrisponde verso il borgo. 2. Porta laterale che corrisponde verso la citta ove fu la facciata vecchia. 3. Altra porta laterale fatta nel muro del choro vecio. 4. Choro e altar maggiore. 5. Altare laterale. 6. Choro vecchio conservato tutto quelo che dimostra l'ombra nera. 7. Simitria del coro vechio che forma la croce. 8. Le due campanile con le sue scale per salire al oratorio. 9. Sacristia con dentro le scale per salire sopra alli oratori. Spiegatione della chiesa vechia: AB Faciata e porta principale che guarda verso la città. C Porte laterale. D Campanile. E Altare laterale di cischeduna parte due ben compendiosi. F Altar di croce. G Altar maggiore. H Sacristia. I Battistero."

Stuttgart, Württembergische Landesbibliothek, Slg. Nicolai, vol. 3, sheet 57, plan.

———, vol. 5, sheet 76, wooden structure within tower roof.

Würzburg, Martin von Wagner-Museum der Universität, Hdz. 50, Auvera's altar project.

12. H. Rott, *Kunstdenkmäler Bruchsal,* p. 26.

13. H. Rott, *Bruchsal. Quellen zur Kunstgeschichte des Schlosses und der bischöflichen Residenzstadt,* Heidelberg, Winter 1914, p. 83, Nr. 329 (*Zeitschrift für Geschichte der Architektur,* Beiheft 11).

K. Lohmeyer, *Neumann an Friedrich Karl von Schönborn,* p. 90.

14. Neumann submitted plans for Münsterschwarzach in the spring of 1727. Cornerstone laid 17 June 1727, choir completed 1730, crossing vaulted in the summer of 1733, plans for the double-tower facade drawn 1736, vaults frescoed 1736–39, facade towers finished 1741, consecration held 8 September 1743, stucco work concluded 1749. Secularized 1803, church and most cloister buildings demolished 1821–41.

Bibliography:

H. Reuther, *Kirchenbauten,* pp. 75–78.

M. H. von Freeden, *Balthasar Neumann,* pp. 21–22, 67.

E. Hempel, *Baroque,* pp. 157–158.

Illustrative material:

*S.E. 54, plan.

S.E. 55, plan.

S.E. 56, two plan variations, cross section through crossing. Burned 1945.

S.E. 57, two plan variations.

S.E. 58, facade elevation.

S.E. 59, north flank elevation.

S.E. 60, north flank elevation.

S.E. 61, longitudinal section.

S.E. 62, longitudinal section.

*S.E. 63, cross section. Burned 1945.

S.E. 64, two plan variations, ground and upper story.

S.E. 65, two plan variations.

*S.E. 66, facade elevation.

*S.E. 67, north flank elevation.

S.E. 68, details of interior and exterior elevations, cross section through a nave chapel, three columns and one pilaster plans.

S.E. 69, half plan, two cross section variations of the dome along the diagonal axis, two corresponding views of the dome.

S.E. 70, facade elevation. Burned 1945.

S.E. 228, east tower elevation and plan of attic story.

S.E. LXXXXV, perspective view with partial longitudinal section. Burned 1945.

S.E. LXXXXVI, plan. Burned 1945.

S.E. LXXXXVIII, perspective view with partial longitudinal section, engraving based on LXXXXV, from dedicatory publication, *Magna Gloria . . . Abbatiae Schwarzacensis,* Würzburg, 1743. Burned 1945.

*Würzburg, Historische Verein, Nr. 84. Burned 1945.

*———, Nr. 1367. Burned 1945.

*———, Nr. 1835. Burned 1945.

*Würzburg, Staatsarchiv, Säkularization, 38/1537, plan. Burned 1945. Munich, Bayerisches National-Museum, model by Neumann.

Würzburg, Mainfränkisches Museum, 19th-century model. Burned 1945.

15. Adolf Kurt Placzek, "Youth and Age in Architecture" in *Perspecta,* 9/10, 1965, pp. 299–302, maintains that historically most architects come into their own about the time they reach forty years of age.

16. Würzburg, Staatsarchiv, Säkularization, 38/1537.

17. The light effects are boldly recorded in S.E. LXXXXV and LXXXXVIII.

18. On 18–20 August 1729 Neumann measured the site in Gossweinstein. Foundations begun 12 May 1730. Roofs finished 1731, vaulting complete 1732, towers under roof by fall 1734. Frescoes and decoration mostly finished by the time of the consecration, 14 May 1739. A fire of 5 August 1746 destroyed the roofs, but left vaults and walls intact.

No design corresponds exactly to the executed church, but the same basic concept informs all the projects for it. S.E. 189 and S.E. 190 largely correspond to the executed building, though in S.E. 189 the crossing is without triangular segments. S.E. 191 re-peats S.E. 189, but without vaulting indications. S.E. 186 and S.E. 187 and Koblenz are projects with single-tower facades. S.E. 186 has a three-bay nave, no chancel bay, and three-quarter engaged columns fronting the crossing piers. S.E. 187 and Koblenz are similar to the executed building, except for the facade and crossing. S.E. 188 contains a two-tower facade, but with two half-side variations.

Originally the church was to have a one-tower facade: Father Dippold to Friedrich Karl von Schönborn on 6 February 1739 reports that, "mann Anfangs des Baus bey Einsetzung der geldmittel die Kirchen mit einer rauen mauern, einen turn und schlechten Faciata zu erbauen entschlossen war" (Staatsarchiv Bamberg, Rep. B49, Nr. 57, Fasc. 20). Neumann suggested one design with the Trinity dedication expressed in three bays and three similar polygonal arms around the crossing (S.E. 186), and a second with nave and crossing-choir area equal in size (S.E. 187, Koblenz). A double-tower facade is proposed in S.E. 188. This interpretation is made definite in S.E. 189 and S.E. 190, but with a change in the crossing shown in S.E. 186, 187, 188, and Koblenz.

Bibliography:

H. Reuther, *Kirchenbauten,* pp. 56–60.

M. H. von Freeden, *Balthasar Neumann,* pp. 46, 67.

E. Hempel, *Baroque,* p. 158.

Joachim Hotz, "Neugefundener Entwurf für die Wall fahrtskirche Gössweinstein" in *Fränkisches Land,* supplement to *Neues Volksblatt Bamberg,* 8, Nr. 6, 1961.

Illustrative material:

S.E. 185, site plan.

*S.E. 186, plan. Burned 1945.

S.E. 187, plan.

*S.E. 188, plan.

S.E. 189, plan.

S.E. 190, facade elevation, plan.

S.E. 191, plan. Burned 1945.

S.E. LXXXVI, frame for a painting.

Bamberg, Staatsarchiv, Rep. B49. Nr.

57. Fasc. 28, site plan of 1629.

————, Rep. B53. Nr. 322. prod. 29, altar project by Küchel.

————, no identification number, altar project by Franz Martin Mutschele, 1762.

Berlin, Kunstbibliothek, Hdz. 5941, facade plan.

Gössweinstein, Pfarrarchiv, terrace in front of church, by Küchel.

Kiedrich, Freiherrn von Ritter zu Gruenstein family archive, project by Freiherrn von Ritter zu Gruenstein.

Koblenz, Staatsarchiv, Abt. 702, Nr. 6542, Sheet 50, half plan, flank elevation, cross section.

19. H. G. Franz, *Böhmen,* pp. 62–64.

20. Vault frescoes were painted in 1743 by Christian Thomas Scheffler. In 1744 Neumann designed the main entrance, in 1745 the high altar, in 1747 the sacristy, in 1752 the side altars. A temporary consecration was given on 4 June 1754, the final one on 6 March 1757.

Bibliography:

H. Reuther, *Kirchenbauten,* pp. 88–89.

M. H. von Freeden, *Balthasar Neumann,* pp. 47, 68.

E. Hempel, *Baroque,* p. 158.

H.-R. Hitchcock, *Rococo,* pp. 122, 161, 210–211, 259–260.

Illustrative material:

Koblenz, Staatsarchiv, Abt. 702, Nr. 248, longitudinal section, portal different from executed work, author anonymous.

————, Nr. 249, copy of Nr. 248.

————, Nr. 250, altar design from Neumann's office.

————, Nr. 251, altar design from Neumann's office.

————, Nr. 252, altar design from Neumann's office.

————, Nr. 253, altar design from Neumann's office.

————, Nr. 254, altar design from Neumann's office.

S.E. XXXI, altar design from Neumann's office. Burned 1945.

21. No similar vault form is to be found in Bohemia (or elsewhere), though Reuther's descriptive term for these, "böhmische Kappengewölbe" (H. Reuther, *Kirchenbauten,* p. 89) suggests a particular geographical prototype. The closest parallel, Christoph Dientzenhofer's monastery church at Brevnov, and his Sv. Mikuláš Malá Strana, Prague, contain vaults which spring from double pilasters set into the nave at an angle to one another, producing a V-shaped form in plan. Consequently, the vault describes a prow-like shape at its springing point, which gradually flattens out as the vault rises to its apex. Furthermore, the Brevnov vault consists of two layers, whereas the Prague vault was designed originally with torsion cross ribs, which were later removed.

22. Preparations for a new building began in 1735 but soon came to a halt because of lack of funds. Material and money were contributed during 1737–38 by Friedrich Karl von Schönborn. Neumann laid out the site in the spring of 1739, and on 18 April of that year the cornerstone was put down. By 17 November 1740 the tower was completed. Christoph Thomas Scheffler's frescoes were begun late in 1741. The structure was consecrated 19 September 1756 after all decoration was completed.

Bibliography:

H. Reuther, *Kirchenbauten,* pp. 61–63.

M. H. von Freeden, *Balthasar Neumann,* pp. 48, 69.

E. Hempel, *Baroque,* p. 158.

Joachim Hotz, "Beiträge zur Kirchenbaukunst Balthasar Neumanns" in *Das Münster,* vol. 14, 1961, pp. 305–320.

Hans Staab, "Die historischen Baudenkmäler Heusenstamms, Die Pfarrkirche St. Cäcilia" in *750 Jahre Heusenstamm. Geschichte und Entwicklung einer jungen Stadt,* Heusenstamm, Heimatverein, 1961, pp. 71–82.

Illustrative material:

S.E. 174, plan, cross section, flank,

facade elevation. Burned 1945.
S.E. 202, plan.
*S.E. 203, plan.
S.E. 204, plan.
S.E. 205, facade elevation.
Koblenz, Staatsarchiv, Abt. 702, Nr. 6542, Sheet 100, plan.

23. On the basis of this one sheet, it is not possible to describe the church in any greater detail.

24. Maria Theresia von Schönborn, widow of Anselm Franz von Schönborn, who died in 1726, was responsible for the mausoleum interpretation. The foundation document for the church, discovered in a tin capsule in the tower, reads in part, ". . . im Jahre 1739, den 18. Tag des April, die alte Pfarrkirche zu Heusenstamm theils wegen Enge des Raumes, theils aber und vordersmast die Ruhestatt obbemelten meines liebsten Gemahles und zwei Söhnen, Lothar Franz und Friedrich Karl, sowie deren Voreltern und Verwandten, desto ansehnlicher zu machen, von Grund hinweggerissen. . . ."

25. Scheffler's vault frescoes, though lighter in tonality than his slightly later work at Trier, remain heavy overall and do nothing to relieve the irresolute quality of the church design. Johann Wolfgang van der Auvera designed the main altar the following year, but work on it was begun only in July 1744. An extraordinarily delicate and airy affair, the altar consists of two life-size angels perched on decorative carving. They turn toward a life-size, crucified Christ on a tall Cross that stands like a shaft at the center of the altar. A dramatic composition in its own right, the altar is so at odds with interior and frescoes that it does not affect the listless Heusenstamm space.

26. Bibliography:
H. Reuther, *Kirchenbauten,* pp. 101–104.

M. H. von Freeden, *Balthasar Neumann,* pp. 46, 68.

E. Hempel, *Baroque,* p. 156.

H.-R. Hitchcock, *Rococo,* pp. 81–82, 115, 209–210, 216, 217, 242, 259.

Illustrative material:

S.E. 286, plans of first and second stories. Burned 1945.
S.E. 288, plan of first story. Burned 1945.
S.E. 289, plan of second story. Burned 1945.
S.E. 290, plan of first story. Burned 1945.
S.E. 291, plan of first story.
S.E. 292, plan of building and site. Burned 1945.
*S.E. 293, plan of basement.
S.E. 294, plan of first floor. Burned 1945.
*S.E. 296, plan of lower mezzanine. Burned 1945.
S.E. 297, plan of second floor. Burned 1945.
*S.E. 298, plan of second floor.
*S.E. 300, plan of upper mezzanine. Burned 1945.
S.E. 301, plan of basement, Hildebrandt. Burned 1945.
S.E. 302, plan of first floor, Hildebrandt. Burned 1945.
S.E. 303, plan of second floor, Hildebrandt. Burned 1945.
S.E. 305, plan of second floor. Burned 1945.
S.E. 307, plan of second floor. Burned 1945.
S.E. 309, plan of upper level of oval church project, von Welsch.
S.E. 310, plan of lower level of oval church project, von Welsch.
*S.E. 311, plan of upper level of oval church project, von Welsch. Burned 1945.
S.E. 312, plans of both levels of oval church project, von Welsch.
S.E. 313, plan and longitudinal section of church in southwest corner. Burned 1945.
*S.E. 319, cross section of roof construction over church. Burned 1945.
*S.E. 323, plan of first floor, Johann Wilhelm Kayser. Burned 1945.
*S.E. 324, plan of first floor, Johann Wilhelm Kayser. Burned 1945.
*S.E. 325, plan of lower mezzanine, Johann Wilhelm Kayser. Burned 1945.
*S.E. 326, partial plan of lower mezzanine.

*S.E. 327, plan of upper mezzanine. Burned 1945.

*S.E. 328, plan of upper mezzanine. Burned 1945.

*S.E. 329, partial plan with oval church project, von Welsch. Burned 1945.

S.E. VII, elevation of high altar, Hildebrandt. Burned 1945.

*S.E. IX, elevation of side altar, Johann Wolfgang van der Auvera. Burned 1945.

*S.E. XVII, elevation of side altar. Burned 1945.

*S.E. XVIII, elevation, two plans of side altar, Hildebrandt. Burned 1945.

*S.E. XX, elevation of altar, Hildebrandt. Burned 1945.

*S.E. XXIII, top of side altar, Antonio Bossi. Burned 1945.

*S.E. XXVII, elevation of two variations of side altar. Burned 1945.

*S.E. XXXVI, elevation of upper high altar, Antonio Bossi. Burned 1945.

S.E. XXXXIII, plan and elevation of oratory. Burned 1945.

*S.E. LI, plan and elevation of altar in two variations. Burned 1945.

*S.E. LVI, plan and elevation of altar. Burned 1945.

S.E. LXVI, plan of church, Hildebrandt. Burned 1945.

S.E. LXVII, view into church from west. Burned 1945.

*S.E. LXIX, view into church from west, engraving based on S.E. LXVII. Burned 1945.

S.E. LXXI, wall elevation of church. Burned 1945.

*S.E. LXXIII, longitudinal section of church with plan of south wall. Burned 1945.

S.E. LXXV, plan and elevation of oratory, Johann Wolfgang van der Auvera. Burned 1945.

*S.E. LXXVI, project for loggia, Johann Rudolf Byss. Burned 1945.

*S.E. LXXVII, two projects for altars. Burned 1945.

S.E. LXXVIII, elevation of east wall with altar, Hildebrandt and Johann Wolfgang van der Auvera. Burned 1945.

S.E. LXXX, plan and elevation of high altar, Johann Rudolf Byss. Burned 1945.

*S.E. LXXXI, plan and elevation of high altar. Burned 1945.

*S.E. LXXXII, project for side altar. Burned 1945.

S.E. LXXXIII, plan and elevation for side altar. Burned 1945.

*S.E. LXXXIV, project for high altar. Burned 1945.

S.E. LXXXVII, plan and elevation for side altar, Johann Wolfgang van der Auvera. Burned 1945.

Bamberg, Staatliche Bibliothek, Plansammlung unbestimmter Provenienz, Nr. 53, elevation, von Welsch.

Berlin, Kunstbibliothek der ehem. Staatl. Museen, Hdz. 4675, facade of oval church project, von Welsch.

———, Hdz. 4677, longitudinal section of Residenz from north to south oval, von Welsch.

———, Hdz. 4679, elevation of north front with oval church entrance facade.

———, Hdz. 4681, plan and cross section of oval church, von Welsch.

———, Hdz. 4687, longitudinal section of church.

———, Hdz. 4688, cross section of church.

———, Hdz. 4689, plan of church.

———, Hdz. 4697, cross section of oval church, von Welsch.

———, Hdz. 4707, plan of second floor.

Koblenz, Staatsarchiv, Abt. 702, Nr. 6542, sheet 48, plan of oval church, von Welsch.

Munich, Bayerisches Hauptstaatsarchiv, plans after 1803.

Paris, Cabinet des Estampes, papers of Robert de Cotte, Nr. 1194, plan of second floor.

———, Nr. 1195, plan of second floor.

———, Nr. 1196, plan of first floor.

———, Nr. 1197, plan of second floor.

Stuttgart, Württembergische Landesbibliothek, Sammlung Nicolai, vol. 2, folio 31, first-floor plan.

———, vol. 3, folio 1, view into

church from west, engraving after
S.E. LXVII.

Würzburg, Schloss- und Gartenverwaltung, three plans of 1816, 1819.

27. This location was first questioned by Friedrich Karl, but later confirmed during the September 1730 conference. See S.E. 294, 296, 297, 298, 299, 300.

28. Even the columns placed close against the wall are not engaged with it. The drawings indicate the balcony passageway wrapping entirely around the church, though it would be very narrow at points.

29. Mirror windows were seen and accepted as an effective illusion. See H. Rott, *Bruchsal. Quellen,* p. 95, point no. 3.

30. A window was planned over the altar to open into the Prince-Bishop's loge. See Karl Heinz Esser, *Darstellung der Formen und Wirkungen der Wallfahrtskirche zu Vierzehnheiligen,* Diss. Bonn, 1940, p. 237.

31. K. H. Esser, *Darstellung,* p. 236, dates the desire to change to 8 April 1731.

32. This raised level includes the transition bay between the two ovals. In the first design, one floor level ran through the whole church.

33. Though Neumann consulted with Hildebrandt at length about the Werneck plans, it is generally felt today that the palace is Neumann's creation. See Bruno Grimschitz's modified position, *Johann Lucas von Hildebrandt,* Vienna, Osterreichische Staatsdrückerei, 1932, pp. 126–134, and the second revised edition, Vienna, 1959, pp. 147–154, as well as M. H. von Freeden, *Balthasar Neumann,* pp. 34–36. Certainly the formal relation between the Würzburg Residenz court church and the Werneck chapel is striking: see the discussion of the former above (pp. 77–82).

The scalloped oval in a rectangle form of the chapel is not yet indicated in the early plans (S.E. 272; Berlin, Hdz. 4746; Würzburg XII B29). It is shown on the undated S.E. 273–276 series. Therefore the final plan must date after the beginning of construc-

tion, spring 1734, and before the completion of the chapel tract, spring 1737.

The present all-white interior of Werneck is very different from the Würzburg court church interior, but the original color scheme has not been determined.

Bibliography:

H. Reuther, *Kirchenbauten,* pp. 97–98.

M. H. von Freeden, *Balthasar Neumann,* pp. 34–36, 68.

E. Hempel, *Baroque,* p. 157.

H.-R. Hitchcock, *Rococo,* pp. 121, 211, 213–214, 218, 261.

Illustrative material:

S.E. 272, plan.

S.E. 273, plan of basement.

S.E. 274, plan of first floor.

S.E. 275, plan of second floor.

S.E. 276, plan of third floor.

S.E. 277, partial plan of tracts toward garden, dated by Neumann 21 March 1735.

*S.E. 278, plan of stairs and adjoining rooms. Burned 1945.

S.E. 279, partial plan of northern tracts. Burned 1945.

S.E. 280, plan of northwest section of palace.

S.E. 281, plan of church.

S.E. C, church plan. Burned 1945.

*S.E. CI, church plan, engraving after S.E. C. Burned 1945.

S.E. CII, perspective longitudinal section of church. Burned 1945.

*Berlin, Kunstbibliothek, Hdz. 4746.

———, Hdz. 4747, elevation, J. R. Tatz?

———, Hdz. 4748, elevation, J. R. Tatz?

———, Hdz. 4749, elevation, J. R. Tatz?

———, Hdz. 4750, elevation, J. R. Tatz?

*———, Hdz. 4751, plan.

———, Hdz. 4752, plan of entire complex.

Frankfurt, private collection, garden elevation by J. R. Tatz, 3 March 1734; differs from executed building primarily in roof forms.

Würzburg, Historischer Verein, XII

B29, plan of palace and gardens, 20 June 1733. Burned 1945.

Chapter IV

1. Designing was begun in 1740, and on 4 June 1741 the cornerstone was laid. Neumann supervised erection of the vault centering in May 1743, and the vault construction was completed in August 1744. Building was finished by May 1745; the consecration ceremonies took place on 17 October.

Bibliography:
H. Reuther, *Kirchenbauten,* pp. 66–67.

M. H. von Freeden, *Balthasar Neumann,* pp. 48–50, 69.

E. Hempel, *Baroque,* p. 252.

Bernhard Rupprecht, *Die Bayerische Rokoko-Kirche,* Kallmünz, Lassleben, 1959, p. 58.

Illustrative material:
*S.E. 206, plan.

S.E. 207, facade, plan, cross section through crossing, longitudinal section. Burned 1945.

S.E. 208, facade, cross section through crossing, two plans.

*S.E. 209, facade, plan, cross section through crossing.

*S.E. LXXXVIII, plan, original drawing for the engraving S.E. LXXXXI, legend on drawing, "Geometrischer Grundriss der nemlichen neuerlich erbauten Catolischen Kirchen zu Kitzingen in Etwashausen. Erbauet und gezeichnet von Balthasar Neumann. Seiner Hochfürstl. Gnaden Ingenieur Architecten und Obristen der Artillerie eines löbl. Fränckischen Creyses." Burned 1945.

S.E. LXXXIX, perspective longitudinal section, original drawings for the engraving S.E. LXXXXIII, legend on drawing, "Scenograffia oder innerlicher Perspectivischer Vorstellung der neuerlich erbauten Chatolischen Kirchen zu Kitzingen in Etwahausen dem Fürstenthumb Wirzburg zugehörig wie dieselbe inwendig erbauet und von Seiner

Hochfürstlichen Gnaden FRIDERICH CARL Bischoffen zu Wirzburg und Hertzogen zu Francken etc. selbsten den 17 Octobris 1745 dem Allerhöchsten Gott geweyet worden. Erbauet und gezeichnet von Balthasar Neumann Seiner Hochfürstlich Gnaden Ingenieur, Architecten und Obristen der Artillerie eines löblichen Fränckischen Creyses." Burned 1945.

*S.E. LXXXX, facade elevation, original drawing for the engraving S.E. LXXXXIV, legend on drawing, "Geometrischer Auftrag oder fordere Faciata der neuerlich erbauten Chatolischen Kirchen zu Kitzingen in Etwashausen den Fürstenthumb Wirtzburg zugehörig und von Seiner Hochfürstlichen Gnaden FRIDERICH CARL Bischoffen zu Wirtzburg Hertzogen zu Francken etc. selbsten den 17 Octobris 1745 den Allerhöchsten Gott geweyet worden, Erbauet und gezeichet von Balthasar Neumann Seiner Hochfürstl. Gnaden Ingenieur Architecten und Obristen der Artillerie eines löblichen Fränckischen Creyses." Burned 1945.

S.E. LXXXXI, plan, engraving after S.E. LXXXVIII, and with same legend. Burned 1945.

S.E. LXXXXIII, perspective longitudinal section, engraving after S.E. LXXXIX, and with same legend. Burned 1945.

S.E. LXXXXIV, facade elevation, engraving after S.E. LXXXX, and with same legend.

Until recently, thirteen drawings and three engravings were connected with Kitzingen. S.E. 210–14 and sheet 58, *"Pläne unbestimmter Provenenz"* in the Bamberg State Library, all illustrate a stubby basilical church containing a tholos-like unit in both nave and crossing. S.E. 206–09 were considered depictions of the executed building, while S.E. LXXXVIII–X constituted the finished drawings for the engravings S.E. LXXXI–IV included in the consecration publication, *Wohlmeinende und Getreue*

Anmerckungen über die bey Einweihung eines neuen Tempel Gottes . . . in der Vorstadt zu Kitzingen . . . jungsthin erbaute Kirchen, Würzburg, 1745. J. Hotz has convincingly reattributed the drawing group S.E. 210–14 and Bamberg, number 58, to the Käppele: see J. Hotz, "Beiträge," p. 317. His reattribution is based on the inappropriateness of the crowning steeple statue of Mary for a church dedicated to the Holy Cross, and of the site description included on S.E. 211, which does not tally with the location of Kitzingen, although it does correspond to that of the Käppele. Other elements further distinguish the two groups of drawings. As will become clear when the Käppele is discussed, S.E. 210–14 and Bamberg, number 58, reveal for interior, facade, and roof a very different concept from that of Kitzingen. In addition, the character of these drawings differs from those definitely associated with Kitzingen. The former consistently illustrate an absolutely empty interior, whereas the latter include an altar arrangement similar to that contained in Kitzingen today. In short, a radical change in concept did not occur in 1740 for Kitzingen (from S.E. 210–14 and Bamberg, number 58, to S.E. 206–09), but in the designs for the Käppele, for which Neumann submitted first thoughts that same year (S.E. 210–14 and Bamberg, number 58), before a new set of plans accompanied the actual building of the church several years later, in 1747–49 (S.E. 45–53).

2. It must be assumed that the vaulting of the entrance and choir arms is the same in both preliminary and final designs, since no longitudinal section survives illustrating the former.

3. Neumann must have undertaken this modification. He maintains that he "alone supervised" construction; he saw to the erection of centering and makes no mention of difficulties in realizing the crossing which may have prompted a change in design. An examination of the vault structure reveals a homogeneous, undisturbed unit. On the other hand, this reduced configuration contradicts the nature of Neumann's approach, which is to intensify counterpoint. In addition, engravings for the project, printed when the building was completed, show the church as it appears in S.E. 207. Neumann kept a close eye on the production of dedicatory engravings. M. H. von Freeden, *Würzburgs Residenz und Fürstenhof zur Schönbornzeit,* Amorbach, Emig, 1961, pp. 46–47, notes that Neumann withdrew two views of the Residenz from Pater Ignaz Gropp's *Würzburgische Chronik* because of their lack of accuracy. In other projects, illustrated and erected monuments correspond exactly. In short, a case cannot be argued convincingly one way or the other. Under the circumstances, I would like to ally myself with the more demanding design. Since the engravings agree with the standing structure except for the crossing, analysis of the interior can be based on this structure, with the exception of the crossing unit. It must be noted, however, that S.E. 207 and S.E. 208 do not agree with the engraving in all respects. The former differs in organ balcony size and the depth of the lower edge of the crossing vault; windows are shown in the crossing corners. The outline plan on the latter contains two windows in each of the cross arm ends, with resulting changes in walls and corners.

4. This arrangement appears in the drawings and engravings of the final project, though in diminutive size. The drawings of the first and final projects illustrate the arrangement as it stands in the church today.

5. Quoted in Georg Lill and F. K. Weyser, *Die Kunstdenkmäler von Unterfranken und Aschaffenburg (Die Kunstdenkmäler des Königreichs Bayern),* II, *Stadt und Bezirksamt Kitzingen,* Munich, Oldenburg, 1911, p. 47. Curiously, the consecration engraving displays cartouches crowning nave and choir windows, while other decorations border the dome edges.

6. This was not the first time that Neumann planned windows in beveled corner walls. He advocated a similar

solution for the pavilions at Werneck, but was voted down by the architectural authority of Vienna. See in K. Lohmeyer, *Neumanns an Friedrich Karl von Schönborn,* the voluminous correspondence from the first half of 1734, following a January conference on the palace in Vienna between Neumann, Hildebrandt, and Friedrich Karl von Schönborn, who was also the patron of Kitzingen.

The plan for the court church in the Bamberg Residenz (p. 62) also has windows placed on the diagonals between each pair of columns. Franz Beer's church in the cemetery at Stephansfeld, begun 1707, contains a similar arrangement, as does the church plan in C. Sturm, *Kirchen,* pl. XXVIII.

7. Curiously, the engravings illustrate these beveled walls as if they were glowing with light; the window is gone, but the masonry appears to be illuminated from within itself.

8. Planned in 1747–48, the cornerstone laid on 5 April 1748, the fabric of the building was already complete by 1749, the vault frescoes approved on 6 April 1750 and completed in 1752. A large chapel, attached to the north transept in 1778, alters the clarity of the building's external shape and influences the internal space. The choir is dominated by a high altar constructed in 1797–99, also well after Neumann's time, and formally distinct from the character of the earlier decoration. The pulpit of 1800 is smaller and less obviously a later addition. An elaborate composition of stairs, terraces, small chapels, and sculpture, begun in 1761 and completed by 1778, is arranged up the side of the steep hill on which the chapel stands. Consecration of the church eventually took place on 21 September 1824.

Neumann's initial project for the Käppele was designed in 1740; see Chapter IV, notes 1 and 17.

Bibliography:
H. Reuther, *Kirchenbauten,* pp. 109–110.

M. H. von Freeden, *Balthasar Neumann,* pp. 61, 69, 70.

M. H. von Freeden, "Balthasar Neumann," in cols. 616–617.

H.-R. Hitchcock, *Rococo,* pp. 128, 211, 218–220, 222, 224.

J. Hotz, "Beiträge," p. 317.

Illustrative material:
*S.E. 45, site plan.
*S.E. 46, plan. Burned 1945.
S.E. 47, plan.
S.E. 48, plan, on verso, "Hierüber währe . . . ein Durchschnid zu machen durch das Creytz, damit man sehen könne, wass dessen in den Riss veränderte Kuppel Des Zeichners Seine Meinung ist Undt wie er gedenkt solche auszuführen. Wirtzburg d.8.Maii 1748."
S.E. 49, longitudinal section.
*S.E. 50, roof elevation. Burned 1945.
S.E. 51, cross section.
*S.E. 52, half plan, two half sections through dome, half cross section through crossing, half cross section through nave. Burned 1945.
*S.E. 53, facade elevation.
*S.E. 201, facade elevation by construction supervisor Balthasar Trexler. Burned 1945.
*Bamberg, Staatliche Bibliothek, VIII D, Nr. 56, plan.
*Würzburg, Historische Verein, XII B 186. Burned 1945.

9. S.E. 46, S.E. 47, S.E. 201, and Würzburg, Historische Verein, illustrate the Käppele as executed. No visual record (reproduction, photograph, etc.) survives for the burned S.E. 50.

10. Indicated on plan is a dome with eight ribs and a lantern; done in different ink from the rest of the drawing and with a dotted line technique never employed by Neumann, it appears to be an addition by another hand.

11. The present tonality of the interior emphasizes the weight and dull light. The colors have darkened; silver, used extensively as a highlight, has blackened. The church was restored 1951–56, using postwar materials that were not stable. This has happened in other Neumann churches as well. An extreme instance is Maria-Limbach, restored

1945–47; the stucco was finished in light gray, which the church priest has scraped away in places to reveal the original coloring, which was gold.

12. The exception is the window-punctured facade. But most of this area is screened from view by the organ and balcony, so that the nave arm is no brighter than the rest of the interior.

13. The Forchheim hospital was built in 1610–12. The Gothic church from the 14th and 15th centuries was baroque-ized in 1688. Neumann's project, as well as that of J. J. M. Küchel, remained unexecuted.

Bibliography:
H. Reuther, *Kirchenbauten*, p. 54.

Tilman Breuer, *Stadt und Landkreis Forchheim*, Munich, Deutscher Kunstverlag, 1961, p. 22.
Traute Knoche, *Johann Jacob Michael Küchel, 1703–1769, ein Beitrag zum deutschen Rokoko*, Diss. Marburg, 1937, pp. 28–32.
Konrad Kupfer, "Ein Kirchenbauplan Balthasar Neumanns für Forchheim" in *Der Fränkische Schatzgräber, Heimatkundliche Beilage zum Forchheimer Tagblatt*, 5th year, 1927, pp. 65*ff*.

Illustrative material:
S.E. 215, in Neumann's hand, "Neyzu erbauende Hospital Kirchen in Vorcheimb. Wirtzburg den 12 Martii 1748. Balthasar Neumann Obrister."
Küchel's project, as was the case at Vierzehnheiligen, is an independent exercise in no way related to Neumann's. See:
*Bamberg, Staatsarchiv, Rep. A 240 R 1172.
*Berlin, Kunstbibliothek, Hdz. 5914, elevations.
*———, Hdz. 5915, sections.
Later projects (1778) by Johann Roppelt include:
*Bamberg, Staatsarchiv, Rep. A 240 R 919.
*Berlin, Kunstbibliothek, Hdz. 6018.
*———, Hdz. 6033.
*Würzburg, Mainfränkisches Museum,

Inv.-Nr. S 39.549.
*———, Inv.-Nr. S 39.550.

14. The plan indicates that a transitional vault segment would be used to join the aisle vault with that covering the cross arms. The nature of this segment cannot be determined. Furthermore, its relation to the aisle remains unresolved, since it appears that both vaults would meet above the window zone; where a wall would seem necessary, there is none. The crossing vault is depicted with several inconsistencies. The north and south crescent-shaped segments are supposedly set higher than the vault itself, yet at the point of intersection, this is not shown. Also, the smaller eastern segment is not drawn in.

15. Altars by Antonio Bossi, 1747–48; organ by Johann Philipp Seuffert, 1749.

Bibliography:
H. Reuther, *Kirchenbauten*, pp. 54–56.

M. H. von Freeden, *Balthasar Neumann*, pp. 49, 69.
E. Hempel, *Baroque*, p. 252.
H.-R. Hitchcock, *Rococo*, p. 261, footnote 113.
J. Keller, *Neumann*, p. 181.

16. For example, E. Lehmann, "Balthasar Neumann und Kloster Langheim," p. 228.

17. J. Hotz, "Beiträge," pp. 317–320, has reattributed S.E. 210–214 to the 1740 Käppele planning. Also see Chapter IV, notes 1 and 8.

Illustrative material:
S.E. 210, two plans, one showing two variations, cross section through nave.
S.E. 211, plan, cross sections through nave and crossing, facade elevation.
*S.E. 212, cross section through nave and crossing, facade elevation.
S.E. 213, plan. Burned 1945.
S.E. 214, facade elevation. Burned 1945.
Koblenz, Staatsarchiv, Abt. 702, Nr. 5821, plan, longitudinal section.

18. Gothic church begun 1264, consecrated 1270, though not complete. Fabric complete by 1744, stuccoes and frescoes begun 1748 and finished 1771.

The church now belongs to the Augustinian Order.

Bibliography:
H. Reuther, *Kirchenbauten,* pp. 100–101.

M. H. von Freeden, *Balthasar Neumann,* pp. 46–47, 69.

E. Hempel, *Baroque,* p. 158.

Illustrative material:
S.E. 226, Neumann's plan superimposed upon the Gothic plan, noted on sheet, "Grund Riss des löbl. Gotteshauses der Herrn P. P. Dominikaner in Wirtzburg. Wirtzburg den 19. Februarii 1741. Balt. Neumann Obristlieut." Burned 1945.

19. Max Hauttmann, *Geschichte der Kirchlichen Baukunst in Bayern, Schwaben und Franken, 1550–1780,* Munich, Praktische Kunstwissenschaft F. Schmidt, 1921, p. 201. This creative attitude should be distinguished from the work of an architect like Giovanni Santini Aichel, who designed an ideocentric "Baroque-Gothic." See H. G. Franz, *Böhmen,* pp. 105–130.

20. Rottenbuch, former Augustinian canon church, built in the 15th century, baroque-ized 1737–44. The pietà statue of 1686 stands in the music choir.

21. Erich Bachmann, "Balthasar Neumann und das Mittelalter" in *Stifter-Jahrbuch,* III 1953, pp. 134–149.

22. M. Hauttmann, *Bayern, Schwaben und Franken,* p. 200.

23. See Chapter III, note 11.

24. E. Bachmann, "Mittelalter," suggests that medieval concepts were deeply ingrained in Neumann's creative personality. He discusses the use of baldachin-like vaults, freestanding support systems, single towers which grow organically from the facade or stand behind the choir, and the qualities of Romanesque space in Gaibach.

25. The 1742 date derives from correspondence by Abbot Mösinger of Langheim with Neumann, requesting the Langheim plans. The 1 June 1742 date was incorrectly read as 1739 by R. Teufel, *Vierzehnheiligen,* 1936 and 1957, but has now been corrected by F. Oswald (see below). Neumann is not mentioned in relation to Langheim in any other correspondence before 1742.

Bibliography:
H. Reuther, *Kirchenbauten,* pp. 69–71.

M. H. von Freeden, *Balthasar Neumann,* pp. 50,.69.

Ferdinand Geldner, *Kloster Langheim,* Lichtenfels, 1961.

Edgar Lehmann, "Balthasar Neumann und Kloster Langheim" in *Zeitschrift für Kunstgeschichte,* 25, 1962, pp. 213–242.

Fritz Oswald, "Zur Vorgeschichte der Wallfahrtskirche Vierzehnheiligen" in *97. Bericht des Historischen Vereins Bamberg,* Bamberg, 1961, Nr. 28, p. 209.

Illustrative material:
S.E. 93, site plan.
S.E. 94, plan, by G. H. Krohne.
S.E. 95, plan, by G. H. Krohne.
S.E. 96, plan, by G. H. Krohne.
S.E. 97, plans, by J. L. Dientzenhofer.
S.E. 98, plan.
S.E. 99, plan.
S.E. 100, plan.
S.E. 101, plan.
S.E. 102, plans.
S.E. 103, plans, by J. L. Dientzenhofer.
S.E. 104, plan. Burned 1945.
S.E. 105, longitudinal section.
*S.E. 106, two cross sections through nave and crossing.
*S.E. 107, two cross sections through nave and crossing. Burned 1945.
S.E. 108, facade elevation.

26. Illustrating the project are the drawings S.E. 102 (three pencil sketches of plans for the church and immediately adjoining cloister buildings), S.E. 98/104, 101 (ground plans of church and cloister, first and second stories), S.E. 99/100 (variation of ground plans for church and cloister, first and second stories), S.E. 105 (longitudinal section related to S.E. 98/104, 101), S.E. 106 (two cross sections, one through the crossing, one through a nave bay, related to S.E. 98/104, 101, 105), S.E.

107 (a copy of S.E. 106), and S.E. 108 (facade elevation).

Lehmann has established that S.E. 98/104, 101 corrects the original projects of S.E. 99/100. In the latter, the cloister atrium cuts into the lower half of the south transept arm. S.E. 98/104, 101 balances this necessary intrusion with a similarly articulated "fill" structure in the north arm. Lehmann would then like to consider the S.E. 102 sketches as Neumann's corrections of S.E. 98/104, 101. Here the transept arms are pulled into line with the nave wall, eliminating the problem of low-set blocks placed in the arms, and tying them more closely to the crossing. Lehmann further considers the wider nave arcades in S.E. 102 (three bays rather than four), and the richer curve of the organ balcony, as additional "improvements" of S.E. 98/104, 101. Hotz, on the other hand, lists S.E. 102 as a sheet of preliminary sketches, but without explanation. The problem of determining Neumann's final design for Langheim is insoluble without additional evidence, but it should be noted that Lehmann's interpretation is based on a sequence through the projects leading directly to Neumann's first designs for Vierzehnheiligen. Since he misdates the 1742 Langheim designs to 1738–39, whereas the Vierzehnheiligen projects originated during the winter of 1741–42, this sequence is inaccurate. In addition, as this essay maintains, such a sequential progression is not characteristic of Neumann's design process, and therefore fails to be convincing. Finally, format and quality of certain drawings among the group indicate which variation was probably definitive. Of all the sheets, only S.E. 104, 105, 106, and 108 are finished presentation renderings, related in format and signature (S.E. 105, 106, and 108 are similarly signed in the lower right hand corner, "Balt: Neumann Obrist von Wirtzburg"). There is no equivalent series related to either S.E. 102 or S.E. 99/100. Acknowledging the possibility of lost or destroyed drawings, the S.E. 104, 105, 106, 108 set seems to record Neumann's final

project for Langheim. S.E. 105 contains questionable sections: the area just inside the main entrance has not been completed, and some of the windows opening the dome would be encased by surrounding roofs, though all are shown as light-filled. The absence of a scale on S.E. 105 and S.E. 108 makes connections tentative.

27. H. Thelen, ed., *Borromini*, Corpus-Nr. 32, considers the significance of a similar motif in Borromini's plan for S. Ignazio in Rome. The author knows of no other building or project employing this arrangement.

28. Cornerstone laid 27 February 1742, consecrated 13 October 1746, given to Mainz University on 6 September 1773 after the dissolution of the Jesuit order, proposed for conversion into a library about 1792, burned out during the night of 28–29 June 1793, demolished 1805–11. Darmstadt stonemason's contract listed in Einsingbach's "Neue Planfunde" (see below).

Bibliography:
H. Reuther, *Kirchenbauten*, pp. 73–74.

Fritz Arens, *Die Kunstdenkmäler der Stadt Mainz*, part 1, *Kirchen S. Agnes bis H. Kreuz (Die Kunstdenkmäler von Rheinland-Pfalz)*, Mainz, Deutscher Kunstverlag, 1961, pp. 267–287.

Wolfgang Einsingbach, "Neue Planfunde zu Balthasar Neumanns Mainzer Jesuitenkirche" in *Mainzer Zeitschrift*, 54, 1959, pp. 33–40.

M. H. von Freeden, *Balthasar Neumann*, pp. 50, 69.

E. Hempel, *Baroque*, pp. 254, 256.

Gerhard Henkes, "Hilfslinien für die Proportionierung des Querschnitts der Jesuitenkirche" in *Mainzer Zeitschrift*, 54, 1959, p. 40.

Illustrative material:
*S.E. 238, site plan. Burned 1945.
S.E. 239, longitudinal section and partial plan. Burned 1945.
S.E. 240, two cross sections through nave and crossing. Burned 1945.
S.E. 241, two plans, one in red super-

imposed upon one in gray. Burned 1945.

*S.E. 242, two plans, by J. V. Thoman. Burned 1945.

S.E. 243, plan (ground and balcony level), longitudinal section.

Marburg, Staatsarchiv, Kartenrepositur C 187 M, Sheet 1, partial plan; Sheet 2, section.

29. S.E. 243 traditionally has been associated with Neumann's project for the Jesuit church in Würzburg; see for example, H. Reuther, *Kirchenbauten,* p. 106 and fig. 47. But the specific character of the spaces around the choir relates it beyond doubt with the Mainz design.

30. Indicated as an office hand by the awkwardness, not to say crudeness, of the rendering. The crossing is tentative, showing major discrepancies between plan and section.

31. Three distinct, overlapping versions of the crossing piers are shown.

1. Massive, richly articulated pier.

2. Wedge-shaped unit connected to the outer wall.

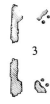

3. Freestanding, wedge-shaped unit fronted by freestanding columns.

The outer wall is shown with curved or angular corners in the crossing area, as a meticulously finished, plastic interpretation in the nave.

32. As in the Basilica of Constantine or Rheims Cathedral, the base of the supports was scaled to superhuman size, so that the spectator would seem located below the building, looking up into it through a transparent floor. In S. Andrea and S. Sebastiano, both in Mantua, Alberti provided a link in this tradition to the 17th and 18th centuries.

33. Gothic chapel taken down in the spring of 1751, cornerstone laid 18 September 1751. South flank foundations of the Gothic church utilized as the facade foundations of the new church. Fabric complete June 1753, consecration 7 September 1755.

Bibliography:

H. Reuther, *Kirchenbauten,* pp. 71–73.

M. H. von Freeden, *Balthasar Neumann,* pp. 64, 71.

Illustrative material:

S.E. 192, Gothic church plan, with half plan variations of the new church partially superimposed upon it.

*S.E. 193, plan, longitudinal and cross section. Burned 1945.

S.E. 194, facade elevation.

*S.E. 195, east flank elevation.

S.E. 196, perspective longitudinal section.

*S.E. 235, upper tower section in elevation, view, cross section and plan, by F. I. M. Neumann. Burned 1945.

S.E. 413, plan, longitudinal and cross section with roof construction, by J. J. Löffler.

S.E. 414, half plan, half working drawings for roof construction, by J. J. Löffler.

34. Design by G. F. von Fackenhofen was in the Dros Collection, Bamberg, but is now missing. J. M. Fischer, Staatliche Bibliothek Bamberg, VIII D, Nr. 67.

35. H. G. Franz, *Böhmen,* pp. 58–62.

36. Hans Reuther, "Die Baugeschichte und Gestalt der Wallfahrtskirche zu Maria-Limbach" in *Das Münster,* 2, 1948–49, p. 363, advances the former, while M. Hauttmann, *Bayern, Schwaben und Franken,* p. 199, suggests the latter.

37. The church's priest has scraped away the gray paint in a number of places to reveal the original gold coloring. See Chapter IV, note 11.

38. The quote is from Niklaus Pevsner, *An Outline of European Architecture,* Baltimore, Penguin, Jubilee edition, 1960, p. 442. Though Teufel recognizes certain affinities between Neumann's personal 1742 project and its 1744 redesigning, Millon, von Freeden, and Hitchcock all state or imply this point of view.

39. The drawings referred to in this and the following paragraph are all illustrated in R. Teufel, *Vierzehnheiligen,* 1957.

Bibliography:

H. Reuther, *Kirchenbauten,* pp. 90–97.

M. H. von Freeden, *Balthasar Neu-*

mann, pp. 50–54, 70.

M. H. von Freeden, "Balthasar Neumann," cols. 615–616.

E. Hempel, *Baroque,* pp. 252–254.

H.-R. Hitchcock, *Rococo,* pp. 14, 17, 171, 208, 215–219, 221–222, 224, 260–261.

Illustrative material:

S.E. 71, site plan.

S.E. 72, site plan. Burned 1945.

S.E. 73, plan with two variations. Burned 1945.

S.E. 74, plan, Neumann's so-called "Privatprojekt."

S.E. 75, plan.

S.E. 76, plan with two variations.

S.E. 77, plan with two variations.

S.E. 78, plan.

S.E. 79, longitudinal section. Burned 1945.

S.E. 80, longitudinal section.

*S.E. 81, elevation of north flank.

S.E. 82, plan.

S.E. 83, plan.

S.E. 84, elevation of facade.

S.E. 85, elevation of north flank.

S.E. 86, longitudinal section.

S.E. 87, plan.

S.E. 88, elevation of facade.

S.E. 89, plan and section of north transept arm and part of choir.

*S.E. 90, plan and section of north transept arm and part of choir. Burned 1945.

S.E. 91, plan above entablature, with roof framework over north aisle, F. I. M. Neumann.

S.E. 92, plan, F. I. M. Neumann. Burned 1945.

Bamberg, Historischer Verein, Inv.-Nr. 210 H, model.

Berlin, Kunstbibliothek der ehem. Staatl. Museen, Hdz. 5908.

Nuremberg, Germanisches National-Museum, HB 23576 b 6, plan.

———, HB 23576 c, facade.

Schwürbitz über Lichtenfels, private collection, model.

40. With the exception of S.E. 90, but this is an exact copy of S.E. 89.

41. Krohne's personal variation of the 1742 designs, according to which he began construction, is too personal to determine which Neumann project it may be based on. It should be noted that on S.E. 77, in the third nave bay, the balcony is shown as a curved form; this was erased and the straight form substituted.

42. Even this is given a curved accent by the use of a torsion arch in the vaulting, which mirrors a similar form in the nave oval.

43. In S.E. 75, the oval is longer, the niches more developed, and pilasters rather than columns are used in the chancel bay.

44. How these would have been vaulted to the west remains unclear. In the plan (Fig.128) a curved line joins the freestanding column in the oval with its crossing counterpart.

45. Andersen divides this material into three projects, a "small," "middle," and "large" one. Three variations exist for the "small" project, plans Berlin, Hdz. 4732 and 4733, in which no church is shown, and 4734. The first two are essentially alike, while the last contains some significant differences in the overall palace layout. The church plan in Hdz. 4734 employs rectangular outer walls within which an oval, oriented lengthwise, occupies two-thirds of the space. A large rectangular area constitutes the choir at one end of the oval, a narrow one the vestibule at the other end. Eight freestanding columns support the oval, grouped in order to establish definite longitudinal and cross axes. Though never engaged with the external fabric, the oval hollows it out along the flanks. An elaborate balcony runs around the entire interior.

Three drawings illustrate the "middle" project, Berlin, Hdz. 4729, 4730, 4731, of which only the plan 4729 contains a church; the other drawings are sections of the stair. Similar in spirit though more elaborate than the "small" project, three ovals are contained within rectangular outer walls—a longitudinal central oval with small cross ovals at either end. These units are placed freestanding within the outer fabric. Four pairs of columns support the central oval, establishing longitudinal and cross axes, while each of the cross ovals rests on four single columns and two square pilasters. The ovoid shapes are repeated on the inner surface of the external masonry. This fabric also is opened along each flank of the longitudinal oval by five close-set window bays. One window bay illuminates the vestibule oval, but the intended arrangement of windows in the choir is not clear in this plan. A richly curved balcony circles the entire church.

Berlin, Hdz. 4726, 4727, 4728 illustrate the "large" project. Site plan 4727 shows the existing buildings with which Neumann had to contend, 4726 is a plan of the entire palace, 4728 plan and section of the church. The additional material listed below, related to the "large" project, sheds no further light on specifics of the church.

Bibliography:
H. Reuther, *Kirchenbauten,* pp. 98–99.

Liselotte Andersen, *Studien zu Profanbauformed Balthasar Neumanns. Die grossen Residenzprojekte für Wien, Stuttgart und Karlsruhe,* Diss. Munich, 1966, pp. 6–30.
M. H. von Freeden, *Balthasar Neumann,* pp. 59, 70.

Illustrative material:
S.E. 376, plan of stair. Burned 1945.
S.E. 377, plan of stair. Burned 1945.
Berlin, Kunstbibliothek der ehem. Staatl. Museen, Hdz. 4725–4734, as discussed above.
Koblenz, Staatsarchiv. Abt. 702, Nr. 2317.

46. In 1747, Abbot Aurelius Braisch of the Benedictine monastery at Neresheim commissioned Neumann to design a new church. Preparation of the site, which necessitated a considerable amount of fill since it dropped off steeply along one side, had been in progress since 1745. On 4 June 1748, the cornerstone for Neumann's church was ceremonially put in place. This new structure was designed to partially occupy the same ground as its Romanesque precursor; the old church was removed as the growth of the new one progressed.

When Neumann died on 19 August 1753, the walls of his church were being erected. By mid-1757 they reached the main entablature and the building was ready for vaults. The need for supervision by a knowledgeable architect was obvious, and Johann Georg Conradi, from Zimmern in Ries, was hired. Maintaining that the walls and supports were too thin to carry stone vaults, Conradi advocated lath and plaster constructions, which were approved. But Conradi soon proved unable to execute his proposals; he was dismissed at the beginning of 1758. Johann Baptist Wiedemann, an architect from Donauwörth, was then engaged, and he completed the building. A combination of structural and financial considerations persuaded the convent to employ vaults lower than those projected by Neumann, and to realize them out of lath and plaster rather than stone (see: J. Keller, *Neumann,* p. 169). By 1764 the vaults were in place; the roof was finished six years later. The facade, in construction from the start, was only completed five years after the roofing. A preliminary consecration took place in 1777 (decoration of the interior was drawn out until the 1790s), thirty years after Neumann's first designs, twenty-four years after he died. Despite this time distance the building remains Neumann's creation. In life, he had achieved a vision so precise and persuasive, that later personalities, the passage of time, modifications and embellishments, did not decisively alter it.

Bibliography:
H. Reuther, *Kirchenbauten,* pp. 78–84.

Balthasar Neumann in Baden-Württemberg. Bruchsal—Karlsruhe—Stuttgart—Neresheim, exhibition catalogue, Staatsgalerie Stuttgart, 28 September to 30 November 1975, pp. 93–140.
M. H. von Freeden, *Balthasar Neumann,* pp. 61–64, 70.
M. H. von Freeden, "Balthasar Neumann," col. 617.
E. Hempel, *Baroque,* pp. 147, 254, 302.
H.-R. Hitchcock, *Rococo,* pp. 16, 171,

215, 220–223, 261.

Hans-Joachin Sachse, *Die barocken Dachwerks- und Gewölbekonstruktionen der Abteikirche zu Neresheim unter der Berücksichtigung der im 19. Jahrhundert durchgeführten konstruktiven Veränderungen,* Diss. Berlin, 1966.

Michael Ullrich, *Untersuchungen zum Tragverhalten barocker Holzkuppeln am Beispiel der Vierungskuppel in der Abteikirche Neresheim,* Diss. Karlsruhe, 1975.

P. Paulus Weissenberger, "Das Fürstliche Haus Thurn und Taxis und seine Grablege in der Benediktinerabtei zu Neresheim," *Jahrbuch des Historischen Vereins Dillingen a. d. Donau,* LXIX, 1967, pp. 81–105.

P. Paulus Weissenberger, "Die Restaurationsarbeiten in der Abteikirch zu Neresheim in den Jahren 1791 bis 1953" in *Zeitschrift für Württembergische Landesgeschichte,* XVI, 1957, pp. 135–190.

Illustrative material:
S.E. 109, plan with two variations.
S.E. 110, plan.
S.E. 111, two plans, one with two variations.
S.E. 112, longitudinal section, cross section through the transept, plan, half cross section through the nave and half elevation of the facade.
S.E. 113, plan.
S.E. 114, plan.
S.E. 115, west facade.
S.E. 116, plan.
S.E. 117, plan.
S.E. 118, partial plan of choir and southeast corner of crossing.
S.E. 119, plan.
S.E. 120, plan, longitudinal section.
S.E. 121, plan.
S.E. 122, plan at two different levels.
S.E. 123, longitudinal section.
S.E. 124, longitudinal section.
S.E. 125, cross section through nave, half cross section through second nave vault from west.
S.E. 126, elevation of facade.
*S.E. 127, elevation of facade.
S.E. 128, half cross section through transept and half elevation of facade.
S.E. 129, construction details for vaulting, F. I. M. Neumann.

Nack, Carl Alois, *Reichstift Neresheim, eine kurze Geschichte dieser Benediktinerabtei in Schwaben und Beschreibung ihrer im Jahre 1792 eingeweihten neuen Kirche,* n.p., 1792, bird's-eye view.

*Neresheim, Benedictine monastery, model of roof structure, Hans Georg Neumayr, 1757.

*———. Bird's-eye view, lithograph, signed: "Neresheim/Verlag von Ch. Hertz in Dillingen."

Regensburg, Fürst Thurn und Taxis Zentralarchiv, Rep. XIV oben III, plan.

———, Rep. XIV, 97, 1, plan.

———, "Schwäbische Akten" Nr. 1178, folio 147/148, longitudinal section, Antonio Giuseppe Sartori, 1775.

———, folio 149/150, longitudinal section, Antonio Giuseppe Sartori, 1775.

———, folio 151/152, pier, pilaster, paired columns of crossing, Antonio Giuseppe Sartori, 1775.

Stuttgart, Württembergische Landesbibliothek, Slg. Nicolai, vol. 3, folio 78, plan.

Wallerstein, Fürstlich Öttingen-Wallerstein'sches Archiv, Ad Neresheim, Kloster- und Kirchenbau VI. 122.5, three plan fragments.

Vienna, Haus- Hof- und Staatsarchiv, Reichshofratsakten, Obere Registratur, page 55, folios 584, 589, 590, 594, 597.

47. Revealed during the course of the extensive restoration, 1966–75: see Norbert Stoffels O.S.B. and Herbert von Moser, "Die Wiederherstellung der Abteikirche Neresheim von 1966–1975" in *Balthasar Neumann in Baden-Württemberg,* pp. 127–133.

48. S.E. 112 (Pl. I) employs balconies in the nave, S.E. 123 in the choir.

49. Shown on S.E. 110 (Fig. 141), 112, 117 (Fig. 143), 119, 120, 121, 122, and the large Regensburg plan.

50. Moved forward in the executed

church.

51. M. H. von Freeden, *Balthasar Neumann*, p. 62.

52. H. Reuther, *Kirchenbauten*, p. 31; H.-R. Hitchcock, *Rococo*, p. 222.

53. M. H. von Freeden, *Balthasar Neumann*, p. 62.

Chapter V

1. If the influence of Georg Dientzenhofer from Bamberg escaped Neumann at precisely the moment of his tutelage by Müller, that of Georg's younger brother, Johann, certainly did not. Having visited Italy (1699–1700), Johann Dientzenhofer was familiar with Roman architecture. His rebuilding of Fulda cathedral (1704–12), strongly reminiscent of Borromini's S. Giovanni in Laterano, demonstrates these affinities. On the other hand, the impact of 17th-century Bohemian work is felt in Johann's designs. His monastery church at Banz combines the Roman basilican format with the Bohemian vocabulary of diagonally placed pilasters, torsion arches, and segmental spaces separating the major units. Johann served as co-supervisor with Neumann for construction of the Residenz from 1722 on. Holzkirchen provided a further point of contact, for which Johann designed a series of centralizing longitudinal interiors, employing torsion arches to distinguish the various units. His different projects utilize circles, cross ovals, and longitudinal ovals, making the central unit in some the largest, in others the smallest element in the interior. After his death in 1726, Neumann succeeded him as architect of Holzkirchen, erecting the existing church, significantly, in a totally different manner. G. Neumann, *Neresheim*, has suggested that Johann was more influenced by Neumann than the other way around. Even if this was so, Johann's presence is significant as one element in a pervasive pattern of exposure to Bohemian architecture.

2. H. G. Franz, *Bauten und Baumeister*, pp. 61–62.

3. B. Grimschitz, *J. L. von Hildebrandt*, pp. 37–40.

4. Hans Reuther, "Die kunstlerischen Einwirkungen von Johann Lucas von Hildebrandt auf die Architektur Balthasar Neumanns," in *Architectura*, 1, 1973, pp. 58–85, reaches a similar conclusion: Hildebrandt never influenced the spatial conception of Neumann's churches, and he provided a decorative overlay only for the Hofkirche and Werneck. Reuther discusses the extensive contact between the two architects, and argues that Hildebrandt did affect the facade compositions of several Schönborn palace projects. These exteriors are not a concern of this study. Reuther also reviews earlier discussions in the scholarly literature of the Neumann-Hildebrandt interaction.

5. Giovanni Battista Gaulli and Andrea Pozzo had transformed the interior of Il Gesù with dramatic, illusionistic paintings and statuary during the last decades of the 17th century.

6. M. H. von Freeden, "Balthasar Neumann in Italien. Neue archivalische Beiträge zur Frühzeit des Künstlers," *Mainfränkisches Jahrbuch für Geschichte und Kunst, Archiv des historischen Vereins für Unterfranken und Aschaffenburg*, 72, 1949. Concerning Neumann's penchant for supporting vaults on columns: Pelegrini's church of S. Fedele in Milan, begun 1569, contains 33-feet-high columns in the nave that carry the vaults.

7. L. Döry, "Balthasar Neumann und die Brüder von Uffenbach," pp. 247–256.

8. K. Lohmeyer, *Neumanns . . . Pariser Studienreise*.

9. Wolfgang Herrmann, *Laugier and Eighteenth-Century French Theory*, London, Zwemmer, 1962.

10. *Verzeichnis der Bücher, Kupferstiche und Handzeichnungen aus der Verlassenschaft des fürstl. Würzburg. Herrn Artillerie-Obersten und berühmten Architekten Franz Ignaz Michael von Neumann, welche zu Würzburg im Gasthofe zum Eichhorn den 18ten Junius und folgende Tage 1804, jedes Mahl Nachmittags von 2–6 Uhr öffentlich versteigert werden. Würzburg, gedruckt bey den Gebrüdern Stahel.*

Würzburg, University Library, Rp. XIV 69. F. I. M. Neumann died in 1785. Presumably his brother, Valentine Franz Stanislaus Neumann, first Kapitular (1771–1775) then Dechant (1775 on) of Neumünsterstift, spiritual advisor and vice-chancellor of the university, inherited his library. Valentine Franz Stanislaus died in the spring of 1803. Due to the turbulent events surrounding the Secularization of 1803, the auction took place only in 1804.

Since Neumann's drawings in the Ekart collection come from this sale (catalogue entries 598, 654, 655, 656, 657, 659, 700, 701, 707, 732, 738, though this constitutes a greater number than the Ekart collection houses today— the location of the missing sheets is not known), it is reasonable to assume that much of the material had been passed on from Balthasar Neumann to his son. Sorting out Neumann's library from the whole can be done with fair certainty. A good half of the volumes date well before 1753, the year of his death. Since Franz Ignaz Michael was born only twenty years earlier, he would not have undertaken any significant buying by this time. It must be kept in mind, however, that older texts could always be purchased if available, much as is the case today. More importantly, the tastes of father and son were different. Franz Ignaz Michael, for example, disliked ornament, whereas Neumann understood it to be an integral part of a building and was concerned with its quality and correct application. It therefore seems reasonable to attribute volumes on ornamentation to the father's holdings. On F. I. M. Neumann, see C. Weiler, "Franz Ignaz Michael von Neumann" in *Mainzer Zeitschrift*, 32, 1937, pp. 1–27.

11. *Verzeichniss der Bücher, Kupferstiche und Handzeichnungen* singles out the Scamozzi as a "rarity" in the introduction.

12. The book is impressively laid out, with large margins and excellent reproductions. A Latin edition also was published in the same year.

13. J. Bergmüller, *Geometrischer Maasstab der wessentlichen Abteilung und Verhältnisse der Säulenordnungen*, n.p., 1752.

14. V. C. Habicht, "Die deutschen Architekturtheoretiker des 17. und 18. Jahrhunderts" in *Zeitschrift für Architektur und Ingenieurwesen*, LXII (vol. XXI of the new series), 1916, p. 261.

15. Sturm divides churches into two types, Catholic and Protestant. Vital to the former, inside and out, is its splendor. Inside, the spectator must be able to see well. Grand domes, great numbers of pilasters and columns, open naves, and many chapels distinguish these buildings. Since hearing and seeing the preacher is crucial to the Protestant churches, balconies are used to concentrate the people around a single spot. Worshippers must be able to take the sacrament, and there must be room for organ and choir. A tower distinguishes these structures. Aesthetic criteria affecting Catholic church design consist of a nave twice as long as wide, dome height between one-third and one-half of its diameter, and the introduction of as much light as possible. The more space between supports, and the thinner the supports without affecting the strength of the church, the better and more beautiful it will be. In articulating the arcade, arches springing from an entablature and supported by paired columns present the greatest beauty. All these characteristics are most effective if revealed gradually as one proceeds into the church, rather than immediately on entering.

16. V. C. Habicht, "Die Herkunft der Kenntnisse Balthasar Neumanns auf dem Gebiete der 'Civilbaukunst,'" in *Monatshefte für Kunstwissenschaft*, IX, 1916, pp. 46–61, saw the works of Sturm and Decker as major sources for several Neumann designs, but his analysis has received little credit. This is hardly surprising. Neumann's buildings can be related to theoretical pronouncements in only the most general way: specific parallels are too farfetched to be convincing. On other occasions, Habicht's incomplete or incorrect knowledge of Neumann's oeuvre nulli-

fies the relationships he suggests from the outset (see, for example, p. 57). Lastly, Habicht considers built structures only to establish these relationships, neglecting Neumann's design process, which in itself contributes to an understanding of the final product.

17. M. H. von Freeden, *Neumann,* p. 41, points out that Neumann was treated, nevertheless, as an equal by some of the most highly placed members of society. Elector Clemens August took Neumann with him on the hunt, had the architect eat with him at his own table, and made him part of his own private society when entertaining foreign dignitaries.

18. The main sources (which include further bibliography) for this discussion are:

R. Benz, *Deutsches Barock, Kultur des Achtzehnten Jahrhunderts,* part I, Stuttgart, Reclam, 1949.

M. Braubach, *Diplomatie und Geistiges Leben im 17. und 18. Jahrhundert,* Bonn, Röhrscheid, 1969.

A. Fauchier-Magnan, *The Small German Courts in the Eighteenth Century,* trans. by M. Savill, London, Methuen, 1958.

Willi Flemming, *Deutsche Kultur im Zeitalter des Barocks,* Konstanz, Akademische Verlagsgesellschaft Athenaion, 2d rev. ed., 1960.

19. W. Flemming, *Kultur . . . Barocks,* p. 321.

20. *ibid.,* p. 315.

21. *ibid.,* p. 317.

22. M. H. von Freeden, "Balthasar Neumanns Tod und Begräbnis" in *Die Mainlande, Geschichte und Gegenwart,* 2, 18 April 1951, pp. 9–10, 15.

1. Balthasar Neumann, painting by Markus Friedrich Kleinert, 1727
(Würzburg, Mainfränkisches Museum).

2. Balthasar Neumann, fireworks display, drawing, 1725 (Stuttgart, Württembergische Landesbibliothek, Slg. Nicolai).

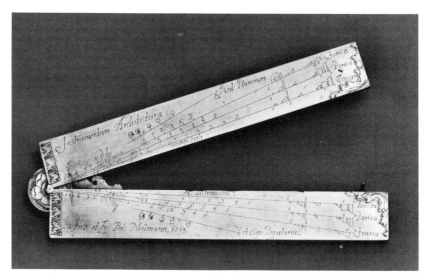

3. Balthasar Neumann, "Instrumentum Architecturae," 1713 (Würzburg, Mainfränkisches Museum).

4. Würzburg, city map, 1723 copy by J. B. Homann from Neumann's drawing of 1722. Residenz shown on left as complete, although work on it was begun only in 1719 (Stuttgart, Württembergische Landesbibliothek, Slg. Nicolai).

5. Würzburg, Stift Haug, Antonio Petrini, 1670–90, view.

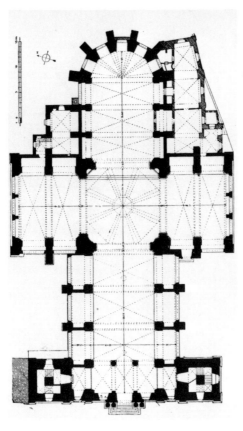

6. Würzburg, Stift Haug, plan.

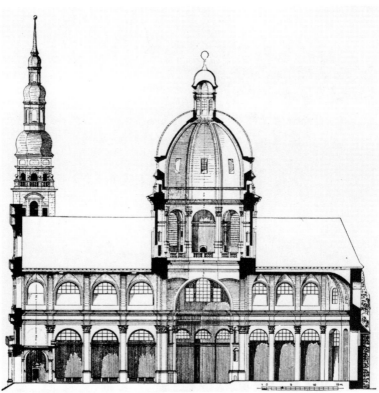

7. Würzburg, Stift Haug, section.

8. Würzburg, the Neumünster,
Josef Greising, rebuilt 1710–19,
facade by Johann Dientzenhofer (?).

9. Ebrach, Cistercian monastery, new construction planned 1714–15, begun
1716, entrance facade.

10. Lothar Franz von Schönborn, oil on copper (Cologne, Wallraf-Richartz Museum).

11. Johann Philipp Franz von Schönborn (Würzburg Residenz).

12. Friedrich Karl von Schönborn (Würzburg Residenz).

13. Die Wies, pilgrimage
church, Dominikus and Johann Baptist
Zimmermann, 1745–54, choir.

14. Isny, SS. George and Jacob the Elder,
Giulliano Barbieri, begun 1664,
interior decoration from the 18th century, choir.

15. Wolf Casper von Klengel, sketch for window frames (Stuttgart, Württembergische Landesbibliothek, Slg. Nicolai).

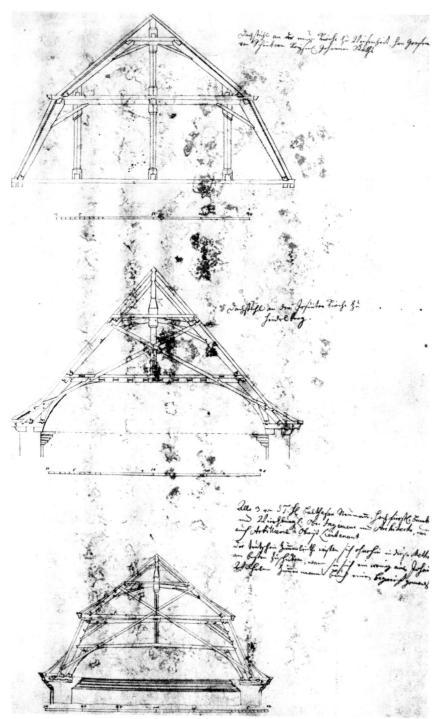

16. Roof trusses, anonymous drawing (Stuttgart, Württembergische Landesbibliothek, Slg. Nicolai).

18. Die Wies, structural detail of main vault
(Hans-Joachim Sachse, *Die barocken Dachwerks- und Gewölbekonstruktionen der Abteikirche zu Neresheim*, 1975).

17. Crane (Johann Wilhelm, *Architectura civilis*, Frankfurt, 1705).

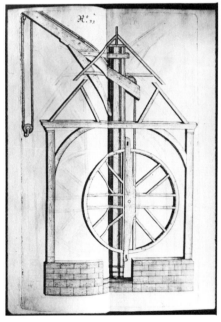

19. Die Wies, view into ambulatory.

20. Ottobeuren, abbey church of the Holy Trinity, planning begun after 1710, construction 1737–55 with the participation of several architects, stucco by J. M. Feichtmayr, 1756–64, frescoes by J. J. Zeiller, 1763, altars and other liturgical fittings completed 1767.

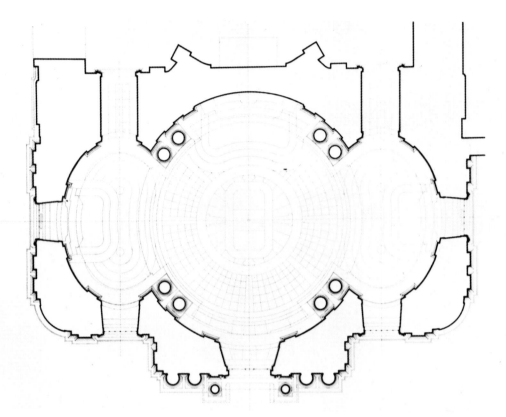

21. Würzburg, Schönborn chapel, project by Maximilian von Welsch
1720–21, reworked by Neumann before April 1721, construction begun
June 1721, plan.

22. Würzburg, Schönborn chapel, cross section.

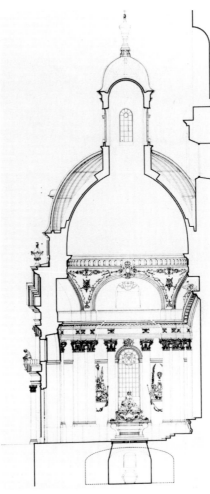

23. Würzburg, Schönborn chapel, longitudinal section.

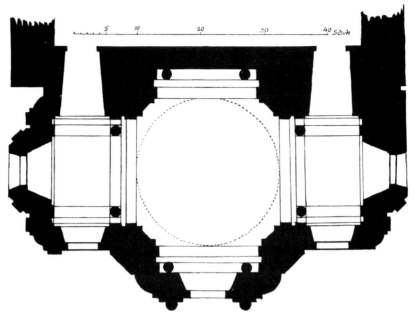

24. Würzburg, Schönborn chapel, von Welsch plan as reconstructed by Boll.

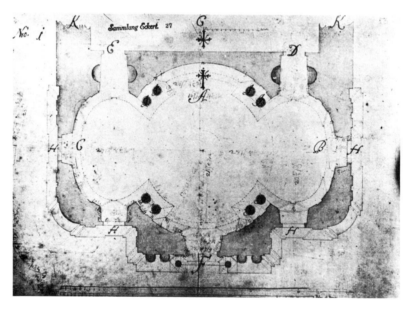

25. Würzburg, Schönborn chapel, Neumann plan of 1721 (S.E. 27).

26. Würzburg, Schönborn chapel,
section and elevation of the plan
in Fig. 25 (S.E. 44).

27. Würzburg, Schönborn chapel, view by Salomon Kleiner, 1724–29.

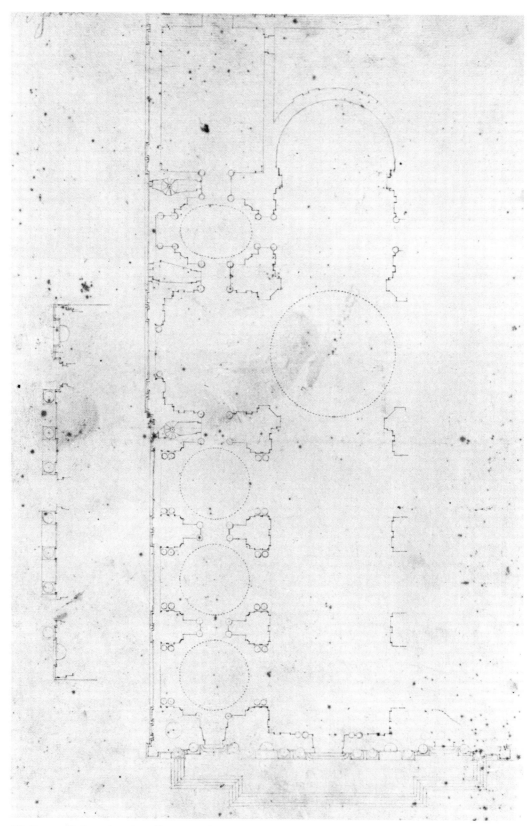

28. Rome, S. Ignazio, plan, Francesco Borromini drawing of ca. 1626 (Vienna, Albertina).

29. Rome, S. Andrea al Quirinale, Gianlorenzo Bernini, 1658–70, interior.

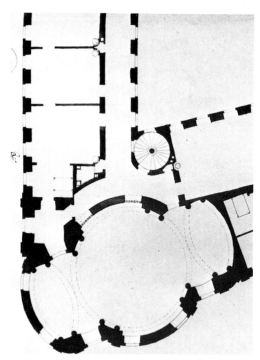

30. Holzkirchen, former Benedictine priory church, plan by Johann Dientzenhofer, before 1726 (Würzburg, Universitäts-Bibliothek, Delin. II/121).

31. Holzkirchen, plan by Dientzenhofer (Würzburg, Universitäts-Bibliothek, Delin. II/115).

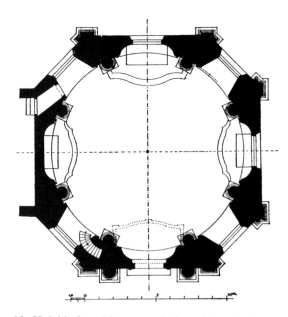

32. Holzkirchen, Neumann design of 1726, plan.

33. Holzkirchen, Neumann design of 1726, exterior elevation (Würzburg, Mainfränkisches Museum, S.E. 199b).

34. Holzkirchen, Neumann design of 1726, section.

35. Holzkirchen, Neumann design of 1726, detail of interior.

36. Bamberg, palace church, second project of 1733, plan (redrawn from a plan in Bamberg, Stadtarchiv).

0   10   20   30   40   50   60   SCHUHE

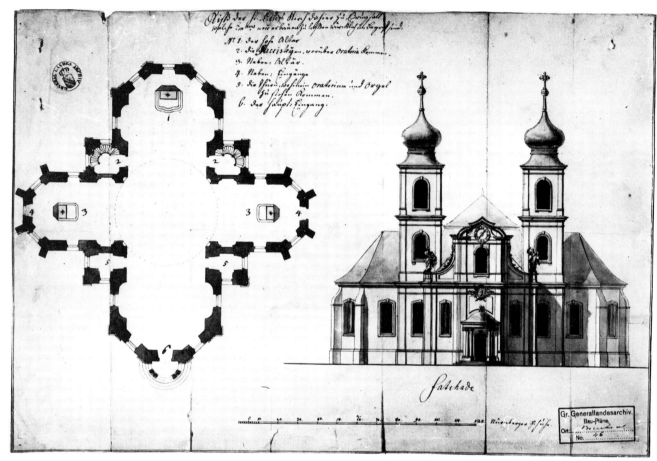

37. Bruchsal, parish church of St. Peter, designed by 1738, plan and facade
elevation, drawing by unknown hand (Karlsruhe, Generallandesarchiv,
Bruchsal Nr. 46).

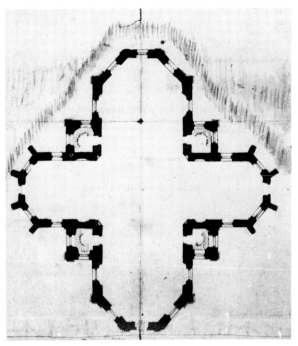

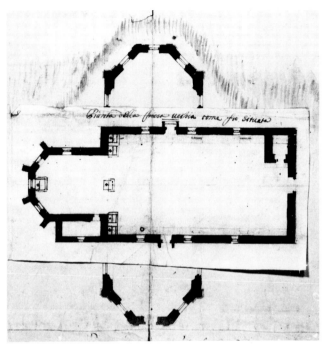

38. Bruchsal, plan of Neumann's church
(Karlsruhe, Generallandesarchiv, Bruchsal Nr. 60).

39. Bruchsal, plan of church replaced by Neumann
(Karlsruhe, Generallandesarchiv, Bruchsal Nr. 60).

40. Bruchsal, view to vaults, stucco completed 1746, paintings 1907.

41. Bruchsal, crossing dome.

42. Bruchsal, springing of dome and view into transept.

43. Bruchsal, main altar, designed by Neumann.

44. Bruchsal, tower bells, scaffolding designed by Neumann.

45. Münsterschwarzach, Benedictine monastery church, begun 1727, demolished 1821–41, lithograph by C. F. Müller, 1825.

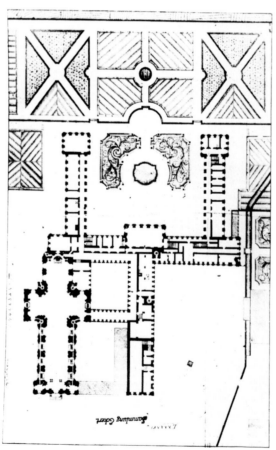

46. Münsterschwarzach, plan
(Würzburg, Mainfränkisches Museum, S.E. LXXXXVI).

47. Münsterschwarzach, perspective elevation and longitudinal section
(Stuttgart, Württembergische Landesbibliothek, Slg. Nicolai).

48. Münsterschwarzach, model, exterior view (Munich, Bayerisches National-Museum).

49. Münsterschwarzach, model, interior view (Munich, Bayerisches National-Museum).

50. Gössweinstein, pilgrimage and parish church of the Holy Trinity, designed 1729–30, facade.

51. Gössweinstein, choir and flank.

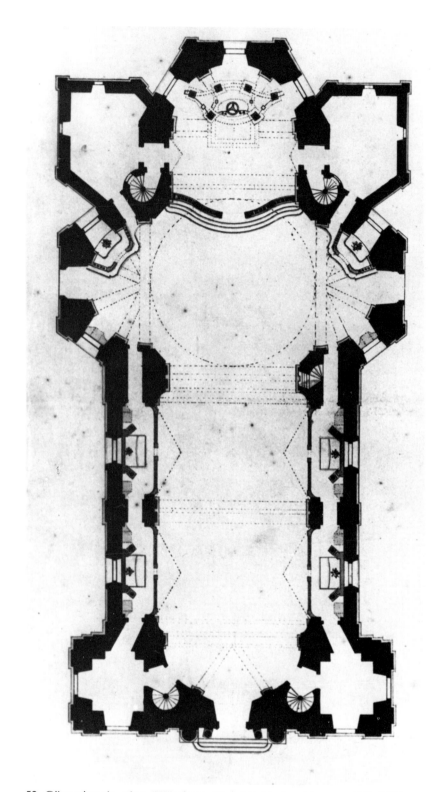

52. Gössweinstein, plan (Würzburg, Mainfränkisches Museum, S.E. 189).

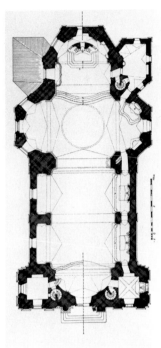

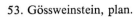
53. Gössweinstein, plan.

54. Gössweinstein, longitudinal section.

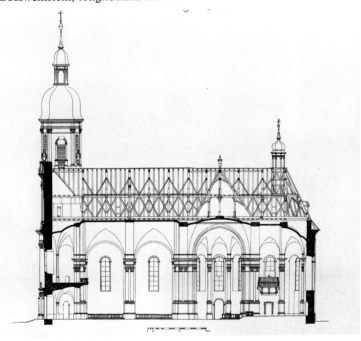

55. Gössweinstein, view to choir, vault stucco by Franz Jakob Vogel, 1733,
vault paintings by Waldemar Kolmsperger, 1928.

56. Gössweinstein, transept arm vault.

57. Gössweinstein, altar by
Johann Jakob Michael
Küchel, designed 1737–38.

58. Trier, St. Paulin, cornerstone
1734, construction 1738–43, facade.

59. Trier, choir and side elevation.

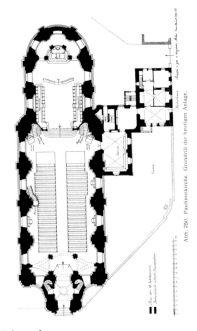

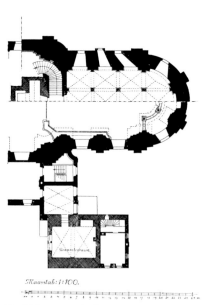

60. Trier, plan.

61. Trier, crypt plan.

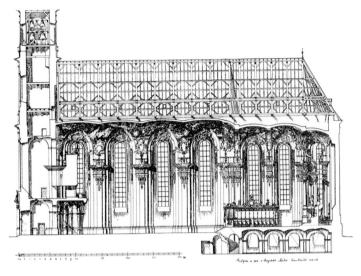

62. Trier, longitudinal section.

63. Trier, view to choir, vault fresco
by Christian Thomas Scheffler,
completed 1743; altar designed by
Neumann, 1745, built by Ferdinand
Tietz, 1755–61.

64. Heusenstamm, parish and mortuary church of SS. Cecilia and Barbara, begun 1739, facade.

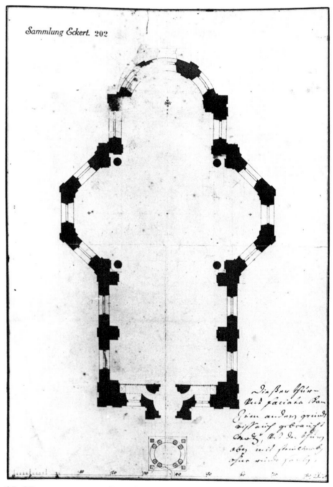

Sammlung Eckert. 202

65. Heusenstamm, plan (Würzburg, Mainfränkisches Museum, S.E. 202).

66. Heusenstamm, view to choir, vault frescoes by Christian Thomas Scheffler, 1741; altar by Johann Wolfgang van der Auvera, designed 1742.

67. Heusenstamm, facade, side elevation, cross section through crossing, plan (Würzburg, Mainfränkisches Museum, S.E. 174).

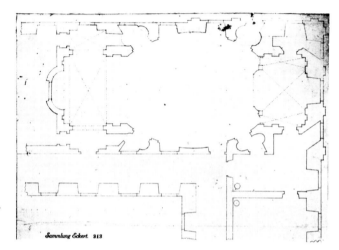

68. Würzburg, palace church
in the Residenz, designed
1732, modified by J. L. von
Hildebrandt, plan (Würzburg,
Mainfränkisches Museum,
S.E. 313).

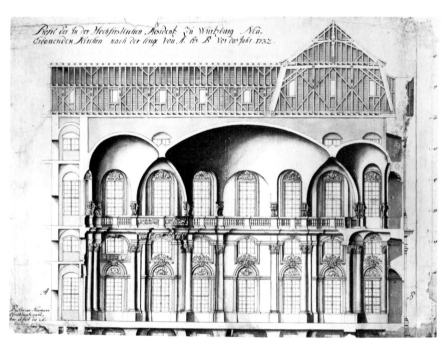

69. Würzburg, palace church, longitudinal section (Berlin, Kunstbibliothek,
Hdz. 4687).

Profil der Hochfürstlichen Residentz Neü=
Erbauenden Kirchen übers Creütz in Würzburg .1732.

70. Würzburg, palace church, cross section (Berlin,
Kunstbibliothek, Hdz. 4688).

71. Würzburg, palace church, main altar.

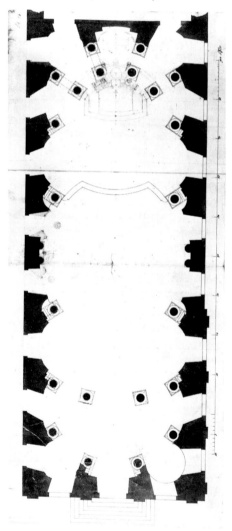

72. Würzburg, palace church, plan (Berlin, Kunstbibliothek, Hdz. 4689).

73. Würzburg, palace church, perspective view to choir (Stuttgart, Württembergische Landesbibliothek, Slg. Nicolai).

74. Würzburg, palace church, view to choir, stucco by Antonio Bossi, paintings by Johann Rudolf Byss, sculpture by Johann Wolfgang van der Auvera.

75. Würzburg, palace church, main vault.

76. Würzburg, palace
church, main vault
from above, showing
brickwork and ribs.

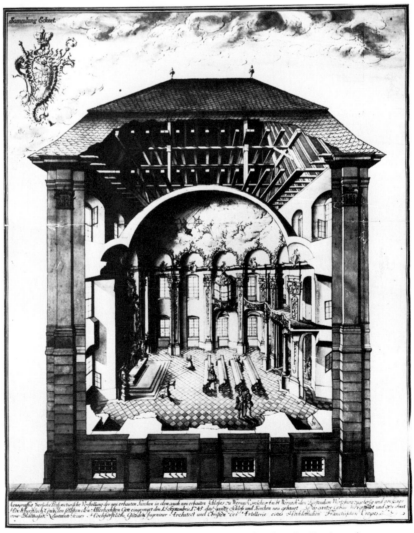

77. Werneck, palace church, 1734–37, perspective longitudinal section
(Würzburg, Mainfränkisches Museum, S.E. CII).

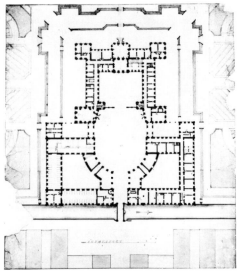

78. Werneck, plan of palace, church located at middle left (Berlin, Kunstbibliothek, Hdz. 4251).

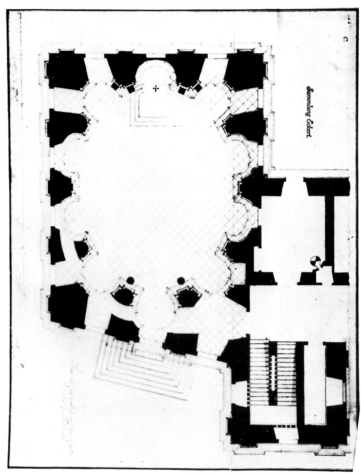

79. Werneck, plan (Würzburg, Mainfränkisches Museum, S.E. C).

80. Werneck, interior to left of main altar.

81. Werneck, view to entrance.

82. Werneck, vault from above, showing brickwork and thicker shell in bottom third of vault.

83. Werneck, framework of roof.

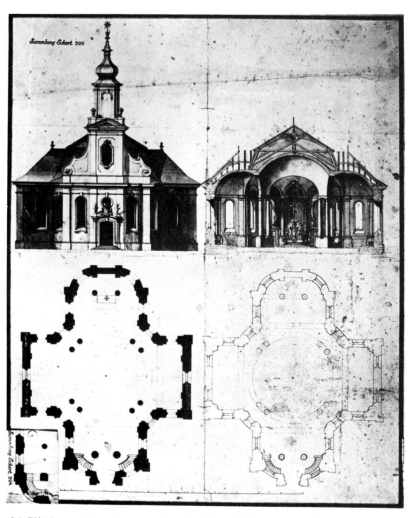

84. Kitzingen-Etwashausen, church of the Holy Cross, designed 1740–41, built 1741–45, facade elevation, cross section through crossing, two plans (Würzburg, Mainfränkisches Museum, S.E. 208).

85. Kitzingen, facade elevation, cross section through crossing, plan
(Würzburg, Mainfränkisches Museum, S.E. 209).

86. Kitzingen, perspective longitudinal section
(Würzburg, Mainfränkisches Museum, S.E. LXXXIX).

87. Kitzingen, view to entrance.

88. Kitzingen, view to choir.

89. Würzburg, pilgrimage church Käppele-Visitation of Mary, designed
1747–48, begun 1748, exterior.

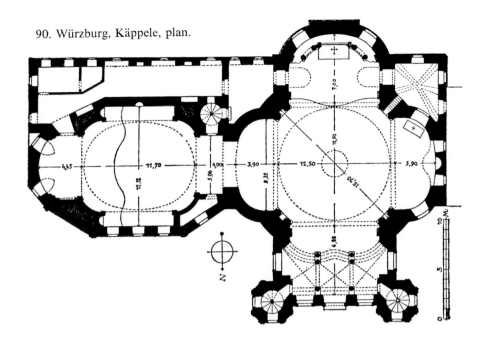

90. Würzburg, Käppele, plan.

91. Würzburg, Käppele, view to entrance.

92. Würzburg, Käppele, view to choir, frescoes by Matthäus Günther, 1750–52; stucco from the circle of Johann Michael Feichtmayr; main altar by Johann Georg Winterstein (?), 1797–99; pulpit by Materno Bossi, 1800.

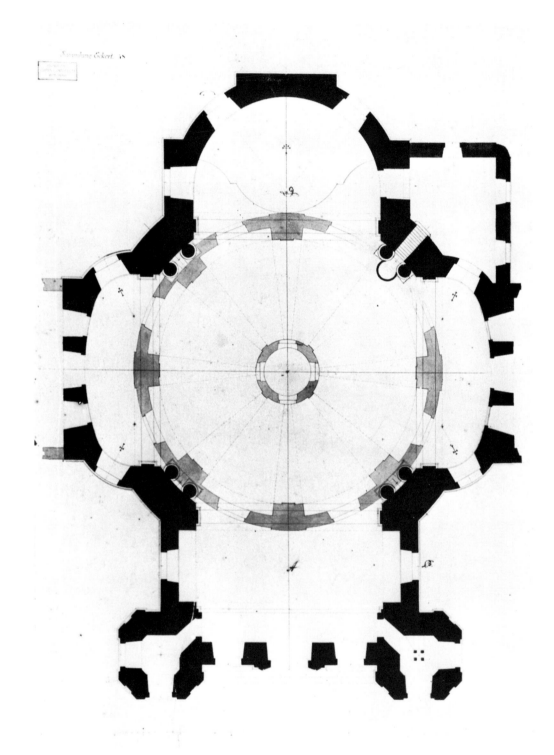

93. Würzburg, Käppele, plan (Würzburg, Mainfränkisches Museum, S.E. 48).

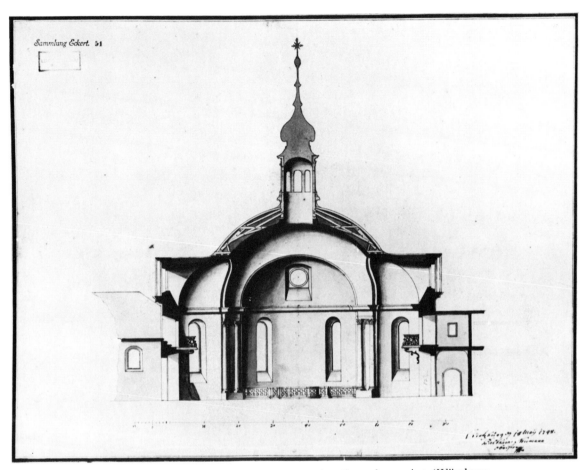

94. Würzburg, Käppele, cross section through crossing (Würzburg, Mainfränkisches Museum, S.E. 51).

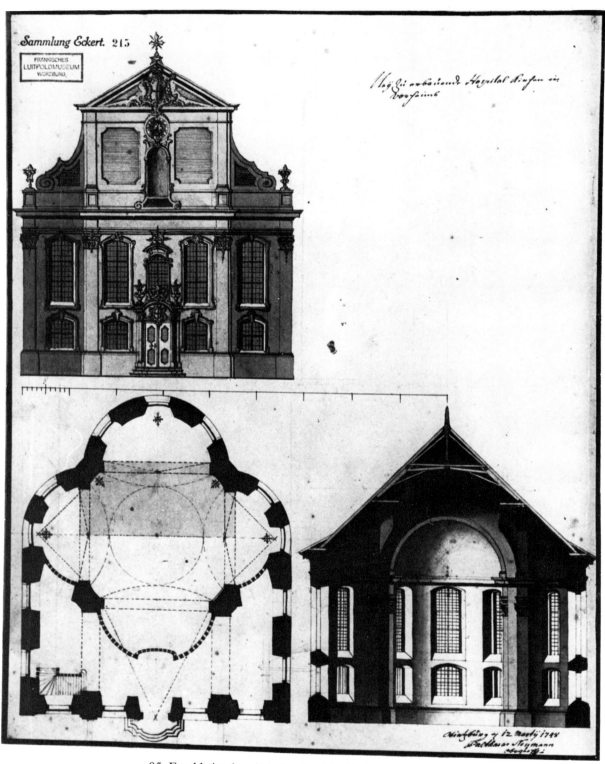

95. Forchheim, hospital church of St. Katherine, facade elevation, plan, cross section through crossing, drawing dated 12 March 1748 (Würzburg, Mainfränkisches Museum, S.E. 215).

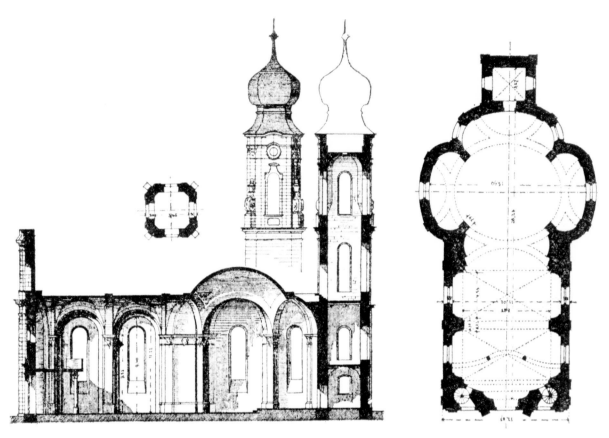

96. Gaibach, parish church of the Holy Trinity, designed 1740, built
1742–49, longitudinal section and plan.

97. Gaibach, facade.

98. Gaibach, nave vault.

99. Gaibach, crossing.

100. Gaibach, transept vault.

101. Würzburg, Käppele, 1740 project, two plans, cross section through nave (Würzburg, Mainfränkisches Museum, S.E. 210).

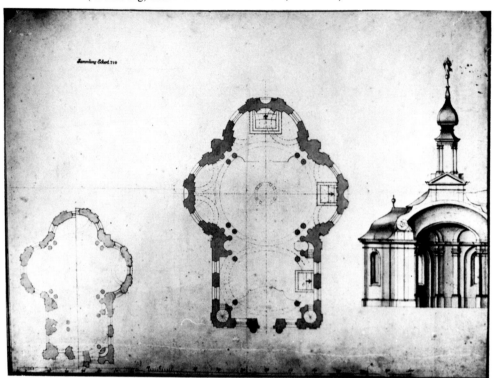

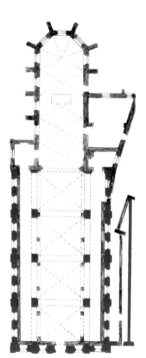

102. Würzburg, former Dominican church, 1741–44, plan.

103. Würzburg, former Dominican church, view to choir, pre-1945, stucco by Franz A. Ermeltraut, Georg Anton Urlaub, Antonio Bossi.

104. Würzburg, former Dominican church, view to choir, post-1945.

105. Rottenbuch, Pietà, 1686, anonymous.

106. Langheim, Cistercian monastery church of SS. Mary, John the Evangelist, Nicolaus, designed 1742, facade (Würzburg, Mainfränkisches Museum, S.E. 108).

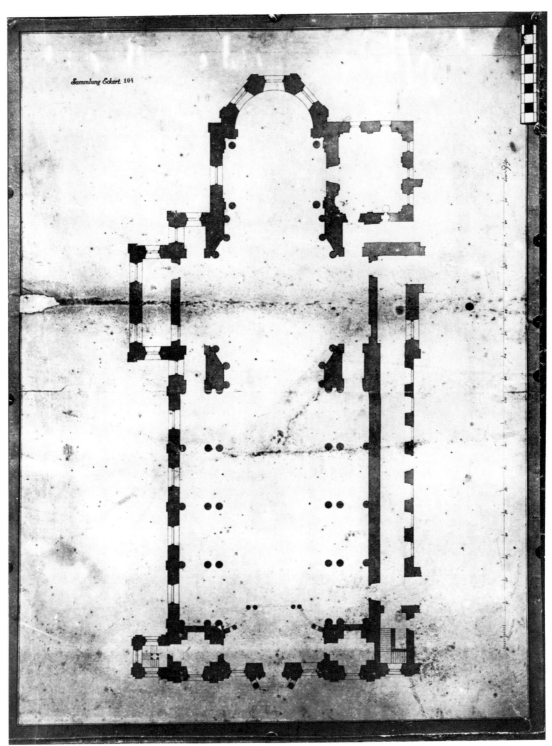

Sammlung Eckert 104

107. Langheim, plan (Würzburg, Mainfränkisches Museum, S.E. 104).

108. Langheim, longitudinal section (Würzburg,
Mainfränkisches Museum, S.E. 105).

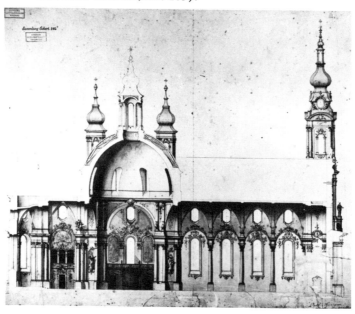

109. Langheim, detail
of Fig. 108, nave.

110. Langheim, detail of
Fig. 108, transept.

111. Langheim, detail of
Fig. 108, choir.

112. Langheim, cross sections through nave and crossing (Würzburg,
Mainfränkisches Museum, S.E. 106).

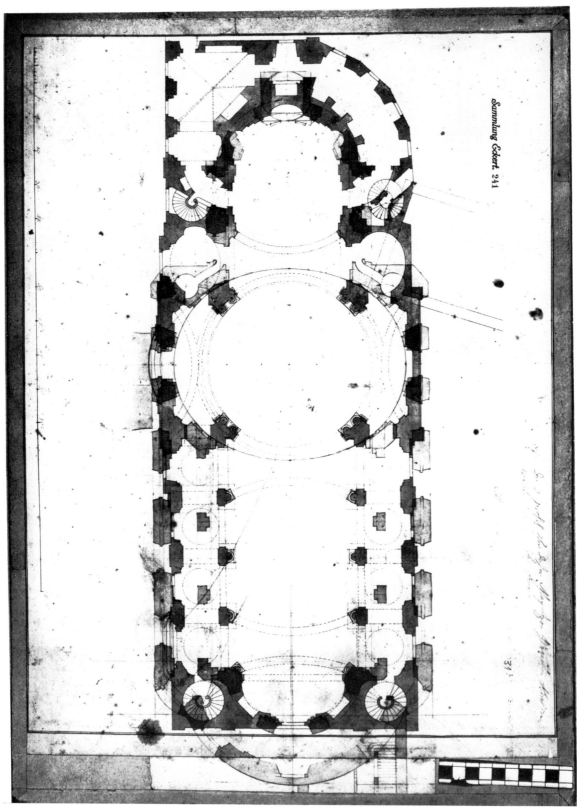

113. Mainz, Jesuit church of St. Ignatius, begun 1742, destroyed by fire
1793, demolished 1805–11, two superimposed plans (Würzburg,
Mainfränkisches Museum, S.E. 241).

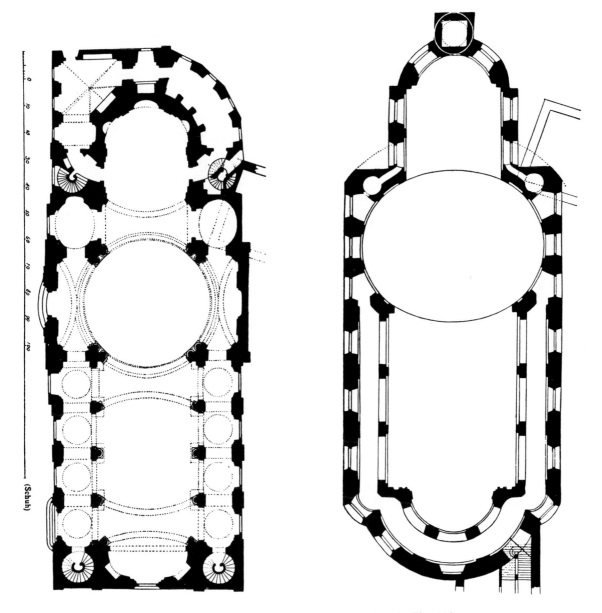

114. Mainz, separation of superimposed plans in Fig. 113.

115. Mainz, longitudinal section (Würzburg, Mainfränkisches Museum, S.E. 239).

116. Mainz, cross sections through nave and crossing (Würzburg, Mainfränkisches Museum, S.E. 240).

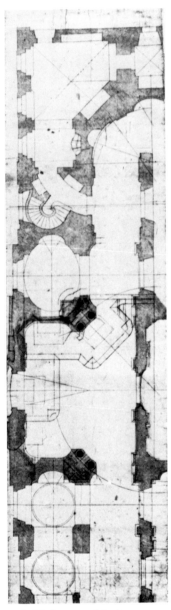

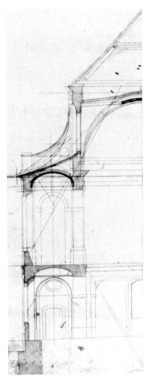

118. Mainz, partial section
(Marburg, Staatsarchiv).

117. Mainz, partial plan
(Marburg, Staatsarchiv).

119. Limbach am Main, pilgrimage and parish church of the Visitation of Mary, called Maria-Limbach, begun 1751, facade.

120. Limbach, perspective longitudinal section (Würzburg, Mainfränkisches Museum, S.E. 196).

121. Limbach, plan second section (Würzburg, Mainfränkisches Museum, S.E. 193).

122. Limbach, detail of nave elevation.

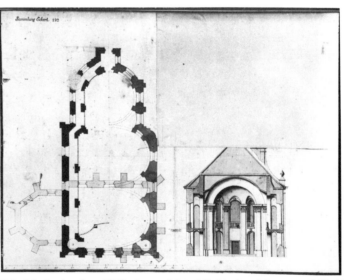

123. Limbach, plan (Würzburg, Mainfränkisches Museum, S.E. 192).

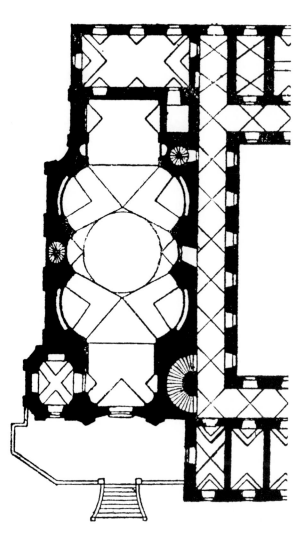

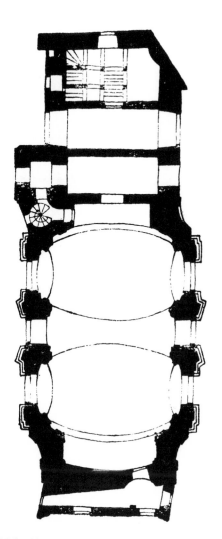

124. Christoph Dientzenhofer, Obořiště, Pauline
monastery church, begun 1702, plan.

125. Christoph Dientzenhofer, Eger (Cheb),
St. Clara, 1707–11, plan.

126. Vierzehnheiligen, pilgrimage church of the Assumption of Mary.
preliminary designs 1742, executed design 1744, longitudinal section
(Würzburg, Mainfränkisches Museum, S.E. 79).

127. Vierzehnheiligen, longitudinal section (Würzburg, Mainfränkisches
Museum, S.E. 80).

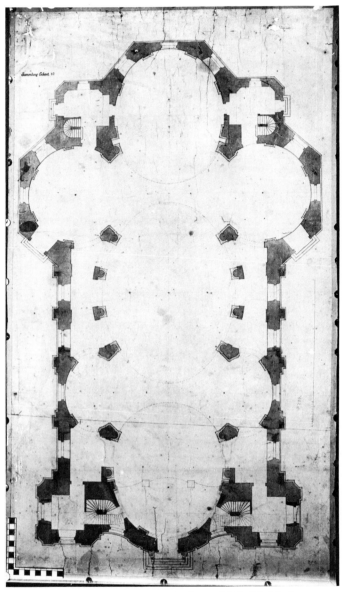

129. Vierzehnheiligen, plan (Würzburg, Mainfränkisches Museum, S.E. 87).

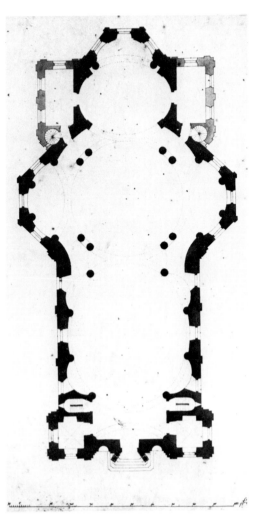

128. Vierzehnheiligen, plan (Würzburg, Mainfränkisches Museum, S.E. 75).

130. Vierzehnheiligen, geometric figures in plan, based on S.E. 83 (Teufel, *Vierzehnheiligen,* p. 201).

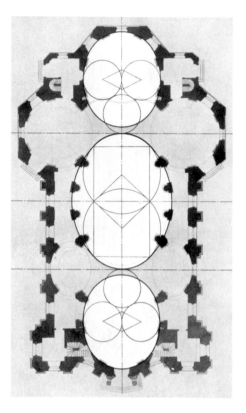

131. Vierzehnheiligen, longitudinal section (Würzburg, Mainfränkisches Museum, S.E. 86).

132. Vierzehnheiligen, model (Bamberg, Historischer Verein).

133. Vierzehnheiligen, view.

134. Vierzehnheiligen, facade (Würzburg, Mainfränkisches Museum, S.E. 88).

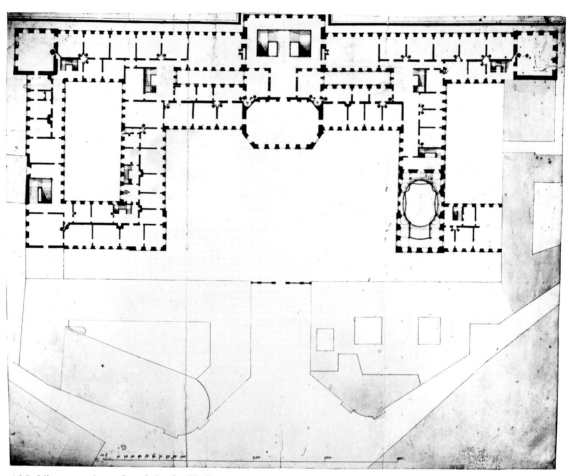

135. Vienna, palace church in the Hofburg,
1746–47, palace plan (Berlin, Kunstbibliothek,
Hdz. 4734).

136. Vienna, palace church plan, detail of Fig. 135,
turned 180°.

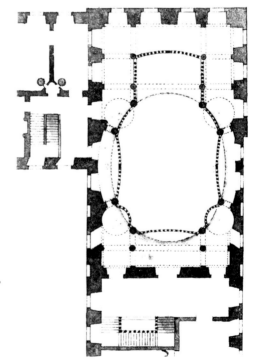

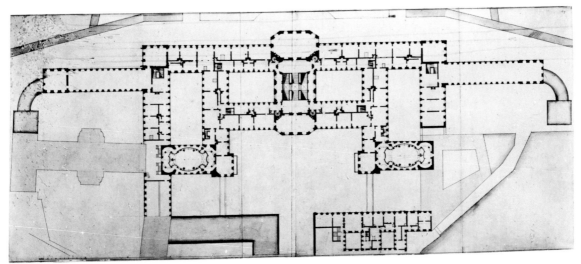

137. Vienna, palace plan (Berlin, Kunstbibliothek, Hdz. 4729).

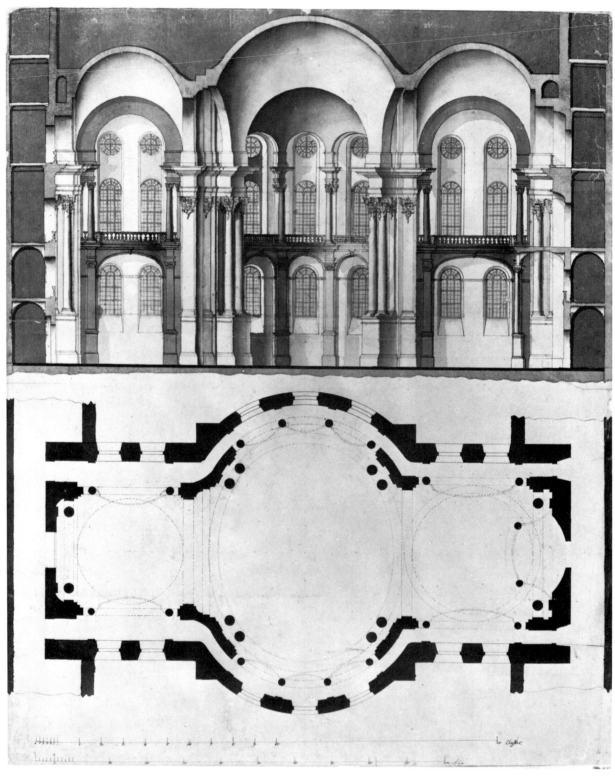

138. Vienna, longitudinal section and plan (Berlin, Kunstbibliothek, Hdz. 4728).

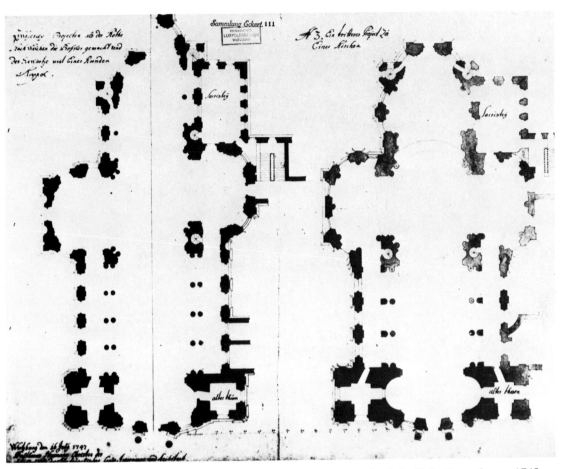

139. Neresheim, Benedictine abbey church of the Holy Cross, begun 1748,
two plans (Würzburg, Mainfränkisches Museum, S.E. 111).

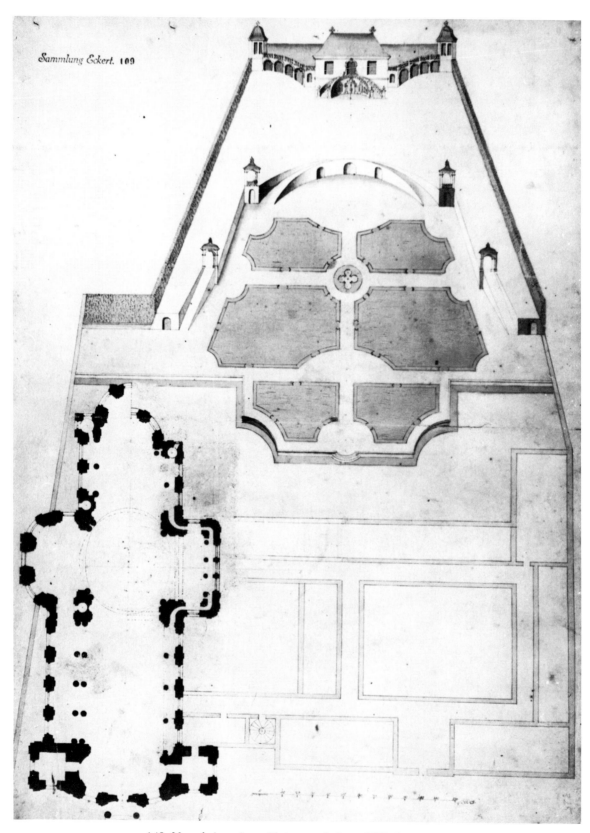

140. Neresheim, plan with two variations (Würzburg, Mainfränkisches Museum, S.E. 109).

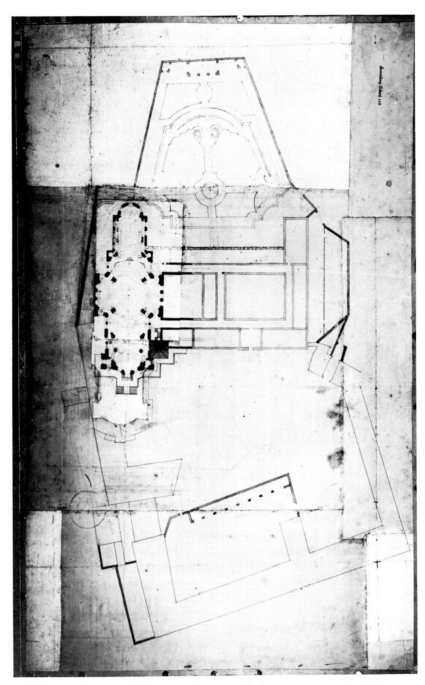

141. Neresheim, plan (Würzburg, Mainfränkisches Museum, S.E. 110).

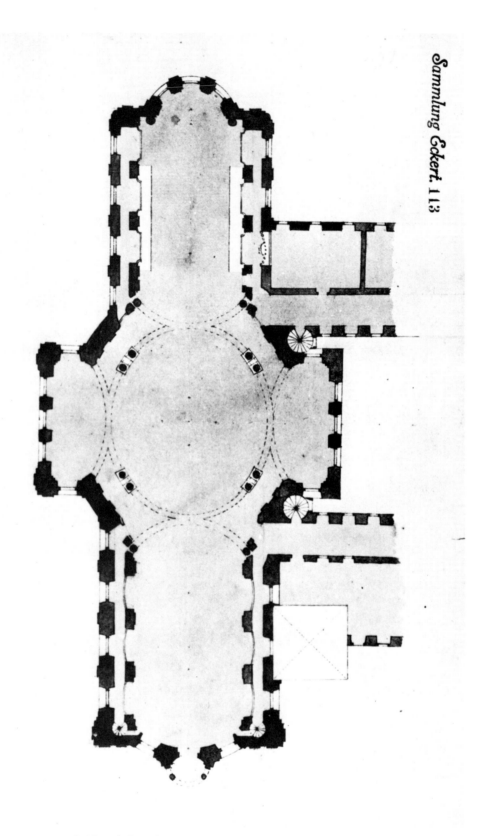

142. Neresheim, plan (Würzburg, Mainfränkisches Museum, S.E. 113).

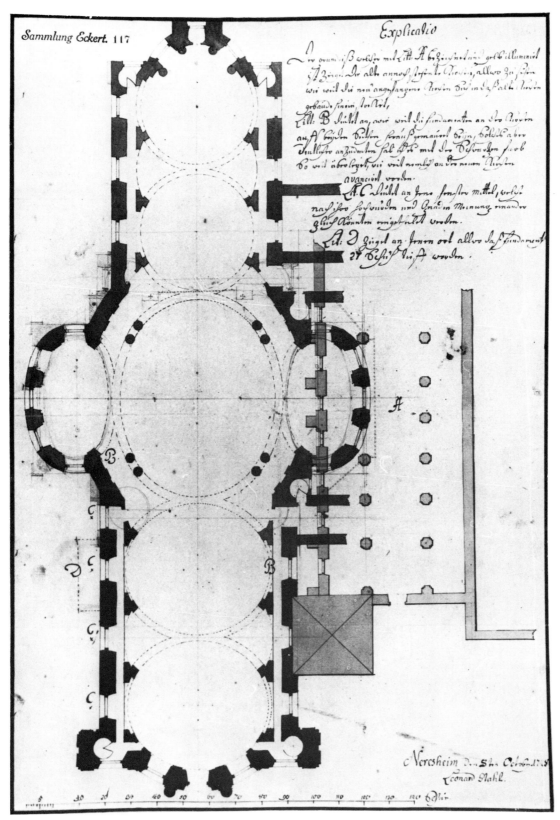

Explicatio

[handwritten German text]

Neresheim d. 5t. Octob. 1738
Leonard Stahl.

143. Neresheim, plan (Würzburg, Mainfränkisches Museum, S.E. 117).

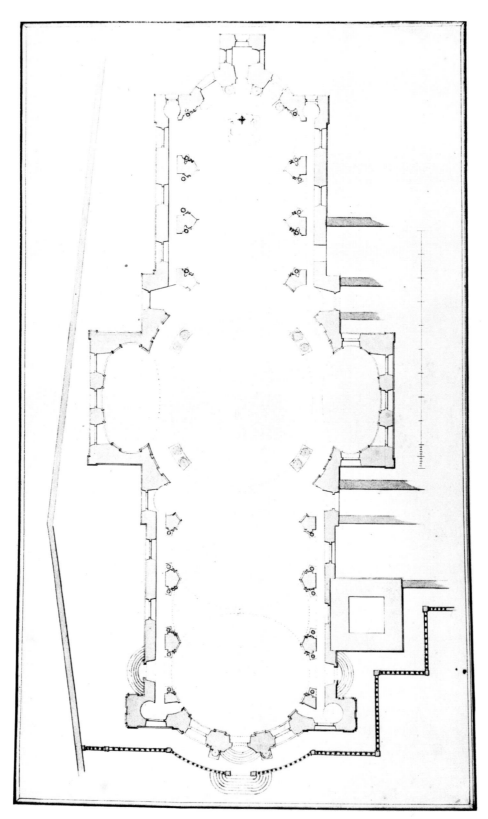

144. Neresheim, plan (Stuttgart, Württembergische Landesbibliothek, Slg. Nicolai).

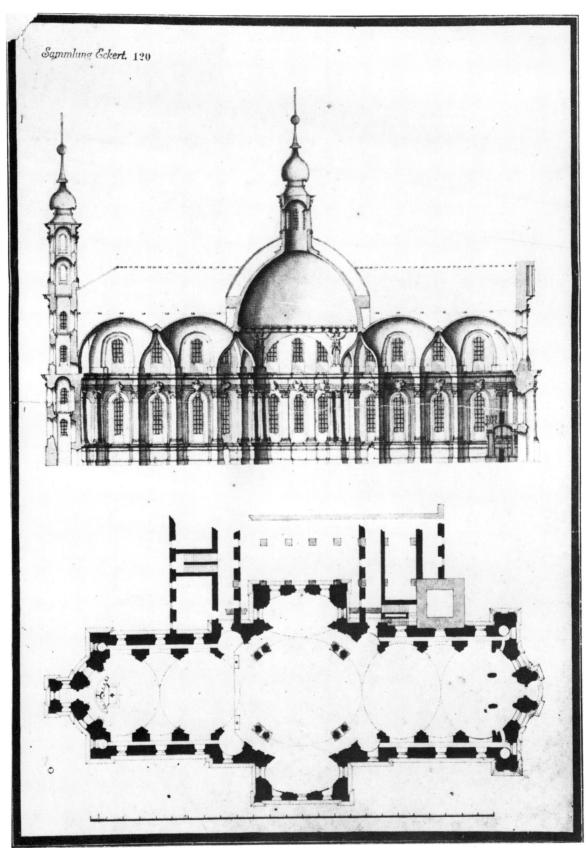

145. Neresheim, plan and longitudinal section (Würzburg, Mainfränkisches Museum, S.E. 120).

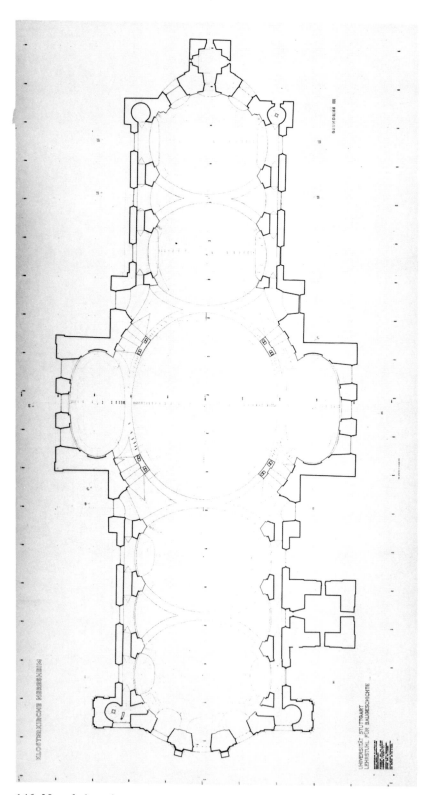

146. Neresheim, plan.

147. Neresheim, view into south transept, frescoes by Martin Knoller, 1770–75; stucco by Thomas Scheithauf, 1776–78; altars and pulpit by Thomas Scheithauf, 1778–92.

148. Neresheim, view into choir during restoration.

149. Neresheim, view of southern nave elevation.

150. Neresheim, nave elevation, vaults, and torsion arches (see p. 156, n. 4).

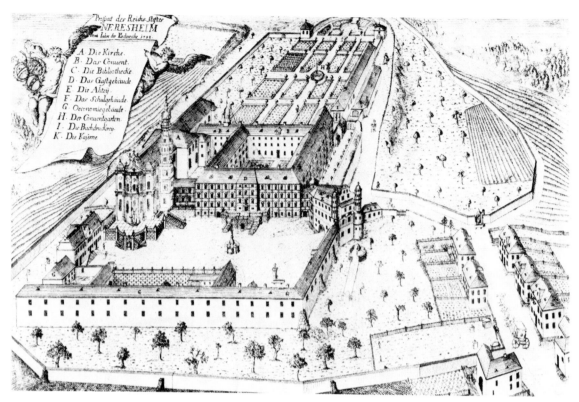

151. Neresheim, bird's-eye view (Carl Alois Nack,
*Reichstift Neresheim,*1792).

152. Neresheim, facade (Würzburg, Mainfränkisches
Museum, S.E. 127).

153. Neresheim, crossing columns.

154. Neresheim, model for roof framework by Joseph Neumaier.

155. Neresheim, plan of roof
framework built by Franz
Joseph Pfeifer, 1763–70.

156. Christoph Dientzenhofer, Eger (Cheb), St. Clara, 1707–11, longitudinal section.

157. Johann Lucas von Hildebrandt, elevation and section of domed church, 1730s (Vienna, Galerie Harrach).

158. Johann Lucas von Hildebrandt,
Gabel, Dominican church of St.
Lawrence, begun 1699, view to choir.

159. Maximilian von Welsch, project
for Vierzehnheiligen, 1744,
longitudinal section (Nuremberg,
Germanisches Museum, HB. 23576a).

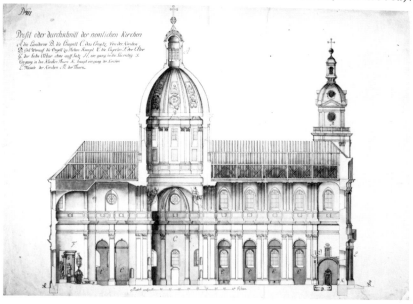

160. Jules Hardouin Mansart, Versailles, palace chapel of Notre Dame, 1689–1710, view to choir.

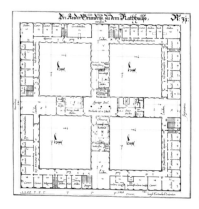

161. Joseph Furttenbach, project for a city hall, plan (*Architectura Recreationis*, Augsburg, 1640, pl. 31).

162. Paul Decker, *Fürstlicher Baumeister,* 2 vols., Augsburg, Wolf, 1711–16, vol. II, Pl. 2.

163. Dominikus Zimmermann, votive painting, 1757.

Bibliography

The Bibliography documents materials used for this study; writings that served a limited purpose in this regard are mentioned only in the Notes. Works of special significance are characterized by brief comments.

The bibliographical and archival material is arranged under four headings:

I. REUTHER'S BIBLIOGRAPHIES

Reuther, Hans, "Die mainfränkische Barockarchitektur. Der gegenwärtige Stand der Forschung" in *Zeitschrift für Kunstgeschichte,* XXII, 1959, pp. 268–286.

———— "Nachtrag zum Balthasar-Neumann-Jubiläumsjahr 1953" in *Kunstchronik,* VII, 1954, pp. 35–37.

———— "Neues Schriftum über Balthasar Neumann" in *Kunstchronik,* VI, 1953, pp. 209–221.

II. WORKS ON NEUMANN

A. MONOGRAPHS

Freeden, Max Herrmann von, *Balthasar Neumann. Leben und Werk,* 2d ed., Munich/Berlin, Deutscher Kunstverlag, 1963.

    Though short, this remains the basic study on Neumann. The material it contains is sound but presented without footnotes or bibliography. It includes many photographs but painfully few plans and drawings. First published in 1953.

———— "Neumann, Balthasar" in *Encyclopedia of World Art,* 15 vols., New York, McGraw-Hill, 1959–1968, vol. X, cols. 611–618.

Keller, Joseph, *Balthasar Neumann. Eine Studie zur Kunstgeschichte des 18. Jahrhunderts,* Würzburg, Bauer, 1896.

    Neumann fell into obscurity shortly after his death. Modern study of the man and his work began with this publication.

Knapp, Fritz, "Balthasar Neumann" in *Zeitschrift für Denkmalpflege,* II, 1928, pp. 165–170.

———— *Balthasar Neumann—Der grosse Architekt seiner Zeit,* Bielfeld, Velhagen, 1937.

Lorck, Carl von, ed., *Balthasar Neumann; Sechzig Bilder,* Königsberg, Kanter, ca. 1940.

Neumann, Günter, *Neresheim.*

    See listing under II, C.

Pröll, F. X., *Kirchenbauten Balthasar Neumanns* (Stilkritische Skizze nach den Plänen der Sammlung Eckert im Fränkischen Luitpoldmuseum Würzburg), diss., Würzburg, 1936.

> Superficial and uninformative.

Reuther, Hans, *Die Kirchenbauten Balthasar Neumanns,* Berlin, Hessling, 1960.

> An important catalogue of Neumann's churches, though with errors and omissions.

Schenk, Clemens, *Balthasar Neumanns Kirchenbaukunst,* Würzburg, 1939.

> Readable, though requiring much updating of scholarship.

———— *Die Kirchenbaukunst Balthasar Neumanns mit einleitenden Betrachtungen über den gesamten Kirchenbau des süddeutschen Barocks und Rokokos,* Würzburg, 1923.

B. SPECIAL STUDIES

Andersen, Liselotte, *Studien zu Profanbauformen Balthasar Neumanns. Die grossen Residenzprojekte für Wien, Stuttgart und Karlsruhe,* diss., Munich, 1966.

> Useful for the history and context of the churches in these projects.

Bachmann, Erich, "Balthasar Neumann und das Mittelalter" in *Stifter-Jahrbuch,* III, 1953, pp. 134–149.

Balthasar Neumann, Leben und Werk. Gedächtnisschau zum 200. Todestage, exhibited in the Würzburg Residenz, 21 June to 18 October, 1953; catalogue produced under the supervision of M. H. von Freeden.

Beck, G., "Balthasar Neumann und Bamberg" in *Bamberger Jahresblatt,* 1938, pp. 94 ff.

Bendel, F. J., "Beiträge zur kirchlichen Bautätigkeit Balthasar Neumanns in den Jahren 1730–1745" in *Archiv des Historischen Vereins für Mainfranken,* LXXI, 1937, pp. 69 ff.

Brinckmann, Albert Erich, *Von Guarini bis Balthasar Neumann,* Berlin, Deutscher Verein für Kunstwissenschaft, 1932.

Coolidge, John, "The Neumann Bicentennial" in *Journal of the Society of Architectural Historians,* XII, December 1953, pp. 12–14.

Döry, Baron Ludwig, "Balthasar Neumann und die Brüder von Uffenbach" in *Stifter-Jahrbuch,* VII, 1962, pp. 247–256.

Eckert, Georg, "Das Würzburger Residenzmuseum und die Balthasar-Neumann-Ausstellung" in *Zentralblatt der Bauverwaltung,* XLI, Berlin, 1921, pp. 401–404.

Franz, Heinrich Gerhard, "Die Klosterkirche Banz und die Kirchen Balthasar Neumanns in ihrem Verhältnis zur böhmischen Barockbaukunst" in *Zeitschrift für Kunstwissenschaft,* I, 1947, pp. 54–72.

Freeden, Max Herrmann von, *Balthasar Neumann als Stadtbaumeister,* Berlin, Deutscher Kunstverlag, 1937.

———— "Balthasar Neumanns Tod und Begräbnis" in *Die Mainlande. Geschichte und Gegenwart,* Würzburg, 18 April 1951, pp. 9–10, 15.

———— "Eine Wiener Studienreise Balthasar Neumanns im Jahre 1729" in *Bamberger Blätter für die fränkische Kunst und Geschichte,* XIII, 1936, no. 5, p. 19.

Habicht, Victor Curt, "Die Herkunft der Kenntnisse Balthasar Neumanns auf dem Gebiete der 'Civilbaukunst'" in *Monatshefte für Kunstwissenschaft,* IX, 1916, pp. 46–61.

Hanftmann, B., "Ein Messinstrument Balthasar Neumanns" in *Archiv des historischen Vereins von Unterfranken,* XLVIII, p. 240.

Hegemann, Hans W., *Die Altarbaukunst Balthasar Neumanns,* diss., Marburg-Lahn, 1937.

Herrmann, H., "J. J. M. Küchel in Bamberg und Balthasar Neumann" in *Bamberger Jahresblatt,* 1939, pp. 63 ff.

Hotz, Joachim, "Beiträge zur Kirchenbaukunst Balthasar Neumanns" in *Das Münster,* XIV, nos. 9–10, September-October 1961, pp. 305–321.
> Basic for the histories of Wiesentheid, Kitzingen-Etwashausen, and the Käppele.

———— "Die Pfarrkirche in Saffig (Kreis Mayen), Ein Werk Balthasar Neumanns" in *Archiv für Mittelrheinische Kirchengeschichte,* XV, 1963, pp. 440–453.

———— "Ein von Balthasar Neumann signierter Entwurf für eine Chorengel in der Abteikirche Münsterschwarzach" in *Würzburger Diözesangeschichtesblätter,* XXV, 1963, pp. 205–207.

Höver, Otto, "Vierzehnheiligen und Neresheim" in *Monatshefte für Kunstwissenschaft,* XV, 1922, pp. 16–22.

Knapp, Fritz, "Werke Balthasar Neumanns (Würzburg Ausstellung)" in *Tag für Denkmalpflege und Heimatschutz Würzburg und Nürnberg,* Berlin, 1929, pp. 43 ff.

Lang, Elmar, "Zu Balthasar Neumanns rheinischen Bauten" in *Jahrbuch der Rheinland-Westfalen Technischen Hochschule Aachen,* Essen, 1950.

Levey, Michael, ed., "Johann Balthasar Neumann. Surviving Works—Mapguide" in *Architectural Design,* XLI, June 1971, pp. 369–370.

Lohmeyer, Karl, "Balthasar Neumann" in *Mannheimer Geschichtesblätter,* 1937.

Reuther, Hans, "Balthasar Neumanns Gewölbebau. Ein Beitrag zur Formgebung und Konstruktion der Gewölbe des mainfränkischen Meisters" in *Das Münster,* VI, 1953, pp. 57–65.

———— "Balthasar Neumann und der Naturstein" in *Der Naturstein,* III, 1948, no. 2, pp. 20–22, no. 5, pp. 36–37.

———— "Die Gewölbesystem von Banz und Vierzehnheiligen, Ihre Konstruktion und Formgebung" in *Bericht über die 22. Tagung für Ausgrabungswissenschaft und Bauforschung vom 16.-20. April 1963 in Bamberg,* Koldewey-Gesellschaft, Vereinigung für Baugeschichtliche Forschung E.V., pp. 78–88.

———— "Die Kirchenmodelle Balthasar Neumanns" in *Heiliges Franken,* I, no. 8, Beilage zu Würzburger Katholischen Sonntagsblatt, 9 August 1953, pp. 29–31.

———— "Die künstlerischen Einwirkungen von Johann Lucas von Hildebrandt auf die Architektur Balthasar Neumanns" in *Architectura,* I, 1973, pp. 58–85.

———— "Die Landkirchen Balthasar Neumanns" in *Zeitschrift für Kunstgeschichte,* XVI, 1953, pp. 154–170.
> The basic catalogue of Neumann's country churches.

———— "Vor 200 Jahren starb Balthasar Neumann" in *Baumeister Zeitschrift für Baukultur und Technik,* XII, 1953, pp. 789 ff.

Schenk, Clemens, "Balthasar Neumann" in *Das Bayerland,* XLVIII, 1937, pp. 225–261.

Schmorl, Th. A., *Balthasar Neumann. Räume und Symbole des Spätbarock,* Hamburg, Claussen und Goverts, 1946.

Spitzenpfeil, Lorenz Reinhard, "Mass und Zahl im Bau" and "Balthasar Neumann, der kühne Raumschöpfer" in *Der fränkische Baumeister,* 1941.

Teufel, Richard, *Balthasar Neumann, sein Werk in Oberfranken,* Lichtenfels, Schulze, 1953.

Zeller, Adolf, "Balthasar Neumann und seine Arbeitsweise" in *Zeitschrift für Bauwesen*, LXXVIII, 1928, pp. 127 ff.

C. STUDIES OF SPECIFIC BUILDINGS (by Site)

Only key monographs on specific buildings are included. Other material can be found in H. Reuther, *Kirchenbaukunst*, the Neumann monographs (II, A), the inventories (III, D), and the appropriate notes. The absence of any monographic study is noted by: "See inventory and notes."

Bamberg

Bartsch, Werner, *Balthasar Neumanns Entwurf zur Hofkirche der neuen Residenz zu Bamberg*, diss., Berlin, 1969.

Bruchsal

Jörg Gamer, "Pfarrkirche St. Peter" in *Balthasar Neumann in Baden-Württemberg*, exhibition catalogue for Europaisichen Denkmalschutzjahr, Staatsgalerie Stuttgart, 28 September to 30 November 1975, Stuttgart, Staatsgalerie, 1975, pp. 31–37.

Forchheim

Kupfer, Konrad, "Ein Kirchenbauplan Balthasar Neumanns für Forchheim" in *Der Fränkische Schatzgräber, Heimatkundliche Beiträge zum Forchheimer Tagblatt*, V, 1927, pp. 65 ff.

Gaibach

See inventory and notes.

Gössweinstein

Hotz, Joachim, "Neugefundener Entwurf für die Wallfahrtskirche Gössweinstein" in *Fränkisches Land, Beilage zum Neuen Volksblatt Bamberg*, VIII, no. 6, 1961.

Schädler, Alfred, "Zur künstlerischen Arbeitsweise beim Bau und bei der Ausstattung der Wallfahrtskirche Gössweinstein" in *Deutsche Kunst und Denkmalpflege*, XV, 1957, pp. 27–39.

Heusenstamm

Knapp, Fritz, "Die Rokokokirche Heusenstamm" in *Altfränkische Bilder*, XL, 1933.

Müller, Otto, "Balthasar Neumanns Pfarrkirche in Heusenstamm" in *Deutsche Kunst und Denkmalpflege*, XIV, 1956, pp. 35 ff.

Holzkirchen

Feulner, Adolf, "Balthasar Neumanns Rotunde in Holzkirchen. 'Konstruierte' Risse in der Barockarchitektur" in *Zeitschrift für Geschichte der Architektur*, VI, 1913, pp. 155–168.

Kitzingen-Etwashausen

Scherf, Andreas, "Die Kreuzkirche zu Kitzingen-Etwashausen" in *Fränkische Monatshefte*, 1932, pp. 138 ff.

Langheim

Lehmann, Edgar, "Balthasar Neumann und Kloster Langheim" in *Zeitschrift für Kunstgeschichte*, XXV, 1962, pp. 213–242.

———— "Zur Baugeschichte des Zisterzienserklosters Langheim im 18. Jahrhundert" in *Zeitschrift für Kunstgeschichte*, XIX, 1956, pp. 259–277.

Limbach am Main

Bendel, Franz J., "Die Wallfahrtskirche zu Limbach" in *Würzburger Diözesangeschichtesblätter*, I, 1933, pp. 9–37.

Reuther, Hans, "Balthasar Neumanns Wallfahrtskirche Maria-Limbach" in *Mainfränkisches Jahrbuch,* V, 1953, pp. 359–362.

———— "Die Baugeschichte und Gestalt der Wallfahrtskirche zu Maria-Limbach" in *Das Münster,* II, 1949, pp. 355–364.

———— *Johann Balthasar Neumanns Kirchenbau zu Maria-Limbach,* diss., T. H. Darmstadt, 1948.

Mainz

Einsingbach, Wolfgang, "Neue Planfunde zu Balthasar Neumanns Mainzer Jesuitenkirche" in *Mainzer Zeitschrift,* LIV, 1959, pp. 33–40.

Henkes, Gerhard, "Hilfslinien für die Proportionierung des Querschnitts der Jesuitenkirche" in *Mainzer Zeitschrift,* LIV, 1959, p. 40.

Münsterschwarzach

Hess, P. Dr. Salesius, O.S.B., "Balthasar Neumanns Kirchenbau in Münsterschwarzach" in *Abtei Münster Schwarzach. Arbeiten aus ihrer Geschichte. Festgabe zur Weihe der Kirche 1938,* pp. 1–76.

Neresheim

Balthasar Neumann in Baden-Württemberg, exhibition catalogue for Europäischen Denkmalschutzjahr, Staatsgalerie Stuttgart, 28 September to 30 November 1975, Stuttgart, Staatsgalerie, 1975, pp. 93–141.

Fuchs-Röll, Willy P., *Die Abteikirche zu Neresheim und die Kunst Balthasar Neumanns,* diss., Stuttgart Technische Hochschule, 1914.

———— "Die Zeichnungen Balthasar Neumanns zur Abteikirche von Neresheim und deren Ausführung" in *Zentralblatt der Bauverwaltung,* XXXVII, 1917, pp. 57 ff.

Neumann, Günter, *Balthasar Neumanns Entwürfe für Neresheim,* Munich, Filser, 1942.

———— "Der Innenraum der Benediktiner Kirche Neresheim" in *Das Bayerland,* XLVIII, 1937, pp. 275–280.

———— *Neresheim,* Munich, Filser, 1947.

     H. Jantzen filled out and edited the manuscript G. Neumann left unfinished when he was killed in 1941. The material on Neresheim from Neumann's 1942 publication is combined with an overview of Balthasar Neumann's church designs, together with comparisons with Guarini and with Austrian and Bohemian structures. The text is extremely difficult to follow, though the analysis of the projects and the executed interior remain the most comprehensive and perceptive to date. On the other hand, Neumann's effort to understand Neresheim as a final synthesis of a theme (the combination of a centralized concept with a longitudinal unit established by freestanding forms) is largely unconvincing.

Reuther, Hans, "Franz Ignaz Michael Neumanns Konstruktionsriss für Neresheim" in *Zeitschrift für Kunstgeschichte,* XXI, 1958, pp. 40–49.

Sachse, Hans-Joachim, *Die barocken Dachwerks- und Gewölbekonstruktionen der Abteikirche zu Neresheim unter der Berücksichtigung der im 19. Jahrhundert durchgeführten konstruktiven Veränderungen,* diss., Berlin, 1967.

Ullrich, Michael, *Unterschungen zum Tragverhalten barocker Holzkuppeln am Beispiel der Vierungskuppel in der Abteikirche Neresheim,* diss., Karlsruhe, 1974.

Weissenberger, P. Paulus, *Baugeschichte der Abtei Neresheim,* Stuttgart, Kohlhammer, 1934.

Trier

See inventory and notes.

Vienna

Andersen, Liselotte, *Studien zu Profanbauformen Balthasar Neumanns. Die grossen Residenzprojekte für Wien, Stuttgart und Karlsruhe,* diss., Munich, 1966, pp. 6–30.

Herrmann, Wolfgang, "Umbauprojekte für die Wiener Hofburg" in *Zeitschrift für Denkmalpflege,* II, 1927–28, pp. 1–14.

Vierzehnheiligen

Eckstein, Hans, *Vierzehnheiligen,* Berlin, Rembrandt, 1939.

Esser, Karl Heinz, *Darstellung der Formen und Wirkungen der Wallfahrtskirche zu Vierzehnheiligen, mit einem Anhang über den "Architektur-Raum" als "Erlebnisraum". II. Anhang: Die Schönbornkapelle. III. Anhang: Die Hofkirche, Würzburg Residenz,* diss., Bonn, 1940.

Mayer, Heinrich. "Neues vom Gnadenaltar in Vierzehnheiligen" in *Das Münster,* V, 1952, pp. 206 ff.

Oswald, Fritz. "Zur Vorgeschichte der Wallfahrtskirche Vierzehnheiligen bis zum Jahre 1743" in *97. Bericht des Historischen Vereins für die Pflege der Geschichte des ehemaligen Fürstbistums Bamberg,* 1961, pp. 201–214.

————— "Zur Wallfahrtskirche Vierzehnheiligen" in *Fränkisches Land, Beilage zu Neuen Volksblatt Bamberg,* VII, nos. 10–11, 1961.

Teufel, Richard. "Der geometrische Aufbau der Pläne der Wallfahrtskirche Vierzehnheiligen" in *Zeitschrift für Kunstgeschichte,* X, 1941–42, pp. 163–187.

————— *Vierzehnheiligen,* 2d. ed., Lichtenfels, Schulze, 1957.

An excellent presentation of the building and its history. An outstanding analysis of the drawings. Many fine insights along the way.

————— "Zur Entstehung des G.... 'naltars in Vierzehnheiligen" in *Zeitschrift für Kunstgeschichte,* XI, 1943–44, pp. 44–53.

Werneck

Hertz, Carmen, *Balthasar Neumanns Schlossanlage zu Werneck,* diss., Würzburg, 1917.

Reuther, Hans, "Die Schlosskapelle zu Werneck und ihre Stellung in der Mitteleuropäischen Barockarchitektur" in *Das Münster,* XXI, 1968, pp. 113–120.

Würzburg

a. Former Dominican church
   See inventory and notes.
b. Käppele
   See inventory and notes.
c. Palace chapel

Eckert, Georg, *Balthasar Neumann und die Würzburger Residenzpläne. Studien zur deutschen Kunstgeschichte,* Heft 203, Strasbourg, Heitz, 1917.

————— "Das Würzburger Residenzmuseum und die Balthasar-Neumann-Ausstellung" in *Zentralblatt der Bauverwaltung,* XLI, 1921.

Esser, Karl Heinz, *Darstellung der Formen und Wirkungen der Wallfahrtskirche zu Vierzehnheiligen, mit einem Anhang über den "Architektur-Raum" als "Erlebnisraum." II. Anhang: Die Schönbornkapelle. III. Anhang: Die Hofkirche, Würzburg Residenz,* diss., Bonn, 1940.

Herrmann, Wolfgang, "Neue Entwürfe zur Würzburger Residenz" in *Jahrbuch der Preussischen Kunstsammlungen,* XLIX, 1928, pp. 111–134.

Sedlmaier, Richard, and Pfister, Rudolf, *Die fürstbischöfliche Residenz in Würzburg,* 2 vols., Munich, Müller, 1923.

d. Schönborn chapel

Boll, Walter, *Die Schönbornkapelle am Würzburger Dom; ein Beitrag zur Kunstgeschichte des XVIII. Jahrhunderts,* Munich, Müller, 1925.

D. PUBLISHED DOCUMENTS

Freeden, Max Herrmann von, "Balthasar Neumann in Italien. Neue archivalische Beiträge zur Frühzeit des Künstlers" in *Mainfränkisches Jahrbuch für Geschichte und Kunst, Archiv des historischen Vereins für Unterfranken und Aschaffenburg,* LXXII, 1949.

———— "Balthasar Neumanns Gesuche an den fränkischen Kreistag" in *Festschrift für Karl Lohmeyer,* Saarbrücken, West-Ost, 1954, pp. 65–69.

———— "Balthasar Neumanns Lehrjahre an Hand Lebensbeschreibung aus Familienbesitz" in *Mainfränkisches Jahrbuch für Geschichte und Kunst, Archiv des historischen Vereins für Unterfranken und Aschaffenburg,* LXXI, 1937, pp. 1–18.

———— "Ein Unbekannter Brief Balthasar Neumanns an Kaiser Franz Stephan" in *Mainfränkisches Jahrbuch für Geschichte und Kunst,* X, 1958, pp. 277–286 (Archiv des historischen Vereins für Unterfranken und Aschaffenburg, LXXXI).

Lohmeyer, Karl, *Die Briefe Balthasar Neumanns an Friedrich Karl von Schönborn, Fürstbischof von Würzburg und Bamberg, und Dokumente aus den ersten Baujahren der Würzburger Residenz,* Saarbrücken/Berlin/Leipzig/Stuttgart, Hofer, 1921.

A collection of major importance for any study of Neumann.

———— *Die Briefe Balthasar Neumanns von seiner Pariser Studienreise 1723,* Düsseldorf, Schwann, 1911.

Morper, J. J., "Unbekannte Briefe Balthasar Neumanns" in *Bamberger Blätter für fränkische Kunst und Geschichte. Beilage zum Bamberger Volksblatt,* IV, no. 1, January 1927, no. 21, October 1927.

Quellen zur Geschichte des Barocks in Franken unter dem Einfluss des Hauses Schönborn. Part I: *Die Zeit des Erzbischofs Lothar Franz und des Bischofs Johann Philipp Franz von Schönborn, 1693–1729,* Anton Chroust, P. Hugo Hantsch, Andreas Scherf, Max Herrmann von Freeden, eds., vol. 1: Augsburg, Filser, 1931; vol. 2: Würzburg, Schöningh, 1950.

The basic compilation of source material dealing with the patronage of the Schönborn.

Renner, Michael, "Ein unbekannter Brief Balthasar Neumanns" in *Mainfränkisches Jahrbuch für Geschichte und Kunst,* XII, 1960, pp. 217–222 (Archiv des historischen Vereins für Unterfranken und Aschaffenburg, LXXXIII).

———— "Unbekannte Briefe und Quellen zum Wirken Balthasar Neumanns 1728–53" in *Mainfränkisches Jahrbuch für Geschichte und Kunst,* XIII, 1961, pp. 129–146 (Archiv des historischen Vereins für Unterfranken und Aschaffenburg, LXXXIV).

Rott, Hans, *Bruchsal. Quellen zur Kunstgeschichte des Schlosses und der bischöflichen Residenzstadt. Beiheft 11 zur Zeitschrift für Geschichte der Architektur,* Heidelberg, 1911.

Siegel, K., "Balthasar Neumann" in *Unser Egerland,* XXXVI, 1932, pp. 85 ff.

Several letters by Neumann.

Verzeichnis der Bücher, Kupferstiche und Handzeichnungen aus der Verlassenschaft des fürstlichen Würzburg'schen Herrn Artillerie-Obersten und berühmten Architekten Franz Michael Ignaz von Neumann, welche zu Würzburg im Gasthofe zum Eichhorn den 18ten Junius und folgende Tage 1804, jedes mahl Nachmittags von 2–6 Uhr öffentlich versteigert werden, Würzburg, Stahel, 1804.

The source for the contents of Balthasar Neumann's library.

Will, Cornelius, "Briefe und Aktenstücke über die Erbauung der Stiftskirche zu Neresheim durch Balthasar Neumann" in *Mainfränkisches Jahrbuch für Geschichte und Kunst, Archiv des historischen Vereins für Unterfranken und Aschaffenburg,* XLIII, 1901, pp. 1–26.

———— "Ein Schreiben des Duc de Silva Tarouca im Auftrag der Kaiserin Maria Theresia an den Artillerie-Oberst und Baudirector Balthasar Neumann zu Würzburg" in *Mitteilungen des Vereins für Geschichte der Deutschen in Böhmen,* XL, 1902, pp. 280 ff.

Wille, J., "Briefwechsel Balthasar Neumanns mit Kardinal Schönborn" in *Zeitschrift für die Geschichte des Oberrheins und Niederfranken,* XIV, 1899, pp. 465 ff.

III. ARCHITECTURE IN SOUTHERN GERMANY

A. GENERAL

Abert, Josef Friedrich, *Vom Mäzenatentum der Schönborn,* Mainfränkische Hefte, VIII, 1950 (Freunde Mainfränkischer Kunst und Geschichte, E.V., Würzburg).

Au, Bodo von der, *Über barocke Dorfkirchen und ihre Baumeister im südhessisch- nordbadischen Gebiet,* diss., Heidelberg, 1953.

Bandmann, Günter, "Ikonologie des Ornaments und der Dekoration" in *Jahrbuch für Ästhetik und allgemeine Kunstwissenschaft,* IV, 1959, pp. 232 ff.

Benz, Richard Edmund, *Deutsches Barock, Kultur des Achtzehnten Jahrhunderts,* Part I, Stuttgart, Reclam, 1949.

Biermann, G., *Deutsches Barock und Rokoko. Im Anschluss an die Jahrhundert-Ausstellung deutscher Kunst, 1650–1800,* 2 vols., Leipzig, Schwaback, 1914.

Boll, Walter, "Zur Geschichte der Kunstbestrebungen des Kurfürsten von Mainz Lothar Franz von Schönborn" in *Neues Archiv für die Geschichte der Stadt Heidelberg,* XIII, 1928, pp. 168–248.

Brinckmann, Albert Erich, *Die Baukunst des 17. und 18. Jahrhunderts,* Berlin, Akademische Verlagsgesellschaft Athenaion, 1919 (Handbuch der Kunstwissenschaft).

Domarus, M., *Rudolf Franz Erwein von Schönborn,* privately printed, 1955.

Fauchier-Magnan, A., *The Small German Courts in the Eighteenth Century,* trans. by M. Savill, London, Methuen, 1958.

Flemming, Willi, *Deutsche Kultur im Zeitalter des Barocks,* 2d. rev. ed., Constance, Athenaion, 1960.

Franz, Heinrich Gerhard, *Bauten und Baumeister der Barockzeit in Böhmen. Entstehung und Ausstrahlungen der böhmischen Barockbaukunst,* Leipzig, Seemann, 1962.

———— "Die 'böhmische Wandpfeilerhalle' im 18. Jahrhundert" in *Zeitschrift für Ostforschung,* XI, 1962, pp. 625–636.

Freeden, Max H. von, *Würzburgs Residenz und Fürstenhof zur Schönbornzeit,* Amorbach, Emig, 1961.

Grashoff, Ehler, W., "Die Schlosskapelle von Anet und die deutsche Barockarchitektur" in *Zeitschrift des Deutschen Vereins für Kunstwissenschaft,* VII, 1949, pp. 123 ff.

Grimschitz, Bruno, "Das kollektivistische Problem der Würzburger Residenz und der Schönbornkapelle am Würzburger Dom" in *Belvedere,* VIII, 1925.

Gurlitt, Cornelius, *Geschichte des Barockstills und des Rococo in Deutschland,* Stuttgart, Ebner + Seubert, 1889.

Haas, Walter, "Die Architekten Retti und La Guêpière am Neuen Schloss in Stuttgart" in *Deutsche Kunst und Denkmalpflege,* XVIII, 1960, pp. 30–38.

Hager, Werner, *Die Bauten des deutschen Barocks, 1690–1770,* Jena, Diederichs, 1942.

Hauttmann, Max, *Geschichte der kirchlichen Baukunst in Bayern, Schwaben und Franken, 1550–1780,* Munich/Berlin/Leipzig, Schmidt, 1921.
> Still the fundamental study of this architecture.

Hempel, Eberhard, *Baroque Art and Architecture in Central Europe. Germany, Austria, Switzerland, Hungary, Czechoslovakia, Poland. Painting and Sculpture: Seventeenth and Eighteenth Centuries. Architecture: Sixteenth to Eighteenth Centuries,* Baltimore, Md., Penguin, 1965.
> The basic survey in English, but because it covers so much material, the presentation is often disjointed and superficial. The information needs updating in places.

Herrmann, Wolfgang, "Deutsche und österreichische Raumgestaltung im Barock" in *Jahrbuch für Kunstwissenschaft,* 1927, pp. 129–158.
> A key evaluation of Southern German Rococo architecture.

Hirschfeld, Peter, *Mäzene, Die Rolle des Auftraggebers in der Kunst,* Berlin/Munich, Deutscher Kunstverlag, 1968.

Hitchcock, Henry-Russell, *German Rococo: The Zimmermann Brothers,* Baltimore, Md., Penguin, 1968.
> An important summary of the historical and social context in which architects like Neumann and the Zimmermans found themselves.

———— *Rococo Architecture in Southern Germany,* New York, Phaidon, 1968.
> Highly informative descriptions of the work of the Asams, Johann Georg Fischer of Füssen, the Schmuzers, Peter II Thumb, with more selective consideration of Johann Michael Fischer and Neumann.

Hoffmann, Ilse, *Der Süddeutsche Kirchenbau am Ausgang des Barock,* Munich, Neuer Filser, 1938.
> An outstanding study of South German architecture during the second half of the eighteenth century.

Hofmann, Walter Jürgen, *Der Neue Bau von Kloster Ebrach,* Neustadt a. d. Aisch, Degener, 1971 (Sonderdruck aus Jahrbuch für fränkische Landesforschung, XXXI, 1971).

———— *Schloss Pommersfelden, Geschichte seiner Entstehung,* Nuremberg, Hans Carl, 1968 (Erlanger Beiträge zur Sprach- und Kunstwissenschaft, vol. 32).

Hotz, Joachim, *Johann Jakob Michael Küchel,* diss., Würzburg, 1963.

Kömstedt, Rudolf, *Von Bauten und Baumeister des fränkischen Barocks. Aus dem Nachlass herausgegeben von Hans Reuther,* Berlin, Hessling, 1963.

Lieb, Norbert, *Barockkirchen zwischen Donau und Alpen,* Munich, 1953; 2d. rev. ed., Munich, Hirmer, 1958.

———— *Münchener Barockbaumeister. Leben und Schaffen in Stadt und Land. Archivalische Vorarbeiten,* Munich, Schnell und Steiner, 1941.

Lippert, Karl-Ludwig, *Giovanni Antonio Viscardi, 1645–1713, Studien zur Entwicklung der barocken Kirchenbaukunst in Bayern,* Munich, Seitz + Höfling, 1969 (Studien zur Altbayerischen Kirchengeschichte, vol. 1).

Lohmeyer, Karl, *Die Baumeister des rheinisch-fränkischen Barocks,* Heidelberg, Kerle, 1931.

Mayer, Heinrich, *Bamberger Residenzen. Ein Kunstgeschichte der Alten Hofhaltung, des Schlosses Geyerswörth, der Neuen Hofhaltung und der*

283

Neuen Residenz zu Bamberg, Munich, Kösel, 1951.
————— *Die Kunst des Bamberger Umlandes,* 2d. ed., Bamberg, Bayerische Vorlagsanstalt, 1952.
Morper, Johann Joseph, "Die Stiftskirche von Waldsassen und ihre böhmische Wurzel" in *Das Münster,* XVI, 1963, pp. 312–315.
————— "Uber die künstlerische Arbeitsweise des 18. Jahrhunderts" in *Die christliche Kunst, Monatsschrift für alle Gebiete der christlichen Kunst- und Kunstwissenschaft,* XXII, 1925–26, pp. 284–289.
Norberg-Schulz, Christian, *Late Baroque and Rococo Architecture,* New York, Abrams, 1974 (History of World Architecture).
Pevsner, Nikolaus, "The Three-Dimensional Arch from the 16th to the 18th Centuries" in *Journal of the Society of Architectural Historians,* XVII, 1958, pp. 22–24.
Pinder, Wilhelm, *Deutscher Barock. Die grossen Baumeister des 18. Jahrhunderts,* Düsseldorf/Leipzig, Langewiesche, 1912.
Powell, Nicolas, *From Baroque to Rococo: An Introduction to Austrian and German Architecture from 1580–1790,* New York, Praeger, 1959.
Reuther, Hans, "Barocke Dachwerke in Mainfranken" in *Deutsche Kunst und Denkmalpflege,* XIII, 1955, pp. 44 ff.
————— "Beiträge zur Natursteinverwendung in der mainfränkischen Barockarchitektur" in *Deutsche Kunst und Denkmalpflege,* XIV, 1956, pp. 128–146.
————— "Das Platzlgewölbe der Barockzeit" in *Deutsche Kunst und Denkmalpflege,* XIII, 1955, pp. 121–139.
————— "Der Gewölbebau des mainfränkischen Barock 1650–1760, seine Formgebung und Konstruktion" in *Kunstchronik,* VII, 1954, pp. 285–287.
————— "Der spätbarocke Kirchenbau im Mainfranken" in *Zeitschrift für Kunstwissenschaft,* XII, 1949, pp. 160–172.
————— "Die Erscheinungsformen der Pendentifkuppel in der Mitteleuropäischen Barockarchitektur" in *Neue Ausgrabungen und Untersuchungen in Nahen Osten-Mittelmeerraum und in Deutschland, Bericht über die Koldewey-Gesellschaft Tagung in Berlin 1961,* 4 to 8 April 1961, pp. 54–57.
————— "Die Wölbformen im mainfränkischen Sakralbau von 1660 bis um 1720" in *Zeitschrift für Kunstgeschichte,* XVIII, 1955, pp. 40–60.
————— *Dome, Kirchen und Klöster in Franken; nach alten Vorlagen,* Frankfurt, Weidlich, 1963.
————— "Johann Jacob Schübler und Balthasar Neumann" in *Mainfränkisches Jahrbuch für Geschichte und Kunst,* VII, 1955, pp. 345–352 (Archiv des Historischen Vereins für Unterfranken und Aschaffenburg, LXXVIII).
————— "Von S. Michael in München zu S. Michael in Würzburg, Ein Uberblick über die Entwicklung der bayerischen Jesuitenkirchen" in *Heiliges Franken, Beilage zum Würzburger Katholischen Sonntagsblatt,* 2, 1954, nos. 9 and 10.
Rose, Hans, *Spätbarock. Studien zur Geschichte des Profanbaues in den Jahren 1660–1760,* Munich, Bruckmann, 1922.
Rupprecht, Bernhard, *Die Bayerische Rokoko-Kirche,* Kallmünz, Lassleben, 1959 (Münchener historische Studien, Abteilung Bayerische Geschichte, vol. 5).
    An excellent analysis of the style and meaning of Bavarian sacred Rococo architecture.
Schmitt, Charlotte, *Ein- und Zweiturmkirchenfassaden im fränkischen Barock,* diss., Frankfurt, 1945.
Schrobe, H., "Zur Mainzer Kunstgeschichte in der zweiten Hälfte des 17.

Jahrhunderts" in *Mainzer Zeitschrift,* II, 1907, pp. 97 ff.

Sedlmayr, Hans, and Bauer, Hermann, "Rococo" in *Encyclopedia of World Art,* 15 vols., New York, McGraw-Hill, 1959–68, vol. XII, cols. 230–274.

Teufel, Richard, "Beiträge zum fränkischen Barock" in *Zeitschrift für Kunstgeschichte,* XII, 1949, pp. 46 ff.

Treeck, Peter van, *Franz Ignaz Michael von Neumann,* Würzburg, Freunde mainfränkischer Kunst und Geschichte E.V., Würzburg, Historischer Verein Schweinfurt, 1973 (Mainfränkische Studien, VI).

Vierl, Peter, *Der Stuck. Aufbau und Werdegang erläutert am Beispiel der Neuen Residenz Bamberg.* Berlin/Munich, Deutscher Kunstverlag, 1969 (Kunstwissenschaftliche Studien, XLII).

Wackernagel, Martin, *Baukunst des 17. und 18. Jahrhunderts. Germanische Länder,* Berlin-Neubabelsberg, Akademische Verlagsgesellschaft Athenaion, 1915 (Handbuch der Kunstwissenschaft).

Zürcher, Richard, *Der Anteil der Nachbarländer an der Entwicklung der deutschen Baukunst im Zeitalter des Spätbarocks. Ars docta,* III, Basel, Holbein, 1938.

B. ARCHITECTURAL THEORY

Berling, Karl, *Entwickelung der Säulenordnungen Vitruvs bei den französischen und deutschen Theoretikern des 16.–17. und 18. Jahrhunderts.*

Forssman, Erik, *Dorisch, Jonisch, Korinthisch: Studien über den Gebrauch der Säulenordungen in der Architektur des 16.–18. Jahrhunderts,* Stockholm, Almqvist und Wiksell, 1961.

Habicht, Victor Curt, "Die deutschen Architekturtheoretiker des 17. und 18. Jahrhunderts" in *Zeitschrift für Architektur und Ingenieurwesen,* 1916: cols. 1–30, 261–288; 1917: cols. 209–244; 1918: cols. 157–184, 201–230.

    The basic collection of material on German architectural theory.

———— "Architekturtheorie" in *Reallexikon zur deutschen Kunstgeschichte,* vol. 1, Stuttgart, Metzler, 1937, cols. 959–992.

Blum
May, Ernst, *Hans Blum von Lohr am Main. Ein Bautheoretiker der Renaissance,* Strasbourg, 1910 (Studien zur deutschen Kunstgeschichte, Heft 124).

Decker
Schneider, E., "Die Zeichnungen Paul Decker d. A. im Germanischen National Museum" in *Anzeiger des Germanischen National Museum,* 1936–39, pp. 175–187.

———— *Paul Decker d. A.* diss., Frankfurt, 1937.

Dietterlin
Ohnesorge, Karl, *W. Dietterlin, Maler von Strassburg,* Leipzig, Seemann, 1893.

Pirr, Margot, *Die Architectura des Wendel Dietterlin,* Gräfenhainichen, no date.

Furttenbach
Berthold, Margot, *Josef Furttenbach von Leutkirch, Architekt und Ratsherr in Ulm (1591–1667).* Reprint from *Zeitschrift für Geschichte und Kunst. Mitteilungen des Vereins für Kunst und Altertum in Ulm und Oberschwaben,* XXXIII, 1953.

Goldmann
Semrau, Max, "Zu Nikolaus Goldmanns Leben und Schriften" in *Monatshefte für Kunstwissenschaft,* IX, pp. 349 ff., 463 ff.

Indau

Ilg, Albert, "Das Wienerische Architekturbuch Johann Indaus von 1686" in *Berichte und Mitteilungen des Altertumsvereins zu Wien,* XXIV, 1887.

Sandrart

Sponsel, Jean Louis, *Sandrarts Teutsche Academie Kritisch Gesichtet,* Dresden, Hoffmann, 1896.

Schübler

Gürsching, Heinrich, "Johann Jacob Schübler, ein Nürnberger Baumeister des Barockzeitalters" in *Mitteilungen des Vereins für die Geschichte der Stadt Nürnberg,* XXXV, 1937, pp. 17–57.

Steingruber

Hausladen, Eugen Maria, *Der markgräfliche Baumeister Johann David Steingruber und der evangelische Kirchenbau,* Ansbach, Brügel, 1930.

Sturm

Bürkner, Richard, *Der Kirchenbau des Protestantismus,* Berlin, 1893.

——— *Grundriss des deutsch-evangelischen Kirchenbaues,* Göttingen, 1899.

Hammitzsch, Martin, *Der moderne Theaterbau,* diss., Dresden, 1906.

Humbert, Abr., "Mémoire sur la vie et les ouvrages de feu M. L. Chr. Sturm" in *Bibliothèque germanique,* XXVII, 1733, pp. 65–85.

Koch, H. K., manuscript on Sturm in Wolfenbüttel Library, Extr. 2558.

Lange, Werner, *Der gerichtete Zentralbau George Bährs. Ein Beitrag zur Geschichte des sächsischen Kirchenbaus,* diss., Berlin, 1940.

C. ARCHITECTURAL RENDERINGS

Bayerische Akademie der Schönen Künste, Zentralinstitut für Kunstgeschichte München, *Plan und Bauwerk. Entwürfe aus fünf Jahrhunderten,* exhibition and catalogue, Munich, Prinz Carl Palais, 30 May to 31 June 1952, Munich, Hirmer, 1952.

Blomfield, Reginald, *Architectural Drawing and Draughtsmen,* London, Cassel, 1912.

Boll, Walter, "Ein architektonisches Skizzenbuch aus der Wende des 17. Jahrhunderts" in *Münchener Jahrbuch für Bildende Kunst,* neue Folge 2, 1925, pp. 250 ff.

Bosch, Ludwig, "Eine Sammlung Barocker Architekturzeichnungen im Bayerischen Nationalmuseum" in *Münchener Jahrbuch der bildenden Kunst,* V, 1954, pp. 188–204.

Bossert, Helmust Th., *Architektur-Zeichnungen,* Berlin, Wasmuth, 1922.

Coulin, Claudius, *Architekten Zeichnen; ausgewälte Zeichnungen und Skizzen vom 9. Jahrhundert bis zur Gegenwart,* Stuttgart, Hoffmann, 1962.

Döry, Ludwig Baron, "Studien zu dem sogenannten 'Skizzenbuch' Balthasar Neumanns" in *Sitzungsberichte, Kunstgeschichtliche Gesellschaft zu Berlin,* October 1961–May 1962, pp. 4–6.

Egger, Hermann, *Kritisches Verzeichnis der Sammlung Architektonischer Handzeichnungen der K. K. Hof-Bibliothek,* part 1: *Aufnahmen Antiker Baudenkmäler aus dem xv.–xviii Jahrhundert,* Vienna, K.-K. Hof- und Staatsdruckerei, 1903.

Frey, Dagobert, "Architekturzeichnung" in *Reallexikon zur deutschen Kunstgeschichte,* vol. 1, Stuttgart, Metzler, 1937, cols. 992–1013.

——— *Die Architekturzeichnungen der Kupferstichsammlung der österreichischen Nationalbibliothek,* Vienna, Hölzel, 1920.

Heckmann, Hermann, *M. D. Pöppelmann als Zeichner,* Dresden, VEB Verlag der Kunst, 1954.

Hempel, Eberhard, "Unbekannte Skizzen von Wolf Casper von Klengel (1630–91), dem Bergünder des sächsischen Barock" in *Abhandlungen der sächsischen Akademie der Wissenschaften zu Leipzig,* Berlin, Akademie-Verlag, 1958, pp. 3–16.

Hirsch, Fritz, *Das sogenannte Skizzenbuch Balthasar Neumanns, Ein Beitrag zur Charakteristik des Meisters und zur Philosophie der Baukunst,* Heidelberg, Winter 1912.

Hotz, Joachim, "Bamberger Baumeisterzeichnungen in der Kunstbibliothek der Staatlichen Museen zu Berlin, 1. Teil: Pläne für bestimmbare Orte und Bauten" in *100. Bericht des Historischen Vereins für die Pflege der Geschichte des ehemaligen Fürstbistums Bamberg,* Bamberg, 1964, pp. 493–516.

———— *Katalog der Sammlung Eckert aus dem Nachlass Balthasar Neumanns im Mainfränkischen Museum Würzburg,* Würzburg, Schöningh, 1965.

Jakstein, Werner, *Alte Bauzeichnungen,* diss., Braunschweig, 1927.

Reuther, Hans, "Balthasar Neumann" in *Fünf Architekten aus fünf Jahrhunderten, Zeichnungen von Hans Vredeman de Vries, Francesco Borromini, Balthasar Neumann, Hippolyte Destailleur, Erich Mendelsohn,* exhibition Kunstbibliothek Berlin, 1976, pp. 63–114.

Schmitz, Hermann, *Baumeisterzeichnungen des 17. und 18. Jahrhunderts in der Staatlichen Kunstbibliothek zu Berlin,* Berlin, Verlag für Kunstwissenschaft, 1937.

Stein, Walter, *Deutsche Architekturdarstellungen im 17., 18. und 19. Jahrhundert,* diss., place and date unlisted.

Watrous, James, *The Craft of Oldmaster Drawings,* Madison, University of Wisconsin, 1957.

D. INVENTORIES

Gall, Ernst, *Handbuch der deutschen Kunstdenkmäler. Oberbayern,* 3d. ed., Munich, 1960.

———— *Handbuch der deutschen Kunstdenkmäler. Ostliches Schwaben,* Munich, 1954.

———— *Handbuch der deutschen Kunstdenkmäler. Westliches Schwaben,* Munich, 1956.

Die Kunstdenkmäler Bayerns, Landkreis Pegnitz, Alfred Schädler, ed., Munich, 1961.

Die Kunstdenkmäler Bayerns, Stadt und Bezirksamt Kitzingen, Felix Mader, ed., Munich, 1911.

Die Kunstdenkmäler Bayerns, Stadt und Landkreis Schweinfurt, Felix Mader and Georg Lill, eds., Munich, 1917.

Die Kunstdenkmäler Bayerns, Stadt Würzburg, Felix Mader, ed., Munich, 1915.

Die Kunstdenkmäler von Rheinland-Pfalz, Vol. IV/1: *Mainzer Kirchen S. Agnes bis Hl. Kreuz,* Fritz Arens, ed., Munich, 1961.

IV. ARCHIVES CONSULTED

Augsburg, Städtliche Kunstsammlungen
Bamberg, Historischer Verein
Bamberg, Staatliche Bibliothek
Bamberg, Stadtarchiv
Berlin, Kunstbibliothek der ehemaligen Staatlichen Museum
Darmstadt, Staatsarchiv

Karlsruhe, Generallandesarchiv
Koblenz, Staatsarchiv
Marburg, Staatsarchiv
Munich, Bayerisches Hauptstaatsarchiv
Munich, Bayerisches National-Museum
Munich, Technische Hochschule
Nuremberg, Germanisches National-Museum
Regensburg, Fürstliches Thurn- und Taxissches Zentralarchiv
Stuttgart, Württembergische Landesbibliothek, Sammlung Nicolai
Würzburg, Historischer Verein
Würzburg, Mainfränkisches Museum, Sammlung Eckert
Würzburg, Mainfränkisches Museum, Sammlung Winterhelt
Würzburg, Martin-von-Wagner Museum
Würzburg, Staatsarchiv
Würzburg, Universitäts-Bibliothek

Index

Italicized numbers refer to figure numbers.

293

Photographic Sources

Anderson, 29
Mark Ashton   cover, 147
Bamberg, Historischer Verein   132
Berlin, Kunstbibliothek   vi, 69, 70, 72, 78, 135–137
Theron Damon   ii
Karlsruhe, Generallandesarchiv   37–39
Marburg, Staatsarchiv   117, 118
Munich, Bayerisches National-Museum   48, 49
Munich, Lamb   19, 163
Nuremberg, Germanisches National-Museum   159
Paris, Documentation Photographique de la Réunion des Musées Nationaux   160
Mark Reinberger   map, 36, 104
H. Roger-Viollet, iii
Stuttgart, Landesamt für Denkmalpflege   13
Stuttgart, Württembergische Landesbibliothek   2, 4, 15, 16, 27, 47, 73, 86, 144
Vienna, Albertina   28
Würzburg, Mainfränkisches Museum   1, 3, 25, 26, 33, 46, 65, 67, 68, 77, 79, 84,
    85, 93–95, 101, 106–113, 115, 116, 120, 121, 123, 126–129, 131, 134, 139–
    143, 145, 152; I
Würzburg, Universitäts-Bibliothek   30, 31
Würzburg, Zwicker   11, 12
All other photographs by author